18.

D1436440

THE
THEATRE OF THE
LONDON FAIRS IN THE
18TH CENTURY

THE
THEATRE OF THE
LONDON FAIRS IN THE
18TH CENTURY

BY

SYBIL ROSENFELD

CAMBRIDGE
AT THE UNIVERSITY PRESS
1960

PUBLISHED BY
THE SYNDICS OF THE CAMBRIDGE UNIVERSITY PRESS

Bentley House, 200 Euston Road, London, N.W. 1
American Branch: 32 East 57th Street, New York 22, N.Y.

©

CAMBRIDGE UNIVERSITY PRESS

1960

Printed in Great Britain at the University Press, Cambridge
(Brooke Crutchley, University Printer)

IN MEMORIAM
LINDA R. CANE

CONTENTS

List of Plates   *page* ix

List of Abbreviations   x

Preface   xi

Chapter I Bartholomew Fair. Early Shows   1

   II Bartholomew Fair. Theatrical Heyday   22

   III Bartholomew Fair. The Decline   44

   IV Southwark Fair. Early Shows to 1735   71

   V Southwark Fair, 1736–1762   97

   VI May Fair   108

   VII Some Lesser Fairs   121

   VIII Plays and Drolls   135

   IX Theatres and Staging   150

List of References   170

Index   177

LIST OF PLATES

I Bartholomew Fair in 1721   *facing page* 26

From the aquatint published by J. F. Setchel. British Museum

II Southwark Fair playbill of the late seventeenth   76
century

From the Corporation of London Records Office

III Southwark Fair in 1733   77

From the engraving after W. Hogarth. British Museum

IV May Fair in 1716   114

From an engraving, after a water-colour, in *London Society* (1863).
British Museum

V A fair balcony   152

From a drawing by Philip Norman, after an undated original,
in W. Rendle and P. Norman, *The Inns of Old Southwark* (1888)

VI Richardson's booth at Greenwich Fair   153

From a water-colour by Thomas Rowlandson. British Museum

VII Two scenes in a puppet booth   156

From Sayer's 'Punch's Puppet Show'. *Theatre Notebook*

VIII Interior of a country fair booth   157

From *Sports of a Country Fair* engraved by Thomas Tegg
after Rowlandson. Author's possession

I am indebted to Messrs Longmans, Green & Co. Ltd., the
publishers of *The Inns of Old Southwark*, for their efforts,
unfortunately vain, to trace the executors of the late Philip
Norman whose drawing is reproduced in Pl. V. I am also
indebted to the Corporation of London Records Office for per-
mission to reproduce Pl. II, to *Theatre Notebook* for lending the
blocks for Pl. VII, and to the British Museum for photographing
Pls. I, III, IV, V and VI from their copies.

LIST OF ABBREVIATIONS

B.F.   Bartholomew Fair
C.G.   Covent Garden Theatre
D.L.   Drury Lane Theatre
L.I.F. Lincoln's Inn Fields Theatre
M.F.   May Fair
S.F.   Southwark Fair
T.C.   Tottenham Court Fair

PREFACE

THE scope of this book is limited to fairs in what is now greater London though in the eighteenth century a few of those included were outside the city. Others abounded throughout the country at various seasons of the year. The most important of these was Stourbridge Fair near Cambridge, whose entertainments I have covered in an article in *Studies in English Theatre History* (Society for Theatre Research, 1952). Provincial fairs were usually visited by the local circuit company which arranged its itinerary so as to be at the towns at the time when they were held and to reap the benefit of the crowds they gathered. In most cases their dramatic history is part of the annals of the circuit company concerned.

Because the fairs had a continuous history, it has not been possible to adhere too strictly to the eighteenth century. In particular some seventeenth-century material has been incorporated in order to show how their drama developed. Bartholomew Fair and others which survived into the nineteenth century underwent a definite transition when travelling showmen such as Richardson, Saunders and Gyngell toured from fairground to fairground with their wagons, providing more elaborate but standardised programmes of melodrama, farce and pantomime. The start of their activities has been touched on but their story remains to be written.

This is in no sense a history of the fairs nor even of their many and varied entertainments. These have been dealt with in: George Daniel, *Merrie England in the Olden Time* (1842); Thomas Frost, *The Old Showmen* (1874); Samuel McKechnie, *Popular Entertainments through the Ages* (1931); Henry Morley, *Memoirs of Bartholomew Fair* (1892; 1st edition, 1857); R. W. L. Muncey, *Our Old English Fairs* [1936]; George Speaight, *History of the English Puppet Theatre* (1955); Cornelius Walford, *Fairs, Past and Present* (1883), and others. In the main I have confined myself to dramatic entertainments. Puppets, rope dancing, and music booths have been included only when

I have found fresh material about them, when they were run by actors, or provided *commedia dell'arte* and other interludes or pantomimes. Freaks and menageries have been entirely omitted, though readers should bear in mind that they were always present.

It remains to express my deep appreciation and warm thanks to Professor A. H. Scouten for supplying me with material in American libraries and to Mr George Speaight for handing over to me references relating to live actors at the fairs.

S. R.

LONDON
1959

CHAPTER I

BARTHOLOMEW FAIR
EARLY SHOWS

THE FAIR AND THE LAW

IT was a jester turned monk who founded the greatest of London's many fairs. In 1133, Henry I granted a charter to Rahere, his former jester, who was then a prior at St Bartholomew's, confirming his right to hold a fair on St Bartholomew's eve, 23 August, St Bartholomew's day, 24 August, and the following day. In Charles II's reign the fair became extended to a fortnight.

As early as 1676 the inhabitants of Smithfield protested to the Court of Common Council against irregularities and petitioned for a limitation to three days,[1] probably without success, as the fair is said to have been held for two weeks up to 1700.[2] Two years later the Court of Aldermen, concerned at the disorders at Bartholomew and Lady Fairs, was seeking means of preventing them.[3] In July 1694 the inhabitants of Smithfield renewed their complaint of irregularities and again petitioned for a limitation to three days.[4] An order was actually granted for the reduction and a counter-petition supporting its continuance for fourteen days was rejected. This must have proved ineffective for, on 14 May 1700, a committee was appointed to consider ways and means of limiting the fair and preventing immorality.[5] By 18 June it had been decided that booths were to be used only for commerce, and that illegal interludes and stage plays would not be permitted.[6] An announcement to this effect was to be inserted in the *Post Man*. A proclamation, dated 25 June, commanded all concerned not to 'Let, Set, Hire or Use any Booth, Shed, Stall or other Erection whatsoever, to be used or imployed

---

[1] Corporation of London Records Office, Journal 62, f. 342.
[2] *Ibid.*
[3] Corporation of London Records Office, Repertory 83, f. 285; Morley, *Memoirs of Bartholomew Fair* (1892), p. 195.
[4] Repertory 98, pp. 395, 400, 410, 419.
[5] *Ibid.* 104, p. 313.   [6] *Ibid.* pp. 376, 390, 469.

for Interludes, Stage-plays, Comedies, Gaming-places, Lotteries, disorderly Musick-meetings'. It was the authorities' first attempt to get rid of the drolls.

The decision was satirised in a mock *Letter from an Actress of the Play House to a Stroler in the Country, concerning...the Suppression of Drolls in Bartholomew Fair.*[1] The writer claims that drolls were condemned, not only for their immoral influence, but also because they ridiculed 'the Grandeur of the City' making 'a Lord-Mayor (as in the Renown'd Play of *Whittington*) beholding to so mean a creature as a Tabby Cat' or hiring a 'Punch gutted Porter' to represent 'an Alderman in a Scarlet Gown'. He protests against the loss to 'poor Strolers, and we the Underlings of his Majesty's servants':

> We Play'rs sure are persecuted worst,
> Whose very Bills are under such Disgrace
> My Lord-May'r pulls 'em down...
> But that which grieves us starving Sinners most,
> Is the great Benefit o' th' Fair we have lost,
> Which keeps us all in decent Reparation,
> And gave us Credit thro' the long Vacation.

Though there is no evidence of actual performances in 1700 and 1701, the players were not deterred by authority for long and were back in 1702 in the face of a renewal of the proclamation in July that summer.[2] The next year the Lord Mayor, following on a presentment by the Grand Jury on 8 July, once again prohibited the hiring of booths for plays.[3] Nevertheless, by 1708 the theatrical booths had been thoroughly established. They were stated to be 'of extraordinary Largeness...used chiefly for Stage Plays, Musick and Tipling'; the cause of frequent disorders and interruption to traders' traffic as well as of lewdness and debauchery.[4] In the teeth of orders to the contrary, the fair continued to be held for fourteen days. The Court of Common Council once again limited it to 23–5 August. There may have been further suppression in 1710 as William Hone mentions a half sheet

[1] *A Pacquet from Wills* (1701).
[2] Order of the Court of Common Council, B.M. press-mark 1851 b. 2 (27).
[3] *Observator*, 18–21 August 1703.
[4] Corporation Records; Journal, 54, p. 692.

octavo[1] published that year entitled 'The Wonders of England, containing Dogget and Penkethman's Dialogue with Old Nick, on the suppression of Bartholomew Fair in Smithfield'. This was a catchpenny title as it contained nothing about the suppression. In 1715 the order of 1708 was read to the Court of Aldermen and the Mayor recommended to see that it was observed.[2] In 1717 the fair was limited to three days owing 'to the Great Vice and Prophaness, occasion'd there by Stage-Plays',[3] yet, on 28 October 1717,[4] the residents of Smithfield found it necessary to protest against the toleration of a show booth within the Rounds and to request its removal; this was duly ordered. A later order of 1735 limiting the fair to three days and prohibiting play booths was more successful as far as the limitation was concerned,[5] and the fair thereafter was usually restricted to three or four days. But the prohibition of play booths lasted only that season, and they were allowed again the following year. Another prohibition was issued in 1744. In July 1750 a petition was presented to the Lord Mayor and Court of Aldermen, signed by over a hundred graziers, salesmen and inhabitants of Smithfield and the vicinity, protesting against the erection of show booths as an annoyance and disturbance to their work and as 'giving the profligate and abandon'd of both sexes, opportunity to debauch the innocent, defraud the unwary, and endanger the public peace'.[6] Alderman Blackford, who was Lord Mayor, then proclaimed in mid-July his determination to reduce the fair to three days and to invoke the Licensing Act of 1737 to punish the actors as rogues and vagabonds.[7] Other prohibitions were issued in 1762, 1769 and 1776. The last caused a riot with many broken windows.

On 3 December 1760[8] the Court of Common Council decided that Bartholomew and Southwark Fairs tended to vice and

[1] *Year Book, 1832*, p. 984. I have not traced a copy.
[2] Repertory 139, p. 233; 'Miscellaneous Papers Relating to Bartholomew and Southwark Fairs'.
[3] *Weekly Journal*, 24 August 1717. [4] Repertory 121, p. 429.
[5] *Ibid.* 139, p. 233; E. A. Webb, *The Records of St Bartholomew's Priory* (1921), vol. I, p. 244.
[6] *Gentleman's Magazine* (July 1750), vol. 20, p. 329.
[7] C. Walford, *Fairs, Past and Present*, p. 227.
[8] Journal 62, p. 180.

immorality and ought to be suppressed. The committee for letting city lands was asked to enquire into the authority by which they were held and to find out who were the interested people involved. This resulted in the suppression of Southwark Fair, but Bartholomew Fair was a harder nut to crack. By 1776 the city marshals succeeded in enforcing the order against play booths for that year.[1] A further attempt to abolish the fair was made by one Powell in 1798. He was opposed by Goodbehere who maintained that the fair had been held quietly for a number of years without so much as a broken head. A proposal to shorten it to one day was opposed on the grounds that the crowds which flocked from all parts of London would then be dangerous; evidence of the great attraction the fair still exercised.[2]

The reasons why the committee for letting city lands did not recommend its closure were, first, that it could not be suppressed without forfeiting the charter of Charles I, and, secondly, that it would need an Act of Parliament since the city was not the sole owner, a moiety being held by a man named Edwards.[3] It was not until 1855 that the fair finally petered out.

THE SEVENTEENTH CENTURY

We may now turn to the strollers and puppets that were to be seen at the fair before the invasion of the players from the theatres at the end of the seventeenth century. Mr Speaight has shown that puppets were given at the fair during the Commonwealth without hindrance.[4] D'Urfey mentions the performance of pieces about patient Grisel, fair Rosamond, and Susanna, eleven years before the Great Fire of 1666.[5] *Patient Grizill* was seen by Pepys when he visited the fair in 1667,[6] and on a second visit he saw Polichinelle, a new character from the *commedia dell'arte*. In 1668 he witnessed 'a ridiculous, obscene little stage-play, called Merry Andrey [Andrew], a foolish thing, but seen

---

[1] *Annual Register*, 19, p. [176].   [2] *Ibid.* 40, p. 57.
[3] Journal 78, p. 83. The actual report is in 'Papers Relating to Bartholomew and Southwark Fairs'.
[4] G. Speaight, *The History of the English Puppet Theatre* (1955), pp. 70–2.
[5] *Wit and Mirth: or Pills to Purge Melancholy* (1719), vol. IV.
[6] *Diary*, ed. H. B. Wheatley and Lord Braybrooke (1904): 30 August, 4 September 1667, vii, 8, 98; 29, 31 August, 4 September 1668, viii, 93, 96, 98.

by everybody', a Polichinelle, and *Bartholomew Fair* 'with puppets'. The *Merry Andrew* was evidently some crude, improvised farce, like that of the mountebank's patter with his fool. It may have been played on a parade in the open air in order to entice customers to a show within. The English and Italian clowns must have been rivals for the crowds' patronage. Of *Bartholomew Fair* Pepys says: 'It is an excellent play; the more I see it, the more I love the wit of it; only the business of abusing Puritans begins to grow stale.' Morley concludes that what Pepys saw was Jonson's comedy with the puppet show in it, and his mention of satire on the Puritans certainly means that he saw more than the puppet show within the play.[1] Whether it was partly performed by living actors or wholly by puppets is not clear; if the former it would be the first post-Restoration play recorded at the fairs, but it seems more likely that 'with puppets' means that the whole show was a puppet one.

The dramatic entertainments of the fair at that time were probably still limited to puppet plays and Merry Andrew farces. By 1676 the former were called 'operas', a term which seems to have been connected with scenic effects. Duffett, in his epilogue to the *Armenian Queen*, says:[2]

> While Author Punch does strange machines prepare
> For their new Opera in Barthol'mew Fair.

A Bartholomew Fair account book in the Corporation of London Records Office lists the amounts paid by stall and booth holders, and among them are the names of many showmen. The famous rope dancer, Jacob Hall, paid £2. 6s. for 47 ft. in 1670; £5 for 45 ft. in 1672; £5 for 50 ft. and £5. 8s. for 54 ft. in 1674; £5 for 50 ft. and £4. 16s. for 40 ft. in 1675; and £5 from 1676 to 1680. The puppet showman, Anthony Devoto[3] (spelt in the MS. Devoes or Devoe) had 50 ft. for £6 in 1672, for £5 from 1674 to 1677. John Devoto, who provided props for the court performance of *Calisto* in 1675,[4] paid £5 for 40 ft. in 1672,

---

[1] *Memoirs of Bartholomew Fair* (1892), p. 194.
[2] *New Songs* (1676).
[3] Devoto held a licence from the Lord Chamberlain, 11 November 1672 (see A. Nicoll, *History of English Drama* (1955), vol. I, p. 250).
[4] E. Boswell, *Restoration Court Stage, 1660–1702* (1932), p. 212.

for 50 ft. from 1674 to 1675, and for unspecified space in 1676. Robert Parker, who visited Stourbridge Fair in 1673,[1] and who had a company of players at Norwich from 1676,[2] was a constant visitor at Bartholomew Fair. In 1672 he hired 25 ft. for £2. 10s.; in 1674, 23 ft. for £2. 5s.; in 1675, 30 ft. for £3; in 1676 he paid £2 and in 1677 the large sum of £6, in 1681–2 only £3. Other showmen who are also found at Stourbridge were Cornelius Saffery, Richard Shore, and possibly John Perin. Saffery had 42 ft. for £5 in 1672; 40 ft. for £4. 8s. in 1675, and paid £4 in 1676–7, only £1 in 1680, £3 in 1681–2. On 22, 27, 29 August 1682 *The Loyal Protestant and True Domestick Intelligence* advertised 'an Incomparable Entertainment call'd *The Irish Evidence, The Humours of Tiege; or The Mercenary Whore*'; with a Variety of Dances at Mrs Saffry's, a Dutch woman's booth, over against the Greyhound Inne in West Smithfield'. Mrs Saffry's first announcement reads 'By an Approved Company', her two others 'By the first New-market Company'. Perhaps this was due to rivalry with Parker who was likewise appearing at the fair and who, in 1680, had called himself 'Master of New-market Companie of Players'.[3]

Richard Shore, who had shows at Stourbridge in 1679 and 1680, paid £5 for space at Bartholomew Fair in 1681 and £5 and £4 in 1682. The case of John Perin is puzzling. A John Perrin paid £1. 10s. for 8 ft. in 1672, 4s. in 1676 and £1. 10s. in 1680. Why did he have so small a space? It may be that he had only a stall and not a booth, in which case he cannot be identified with the John Perin who was manager of the Nursery and master of the Duke of Monmouth's company in 1673 and who took his company to Stourbridge in 1676. Lastly, John Coysh (or Cosh) paid £6 in 1682. Coysh had been an under-actor at Drury Lane up to 1681 and was in Norwich in 1683. With the exception of the one advertisement for Mrs Saffry, we do not know what drolls or other entertainments these strolling players gave.

Nearly all the plays known to us until towards the end of the

---

[1] *Studies in English Theatre History* (Society for Theatre Research, 1952), p. 26.
[2] S. Rosenfeld, *Strolling Players and Drama in the Provinces, 1660–1765* (1939), pp. 38 ff.   [3] *Ibid.* p. 40.

century were political squibs. Mrs Saffry's *Irish Evidence* must have had its echoes of the Popish Plot; anti-Catholic also was *The Coronation of Queen Elizabeth* acted in 1680 at both Bartholomew and Southwark Fairs and described at length by Morley.[1] This may also have been one of Saffry's drolls as he was at the fair that year. Morley gives an account of another piece entitled *The Royal Voyage, or The Irish Expedition* which he follows Macaulay in assuming was a fair play.[2] But there is no evidence for this. Performance at the fairs was usually announced on title-pages and the words on this one, 'acted in the years 1689 and 90', simply mean that the events it relates took place then. There were several other political plays at the Revolution of the same kind. These topical pieces, when they were performed, gave opportunity for gagging by the comedians. Thus when Admirals Killigrew and Delaval abandoned convoying the Smyrna merchant ships, they were made the subject of attack in a crude droll at the fair in which 'the office of Chorus was performed by a Jack Pudding who expressed very freely his opinion of the naval administration' until he went too far and caused the whole troupe to be arrested.[3]

Montague Summers lists *The Prince's Ball; or The Conquest of Queen Judith* as acted at the booth next to the Greyhound in 1682,[4] but I have been unable to trace this piece in any advertisement.

A description of the fair entertainments at this time is to be found in a poem entitled 'Bartholomew Fair':[5]

> Here's the Whore of *Babylon* the Devil and the Pope,
> The Girl is just agoing on the Rope
> Here's *Dives* and *Lazarus* and the World's Creation,
> Here's the Tall *Dutch* Woman the like's not in the Nation,
> Here is the Booth where the *High-Dutch* Made is
> Hear are the Bears that daunce like any Ladies,
> Tat, tat, tat, tat, tat says the little penny Trumpet
> Here's *Jacob Hall*, that does so jump it, jump it.

[1] *Op. cit.* pp. 197–217.   [2] *Ibid.* p. 233.
[3] Macaulay, *The History of England* (1858), vol. v, p. 425.
[4] *A Bibliography of the Restoration Drama*, p. 18.
[5] *Wit and Drollery* (1682), p. 304. It is also printed as a song, with music by Henry Purcell, in an undated supplement to Playford's *Musical Companion* (1673).

The Whore of Babylon, the Devil and the Pope was a droll acted by Jo Haines in his booth, for which indiscretion he was summoned before Judge Pollixsen and admonished.[1] *Dives and Lazarus* and *The World's Creation* were famous puppet shows. Four years later 'The Second Part of Bartholomew Fair'[2] refers to 'valiant *St George and the Dragon*, a farce' and '*Vienna Besieg'd* a most delicate thing'. The former may have been a puppet play or a droll, the latter sounds like a piece of machinery.

Rope dancing and music booths competed with players and puppets for the custom of the thronging crowds. Morley has given some samples of the kind of entertainments offered at the former;[3] and George Daniel has written of the activities of the latter.[4] There are five large, undated music-booth bills in Harvard University Library Theatre Collection, which are probably those seen by Daniel.[5] They are for: (1) The Kingshead and Mitre Music Booth in Smithfield Rounds kept by Michael Root from the Kings-head at Ratcliff-cross and Elnathan Root from the Mitre in Wapping; (2) Ditto with a slightly different programme; (3) Root's booth at the King Charles Head kept by Powel from Russel Court and Lussingham from the Cyder-Cellar in Covent Garden; (4) The Whelp and Bacon Musick Booth kept by John Sleep from the Rose in Turn-mill-street; (5) The Old Kensington-Court Musick House at the Red-Lyon in Hosier Lane. The booths, it is obvious, were attached to taverns and run by publicans. Their entertainments consisted of singing and dancing. The dances and dancers were often foreign: Indians with castanets, a Spanish saraband with the same, Scaramouches, Irishmen, Italian posture dances, Dutch dancers in costume and the like; or there were trick dancers such as a woman who danced with sixteen glasses on the backs and palms of her hands, or the girl who made play with naked rapiers over various parts of her body. The songs, sometimes dialogues,

---

[1] A. Aston, *A Brief Supplement to Colley Cibber*, p. 20. Aston dates Haines's appearance as in the first year of James II's reign, i.e. 1685, so he may have used a droll already known.

[2] Playford's *Second Book of the Pleasant Musical Companion* (1686).

[3] *Op. cit.* p. 263.

[4] *Merrie England in the Olden Time* (1842), vol. II, pp. 25 ff.

[5] Professor A. H. Scouten drew my attention to these and copied them for me.

sometimes catches, frequently accompanied the dances. The 'merry Jests of Bob the Miller, Billey and Joan, Simpleton the Smith'[1] must have contained the kind of material that was later attached as comic underplot to the drolls.

1698–1699

A great change came over the theatrical booths when the actors from the patent theatres saw in them an opportunity of earning money during the closure of the theatres in the long vacation. As the companies were on shares, the actors received no pay when they were not acting, which was often for several weeks.[2] Bartholomew Fair was held from 23 August and Southwark Fair followed on 7 September, so that a scratch company could go on from one to the other and have a month's continuous work up to the time when the limitation to three days was enforced. Thus it was well worth while to erect booths. It was not surprising that the low comedy actors led the way, for their talents would appeal most to crowds accustomed to Merry Andrews and Jack Puddings.

To William Penkethman of Drury Lane must be given the credit of being the first of His Majesty's Servants to exploit the resources of the fair. An advertisement in the *Post-Boy* of 18 August 1698[3] announced that *Jephtha's Rash Vow*, which had been given the previous year at Blake's booth, would that year be at Blake and Penkethman's. The comedian wisely started his fair career as a partner of an experienced entertainer there. Sorbière wrote about this droll and *The Siege of Namur*.[4] The latter is also mentioned in an undated letter of Walter Moyle's: 'We had the satisfaction to see that the Town was taken, and

---

[1] *Simpleton the Smith* is one of the drolls in F. Kirkman's *The Wits*.

[2] We do not know exactly how long the theatres closed in the first years of the eighteenth century, as advertisements are irregular. In 1701, when booths were probably prohibited, the company at Drury Lane acted three times a week during the fair (*Post Man*, 19–21 August) but in 1702 they did not play after 22 August until after the fair was over (*Daily Courant*, 22 August). In 1704, Drury Lane was shut 24 August–11 September; Lincoln's Inn Fields 17 August–2 October; in 1705, D.L. 28 July–22 September; L.I.F. 14 August–12 September.

[3] Guildhall Library, a collection of cuttings, playbills, etc., MS. 1514.

[4] *A Journey to London in the Year 1698*, p. 27.

the whole Siege was carry'd on as Sieges generally are, with a great deal more noise than Mischief.'[1]

Miller had a droll booth next to Barnes and Appleby's rope dancers in 1699,[2] and in this year other actors followed Penkethman's lead. Ned Ward relates how he went to see a play at Drury Lane but found that the actors had migrated to Bartholomew Fair: 'After Strugling with a Long *Se Saw*, between *Pride* and *Profit*, and having Prudently consider'd the weighty difference between the Honourable Title of one of his *Majesties Servants*, and that of a *Bartholomew-Fair-Player*, a *Vagabond* by the Statute, [they] did at last, with much difficulty, conclude that it was equally reputable to Play the Fool in the *Fair*, for Fifteen or Twenty Shillings a Day as 'twas to Please Fools in the *Play-house*, at so much *per* Week.'[3]

Ward goes on to describe the scene on the parade of a typical droll booth: 'The first Objects. . . that lay within our Observation, were the Quality of the Fair, Strutting round their Balconies in their Tinsy Robes, and Golden Leather Buskins; expressing that Pride in their Buffonery Stateliness, that I could reasonably believe they were as much Elevated with the thoughts of their Fortnights Pageantry, as ever *Alexander* was with the Glories of a new Conquest; look'd with as much contempt from their Slit-Deal-Thrones, upon the admiring Mobility, who gazing in the Dirt at their Ostentatious Heroes, and their most Superbitical Doxies who look'd as Awkward and Ungainly in their Gorgeous Accouterments as an Alderman's Lady in her Stiffen-body'd Gown upon a City Festival.' When they had paraded the length of the gallery 'each ascended to a Seat agreeable to the dignity of their Dress'. The conjuror or Merry Andrew entered, blew his nose over the people, who regarded it as a great joke, then picking out one of the actors began 'a Tale of a Tub,[4] which he Illustrates by abundance of Ugly Faces and Mimical Actions, for in that lay the chief of the Comedy, with which the Gazers seem'd most to be affected. Between these two, the Clod-

---

[1] John Dennis, *Select Works* (1718), vol. II, p. 512. I owe this reference to Mr George Speaight. *The Siege of Namur* had been given at May Fair in 1699, below, p. 108.

[2] *Post Man*, 17 August 1699.

[3] *London Spy* (August 1699), p. 10.

[4] A cock and bull story.

skull'd *Audience* were Lug'd by the Ears for an Hour, the Apes blundering over such a parcel of Insignificant Nonsense, that none but a True *English* unthinking Mob could have laugh'd.' As epilogue the Merry Andrew called out, '*Walk in, Gentlemen, and take your places whilst you may have 'em; the Candles are all Lighted, and we are just agoing to begin*'. Then he 'struts along before the Glittering Train of Imaginary *Heroes*, and their *Water-Lane-Beauties*, leading them to play the Fool within-side in answer to his performance without'.

This passage is of interest as showing that the galleries were used as in the French fairs, not only for the actors to parade, but for farcical dialogues. Though the hour may have been a gross exaggeration, the entertainment was evidently of some little duration because those spectators who could not or would not afford the entrance fee to the booth went away satisfied. These parade farces never developed in England as they did in France where some of them were published in *Théâtre des Boulevards*, nor do they seem to have had the same connection with the *commedia dell'arte*. This duologue at any rate was merely between a clown and one of the actors.

The mixture of heroical and low comic was a foretaste of what the audience could expect to find within. Ward later visited a 'Dwarf *Comedy*, Sir-nam'd a *Droll*' entitled *The Devil of a Wife*, which may have been taken from Jevon's piece of that name. He found the booth pretty full of good, sober citizens though there were ten men to one woman. 'The Minstrels', he continues, 'Scratching over a Concise Piece of Unintelligible Discord, call'd a Flourish, the Curtain was drawn up.' The acting was crude: 'everything was done to such a Perfection of Uncoothness' that, had the actors been puppets, he could not have laughed more at 'their awkward and ridiculous Imitations; every one looking, notwithstanding his Dress, like what he really was, and not like what he represented'. Their tones were unalterable as though they were crying wares, and the entertainment was 'the strangest Hodg-Podg that ever was Jumbled together; and is an excellent Farce to please an Audience of such Fools, who are apt to Admire that most, which they least Understand'.

So great was the press of people that Ward could not get out until the piece ended abruptly and the curtain fell. He returned to the fair in the September issue of the *London Spy* to see the comedian 'who had Manfully run the hazard of Losing that Reputation in the Fair, which he had got in the Play-house' as Ralph in *Fryar Bacon*. This was Thomas Doggett. George Daniel quotes an advertisement for Parker and Doggett's booth near Hosier-Lane-End, where a new droll was presented called *Fryar Bacon; or The Country Justice; with the Humours of Tollfree the Miller, and his Son Ralph*, acted by Doggett, 'With Variety of Scenes, Machines, Songs and Dances. Vivat Rex. 1691.'[1] This date must be incorrect because Queen Mary was alive and the final words would have read 'Vivant Rex et Regina'. It seems to be an obvious error for 1699. It may be the same fair playbill of Doggett's that was possessed by a contributor to Hone's *Table Book* (p. 293) in 1827 and had 'W.R.' in the corners and the royal arms in the centre. Acceptance of the date 1691 has led writers to state that Doggett commenced his career in the fair and that he may have been the first patent theatre actor to have a booth there.[2] But by 1699, as Ward points out, he was an actor of reputation; and Penkethman had been at Smithfield the previous year.

Ward again describes the balconies crowded with a 'Number of Kings, Queens, Heroes, Harlots, Buffoons, Mimicks, Priests, Profligates and Devils', leading patrons to believe that all might be seen within; but the booth was so small that, had they been, there would have been room for only a slender audience. Ward put his pence into the master's pocket and entered the pit 'where several of the Top Quality' women sat cracking nuts and looking round for admirers. Now and again they would call out for the show. The curtain finally drew up to reveal 'a Trunk-Breeches-King, in a Fool's Cap, and a Feather in it, attended with his Cringing Nobility, some Court Jilts, and Two or Three Flattering Priests'. After some 'Fustian Confabulations' the scene shifted to a library where Friar Bacon had projected his brazen

---

[1] *Merrie England*, vol. II, p. 17 n. Followed by Montague Summers, *A Bibliography of the Restoration Drama*, p. 137.
[2] See *D.N.B.*; Leo Hughes, *A Century of English Farce* (1956), p. 183.

head. 'When he had Rav'd and Strutted about a little, with his *Magicians* Wand' and made an oration in praise of the head, 'the Scene chang'd and shut him up in his Study to Consult the Devil a little further'. The comic sub-plot of the miller and his idiot son Ralph then occupied the forestage. Of this latter role Ward comments 'it was the *Comedian* only, and not the *Poet*, that render'd the Character diverting'; both actors, he continues, well became their roles of fool and knave. The next part portrayed the indiscretions of a country justice. These characters were ' Jumbled confusedly together; with a Flying Shoulder of Mutton, dancing and singing Devils, and suchlike pieces of conjuration by the diabolical Friar *Bacon*, With whose Magical Pranks the *Mob* were wonderfully pleas'd, as well as greatly astonish'd'. The droll lasted about three-quarters of an hour and concluded with an assemblage of lords and ladies. From the 'glittering Assembly, one of the best-mouthed Orators steps to the front of the Stage, and with a Cringing piece of formality, promises the Audience to begin again in half an hour'.

Ward's descriptions are the fullest we have of a fair booth in action and, albeit one must allow for satirical intent, they prove that the shows were a crude mixture of fustian and farce and that the rough audiences enjoyed the fancy costumes, the bombast, and the by-play and mimicry of the comics, without caring much for plot or sense. Whether the actors improvised their parts is not known, though it is possible, since this was the practice of strollers at fairs up to the middle of the nineteenth century.[1]

Another visitor to Smithfield in 1699 was the hack writer Tom Brown who printed a letter from the Gun-Musick-Booth, dated 28 August 1699.[2] Brown notices the development of the dramatic offerings in the fair and the introduction of more elaborate scenic effects, and uses them as a whipping-post for the theatres. 'This noble *Fair*', he says, 'is quite another thing than what it was in the last Age; It not only deals in the humble Stories of *Crispin* and *Crispianus*, *Whittington's* Cat, *Bateman's* Ghost, with the merry Conceits of the little Pickleherring; it produces *Opera's* of its own growth, and is become a

---

[1] *Mayhew's Characters*, ed. Peter Quennell (1951), pp. 213 ff.
[2] *Works of Monsieur Voiture* (1705), p. 97.

formidable Rival to both the Theaters. It beholds *Gods* descending from *Machines*, who express themselves in a Language suitable to their Dignity: It trafficks in *Heroes*, it raises *Ghosts* and *Apparitions*; it has presented the *Trojan Horse*...it has seen St *George* encounter the Dragon, and overcome him. In short, for *Thunder* and *Lightning*, for *Songs* and *Dances*, for *sublime Fustian* and *magnificent Nonsence*, it comes not short of *Drury-Lane* or *Lincoln's inn-Fields*.'

Brown also saw the puppet show of *The Creation of the World and Noah's Flood* which was mentioned, with its appendage *Dives and Lazarus*, as an entertainment at the fair in 1682.[1] It held the fair stage for many years and was given by both Matthew Heatley and William Crawley in the early years of the eighteenth century.[2] Anthony Aston relates[3] an anecdote about Betterton taking a rustic tenant of his to Crawley's puppet show. Betterton offered the liberal sum of two shillings for their entrance but Crawley refused it because '*we never take Money of one another*'. The great actor was naturally affronted at being put on the level of a fair showman and threw down the coins. His rustic companion was much diverted with Punch and, not realising he was a puppet, invited him to have a drink with him.

1701–1706

Tom Brown, in another letter dated 10 January 1701,[4] adds *The Prodigal Son* to the list of fair drolls, a subject also favoured in puppet shows. He refers to the performance of the famous low comedian, Jo Haines, and laments the order of the city magistrates by which 'all the Drolls of Glorious Memory are routed, defeated and sent to Grass without any hopes of a reprieve'. As a result of this order of 1700 the entertainments of the fair that year were restricted to rope dancing. The Lord Mayor, when proclaiming the fair, ordered two music booths to be pulled

---

[1] Above, p. 7. A licence was issued in 1662 to George Bayley for playing *Noah's Flood* (see W. Hone, *The Table Book* (1827), p. 67).

[2] Handbills, B.M., Bagford, Collection of titlepages, Harl. 5931, nos. 272, 274. For descriptions: Morley, *op. cit.* p. 274; George Speaight, *op. cit.* p. 165; below, p. 160.   [3] *Op. cit.* p. 5.

[4] *Letters from the Dead to the Living* (1702), p. 39.

down.[1] In 1701 the rope dancers' booths were supplemented by Penkethman's 'Medley' of vaulting and puppets,[2] and a puppet show of *Jephtha's Rash Vow*,[3] and in 1702 the players were back.

An Account of the Last Bartholomew Fair, printed that year, describes how the actors sent advance parties to take possession of their stations, erect pavilions and display show cloths against the arrival of the main bodies. The city orders, which had been posted according to the Common Council's decision, had been spirited from the street posts or capped by droll bills and 'the Booths are up again in *Smithfield*, and their Bills all the Town Over'.[4] The writer, who is virulently anti-player, confirms the growth of the drolls 'into Comedies, highly advanc'd in Wit, and as much in Wickedness, by Parties detach'd (in Vacation-time) from the Play-Houses, to be *Zaneys* at the Fair, and Inter-lope with the Strollers. 'Tis therefore no wonder that the Droll has (of late) been so Edifying, since its Acquaintance with the *Drama*, and the Discipline of the Booth Improv'd by the Morals of the Theatre'. He mentions a droll entitled *A Cure for the Spleen* and a printed song which was originally sung at the play-house. Doggett had a booth but was supported by a poor company:[5] 'The curtain drew, and discovered a nation of beauish machines; their motions were so starched, that I began to question whether I had mistaken myself, and Dogget's booth for a puppet show...they advanced towards the front of the stage, and making a halt, began a singing so miserably, that I was forced to tune my own whistle in romance ere my brains were set straight again. All the secret I could for my life discover in the whole grotesque, was the consistency or drift of the piece, which I could never demonstrate to this hour.' Afterwards came a 'hobletehoy of a dance, and Dogget, in old woman's petticoats and red waistcoat...it would have made a stoic split his lungs, if he had seen the temporary harlot sing and weep both at once'.

---

[1] *Post-Boy*, 15–17 August; *Flying Post*, 13–15 August; *Post Man*, 22–4 August.

[2] *Post Man*, 21–3 August 1701; *Post-Boy*, 19–21 August 1701. A playbill, in Mr H. R. Beard's collection, for rope dancing at Barnes and Finley's booth may be dated this year from comparison with the newspaper advertisements.

[3] *A Walk to Smithfield* (1701); see Morley, *op. cit.* p. 273.

[4] See also *Observator*, 21–5 August 1703.

[5] *Secret Mercury*, 9 September 1702.

The rest of the show consisted of vaulting and the antics of Merry Andrew and Pickle-herrings.

An undated playbill,[1] which must belong to about this time, was from Miller's booth over against the Cross-daggers near the Crown Tavern, and advertised a new droll, *The Tempest: or, the Distressed Lovers, with the English Hero and the Island Princess, with The Comical Humours of the Inchanted Scotchman: or Jockey and the Three Witches*.[2] The chief scenic effect was 'Neptune with his Tritons in his Chariot drawn with Sea-Horses and Mermaids singing'. Here were all the popular ingredients: romance, spectacle, singing and knockabout farce.

A second handbill for Miller's booth must belong to another year since the booth was situated between the Hospital Gate and the Crown Tavern next to the rope dancers.[3] As the bill is torn after the 'Vivat' we cannot assign it to a reign. The droll presented was *Loves Mistress or, the Court of Cupid. With the Comical Humours of Old Grim and his Daughter Peggy;* in addition there were entertainments of dancing and singing, and vaulting on the horse by Simpson, recently returned from Italy.

Doggett was in partnership with Parker at the booth near Hosier Lane End in 1703[4] and there showed the *History of Bateman or the Unhappy Marriage,* with the comical humours of Sparrow his man, who was played by Doggett. A variety of scenes and machines, singing and dancing never previously seen at the fair was announced. It is possible that Doggett was the comedian who deserted the company which was entertaining Queen Anne at Bath, for the lure of a £30 bag at the fair.[5]

At Parker's booth, between two rope dancers, *The Famous History of Dorastus and Fawnia* was given as well as 'pleasant Dialogues and Antick Dances. Never before seen in the Fair.' This droll was taken from Greene's *Pandosto* which was also the source of *The Winter's Tale.* At the rope dancers' booth Scaramouch and Harlequin appeared on 'the great Stage—built after

---

[1] B.M. Harl. MS. 5931.   [2] For further description see below, p. 142.
[3] I owe this reference to Professor A. H. Scouten, who kindly copied out the bill from the extra illustrated copy of Doran, *Annals of the English Stage,* p. 425, in Harvard Theatre Collection.
[4] *Daily Courant,* 21 August 1703. Morley, *op. cit.* p. 283, incorrectly gives 1704.
[5] S. Rosenfeld, *Strolling Players* (1939), p. 169.

the Italian manner'.[1] Penkethman was with Bullock and Simpson over against the Hospital Gate and presented *Jephtha's Rash Vow or the Virgin's Sacrifice. With the Comical Humours of Nurse and her Sons Toby and Ezekiel. Together with the Pleasant Manner of Didimo, Toby's Man.* The comedy was 'all new writ'. Penkethman and Bullock acted the comics Toby and Ezekiel. Steele in a humorous passage has compared the acting of these two comedians.[2]

No advertisements are available for 1704.[3] In 1705 the widow Barnes had a rope-dancing booth at which Pickle-herring 'the chief of all his imitating brethren' appeared.[4] Doggett also performed.

The Wandering Spy visited the fair and described it as though he were a country simpleton: 'I saw many great things like boarded Barns, but instead of honest Fellows with Pitch-Forks, I saw walking round the Balconies, a parcel of Folks most deadly fine dress'd, strutting about, and look'd as furiously as so many Geese on a common, one man dress'd like a Spaniard, a second like a Turk, a Third like a Lord, a fourth like a Fool and all like Sharpers; and the women, what with their painting and patching, their long Trails and plumes of Feathers, their sets of Bristol stones and sham pearls'.[5] It is noteworthy that the two varieties of foreign theatrical costume—those of the Spaniard and the Turk—are both mentioned. At Doggett's booth, he goes on to say, 'you are presented with a new droll called the Distressed Virgin, being a true history of the fair Maid of the West'. An undated handbill of the droll is to be found in Harl. 5931 where it is called 'The Distress'd Virgin or the Unnatural Parents. Being a True History of the *Fair Maid* of the WEST: or, The Loving Sisters. With the Comical Travels of *Poor Trusty*, in Search of his *Master's Daughter*, and his Encounter with Three Witches.'[6] Scenes and machines were announced as never seen

---

[1] *Daily Courant*, 23 August 1703. [2] *Tatler*, no. 188.
[3] *Post-Boy* is missing in the B.M. for 1704–5.
[4] *Daily Courant*, 23 August 1705.
[5] B.M., T. H[aslewood], Collections relating to the drama, vol. IX, f. 72, copied from *The Wandring Spy, or the Way of the World inquired into*, 1–8 September [1705].
[6] For further description of this droll, see below, p. 142.

before. The Spy tells how Merry Andrew and an actor 'fell into a Discourse without Head or Tayl, and said many things to very little purpose and had much talk without any sense in it, when all of a sudden a whistle rattles within the Booth, upon which they all run in, in a mighty hurry, with a pray gentlemen walk in and take your places for upon my word we are just going to begin; and to close all, Andrew he cries, do Gentlemen be rul'd by a Fool for once and come in all of you do, there's good Boys, do now: — For they were no more going to begin than I was about to eat a Toad; this was only to decoy People in, and so to fill their Booth, for they all came out again presently, and told the same story over.' According to Spy: 'every gang had its Fool or Merry Andrew, down from Dogget's Booth, to the Creation of the World, where they have Granny, a she Fool and who is indeed a mere fool, well known all over the Town'. He mentions the rope-dancing booth, a waxwork and 'a Booth full of outlandish monsters'.

In 1706 Penkethman brought out *The Siege of Barcelona or the Soldier's Fortune. With the Taking of Fort Montjouy; containing the Pleasant and Comical Exploits of that Renown'd Hero Captain Blunderbuss and his Man Squib.* The bill adds: 'His adventures with the Conjurer, and a surprising Scene of the Flying Machine, where he and his Man Squib are Enchanted; Also the Diverting Humours of Corporal Scare-Devil.'[1] Bullock played Blunderbuss, Jubilee Dicky Norris (whose first appearance at the fair this seems to have been), Squib, and Bickerstaff, Scare-Devil. Mills who took the hero, Captain Lovewell, was in all probability John Mills, a more serious actor than the low comedians who had hitherto appeared. For the first time the troupe from the theatres included two actresses, Mrs Willis and Mrs Baxter. The droll had topical significance as the capture of Fort Montjuich by the Earl of Peterborough was a celebrated action of the previous year. The conjuring scenes recall similar popular ones in *Friar Bacon.*

---

[1] *Post-Boy*, 24–7 August 1706; B.M. Harl. 5931, no. 275. Morley, *op. cit.* p. 281, failed to date this droll.

1707–1709

The most famous and elaborate of all drolls was first seen at Bartholomew Fair in 1707. It was presented by Mrs Mynns at her booth over against the Hospital Gate, in the Rounds in Smithfield. Of Mrs Mynns we know little except that she had a strolling company of players. They acted at the Cock-Pit in Epsom during Whitsun, 1708,[1] and advertised themselves as 'that Company of Players who perform'd the Siege of Troy with so much Applause last Bartholomew Fair, and who have had the Honour for several Years to play at Windsor for the Entertainment of the Nobility, being by long Travel together able to act near Fifty Plays perfect'. The company, then, was not from the London theatres but had been on the road for some time. Anthony Aston mentions that he 'travell'd with Mr Cash, Dogget, Booker, Mins'[2] and it is possible that this last was Mrs Mynns's husband. Mynns or Mynn joined the Haymarket when it opened in 1705[3] and his wife may then have taken over the company of strollers. However that may be, Mrs Mynns's company suffered in the fair from the competition of the troupes from the London theatres and spent ten months getting up this elaborate show to prove that they could rival the 'operas' of the patent theatres. The droll was printed and sold at the booth[4] and, in a preface to the readers, the proprietors hope 'That as they yearly see some of their happier Brethren, Undertakers in the FAIR more cheaply obtain even the Engrost Smiles of the Gentry and Quality at so much an easier Price; so on the other side their own more costly projection (though less Favourites) might possibly attain to that good Fortune, at least to attract a little share of the good graces of the more Honourable part of the Audience; and perhaps be able to purchase some of those smiles which elsewhere have been thus long the profuser Donation of particular Affection and Favour'. Mrs Mynns employed Elkanah Settle to write the droll. According to Theophilus Cibber,

---

[1] *Daily Courant*, 5 May 1708.
[2] *The Fool's Opera...A Sketch of the Author's Life* [?1731].
[3] A. Nicoll, *History of English Drama* (1952), vol. ii, p. 289.
[4] Guildhall Library has a copy; Morley, *op. cit.* p. 284.

Settle 'was the best contriver of machinery in England and for many years of the latter part of his life received an annual salary from Mrs Minns and her daughter Mrs Leigh, for writing Drolls for Bartholomew and Southwark Fairs, with proper decorations, which were generally so well contrived, that they exceeded those of their opponents in the same profession'.[1]

Settle had long had connections with Bartholomew Fair, and satirical references to his employment as a hack writer there are found as early as 1683.[2] He even appeared on the stage in his old age when he played the dragon, encased in green leather of his own designing, in a droll of *St George and the Dragon*,[3] thereby earning immortality in Pope's *Dunciad*.[4] A further allusion to this is made by Young in his first *Epistle to Mr Pope* (1730):

> Poor Elkanah, all other changes past,
> For bread in Smithfield dragons hiss'd at last,
> Spit streams of fire to make the butchers gape,
> And found his manners suited to his shape.

Morley has given a full account of *The Siege of Troy* which was little superior to others of its kind as far as the text was concerned, but was much more elaborate scenically.[5] This aspect of it is considered in another chapter.[6] The epilogue claimed that hundreds had been expended on it; though doubtless an exaggeration (for how could a strolling company afford such sums?) it must nevertheless have been a highly expensive production. It is curious that, though some of the scenic effects were used in other drolls, it was not revived until it was given at Southwark Fair in 1715.

Penkethman put on an 'opera' with dancing dogs this year which he had previously shown at May Fair. The *Post-Boy* for 28-30 August 1707 advertises the publication of 'The Fair in an Uproar, or a Prologue to the Dancing-Dogs. With their Figures exactly Engrav'd on Copper Plates, as they perform in Pinkeman's Opera in Bartholomew Fair.' I have been unable to trace a copy of this.

[1] *Lives of the Poets* (1753), vol. III, p. 352.
[2] See. F. C. Brown, *Elkanah Settle, his Life and Works* (1910), p. 35.
[3] *Biographia Dramatica* (1812), vol. I, p. 641.
[4] Book III, l. 286.   [5] *Op. cit.* pp. 284 ff.   [6] Below, p. 161 ff.

An extant but undated handbill advertises Mrs Mynns's company at Ben Johnson's[1] booth in the Rounds in *Whittington, Lord Mayor of London*.[2] The chief parts were taken by actors from the London theatres so that Mrs Mynns's strollers must have played only the minor roles. Again it was an elaborate spectacle: 'The Preparation and Decoration of which infinitely exceed both in Expence and Grandeur, all that has ever been on a Stage in the Fair.'[3] If this too was written by Settle, he was in his element with the reproduction of a Lord Mayor's Show, since he had prepared all the actual pageants from 1691 to 1702.

There is a gap in fair advertisements from 1707 to 1719. We know that Penkethman, who had been the first of the patent theatre actors to attend the fair regularly, deserted it for Greenwich in 1709.[4] Other players continued to entrench themselves and, as we have seen,[5] larger booths than ever were erected.

[1] Benjamin Johnson, 1665–1742, a well-known comedian.
[2] B.M. Harl. 5931, no. 278. The date, 1708, is given by T. Frost, *The Old Showmen* (1874), p. 88, but without evidence.
[3] Below, p. 166.   [4] S. Rosenfeld, *op. cit.* p. 266.
[5] Above, p. 2.

CHAPTER II

BARTHOLOMEW FAIR
THEATRICAL HEYDAY

In 1715 'one great playhouse' was erected 'in the middle of Smithfield for the King's players (as they are called). The booth is the largest that ever was built, and abundance of puppet-shews and other shews are set out in the houses round Smithfield...so that the Fair is almost as much resorted to as formerly.'[1] That drolls were being regularly given at the fair, both by players from the theatres and strollers, is evident from *Bartholomew Fair: An Heroi-Comical Poem* published in 1717. In the Preface it is stressed that the satire does not apply to the former but 'only to the low brew of Performers who *ape* Actors so intolerably, that they burlesque the Occupation of *Acting*, and deserve no other Reward from a discerning Audience than a Bastinado'. The account of the performances is as follows:

> Here deathless Actors their Portraitures show,
> And grand Comedians stand in graceful Row.
> Here *Pinkethman* and *Bullock* dauntless sat;
> In fam'd Grimace they fondly emulate.
> A comic Droll here ev'ry Hour is shewn;
> Here *Robin Hood* and *Little John* are known:
> A City Rake, a noble King appears;
> His Tinsel Dress each gazing Clown reveres.
> A Porter here is dress'd in sacred Gown,
> And round his Arms the fine Lawn Sleeves are thrown....
> With tawdry Dress the Royal Consort clad,
> A Crown and Scepter for the Fair is made,
> And Paint Inch-thick on her wan Cheeks is laid;...
> A *Little John* is seiz'd within the Crowd
> To act on Stage he's not a little proud...
> These strolling Actors, with an awful Tread,
> They fill the fond Spectators with a Dread.

[1] *Dawks's Newsletter*, 27 August 1715. Quoted from J. P. Malcolm, *Anecdotes of the Manners and Customs of London during the Eighteenth Century* (1808), p. 325.

Apprentice-Boys, and Chamber-Dam'sels neat,
Th' admiring Audience hourly here compleat....
While Bagpipe plays, and the harmonious Strum,
And Frying-Pan is us'd for Kettle-Drum.
The Play's applauded with judicious Skill,
And loud Huzza's the lofty Play-house fill....
Tho' dull the Scene, th' approving Throng they ring,
And clap aloud the *Exit* of the King.

Rope dancers and puppets are also described. The poetaster suggests that the strolling companies pressed amateurs into their service even for leading parts, and we remember the porter who was dressed as an alderman.[1] Confirmation that a farce called *Robin Hood and Little John* was acted this season is to be found in Nicholas Blundell's *Diary*.[2] He also saw 'A Poppy Play called Patient Grissell & the Babes in the Wood' on 10 August. Perhaps because of the limitation of the fair to three days in 1717, Penkethman showed only his musical picture of the British Court with the Muses above, a machine in a cabinet, painted by the Antwerp artist, Pieter Tillemans.[3]

Mrs Mynns died about this time and her daughter, Mrs Lee, prepared a booth for the fair of 1718.[4] In 1719 another Mrs Leigh, the widow of Francis Leigh, carried on her husband's previous partnership with Bullock.[5] Their booth was in the Greyhound Inn Yard[6] and their new droll was *The Constant Lovers, or the False Friend. With the Comical Humours of Sir Timothy Timberhead and his Man Pismire*. These two comics were played by Bullock and Dicky Norris whilst other parts were filled by Griffin, Ogden, H. Bullock and Mrs Willis, all from Lincoln's Inn Fields Theatre.

Penkethman, who had opened a theatre at Richmond in 1718, was back at the fair in 1719 when he shared a booth with Miller at Horn Inn, Pye Corner. This was probably not the Miller who had been a booth holder in the fair in 1699 and at the beginning of the century,[7] but the notorious Joe Miller of jest fame who

---

[1] Above, p. 2.   [2] Ed. Margaret Blundell (1952), p. 181.
[3] *Mist's Weekly Journal or Saturday's Post*, 10 August 1717.
[4] *Weekly Journal or British Gazetteer*, 23 August 1718.
[5] At Southwark Fair, 1717. See below, p. 79.
[6] *Daily Courant*, 22 August 1719.   [7] Above, pp. 10, 16.

was a regular actor at Drury Lane at the time. They presented the droll of *Jane Shore*: 'shewing the Pomp and Grandeur she lived [in] in King Edward the IVth's time, and the Misery she fell into upon Richard Duke of Gloucester's being made Protector. How she was oblig'd to do Penance in a white Sheet, carrying a lighted Torch bare Foot thro' the City, and then turn'd out to Starve; as also how she wandering met with her Husband, and the Tragick End of them both.' Tagged on to this were 'diverting Humours of Sir Anthony Noodle, a foolish Courtier, and his Man Weazel'. The droll has no connection with Rowe's tragedy of the same name. The King was played by Williams, Shore by Wilks junior, Captain Ayres by Oates, Noodle and Weazle by Miller and Penkethman, and Blunderbuss, another comic character, by Shepherd.

A third theatrical booth was that of Spiller and Lee.[1] James Spiller, a well-known comedian, was at that time in Rich's company at Lincoln's Inn Fields and Lee was probably Mrs Mynns's son-in-law. They presented *King Egbert, King of Kent and Monarch of England; or the Union of Seven Kingdoms*. The Prince of Wales, accompanied by a nobleman and footman, visited the booth incognito, and rewarded the actors with a liberal douceur before he returned to Richmond. This is the earliest occasion that we hear of royalty at a theatrical fair booth.

1720

The widow Leigh and Bullock continued their partnership when they brought out another new droll, *Love's Triumph, or the Happy Fair One* in which Bullock himself, Diggs, Coker, Ogden, H. Bullock, Phipps, Mrs Gulick and Mrs Hobbs acted.[2] All except Phipps and Mrs Hobbs, who were probably strollers, were from Lincoln's Inn Fields. Dancing was by the Misses Bullock and Francis and singing by Dyer and others. This is the last time the widow Leigh is heard of at the fair.

Penkethman and Miller were joined this year by Dicky Norris[3] and their droll was *Maudlin, the Merchant's Daughter of Bristol*.

[1] *Mist's Weekly Journal or Saturday's Post*, 29 August 1719.
[2] B.M. Add. MS. 32249 (Latreille).
[3] *Weekly Journal or British Gazetteer*, 20 August 1720.

With the Tragi-comical Humours of Roger, Antonio's Man, thus cast: Money-Taker, Penkethman; Merchant, Norris; Antonio, Wilks; Grand Turk, Williams; Captain of the Ship, Shepherd; Roger, Miller; Merchant's Wife, Mrs Willis; Maudlin, Mrs Knapp. This again was not the usual mixed band of comedians from both the theatres for all, except Mrs Knapp, came from Drury Lane.

A satirical description of the preparations refers to a stable 'transmography'd for the Residence of Copper Kings, Princesses, Lords, Knights and Ladies...a Manger transform'd into a *Palace*, and a Lestol into and [*sic*] Enchanted Castle, or a fragrant Bower'.[1] It foresees the resort to Penkethman's of the 'mob quality' in hackney coaches, and the South Sea squires and ladies in their own.

1721

Penkethman, who was again in partnership with Miller and Norris,[2] enlarged the boxes in his booth for the comfort of the quality. The players were out to attract a better-class audience, though their entertainments continued to consist of unsophisticated drolls with a large admixture of comic clowning. This season the droll was *The Injur'd General; or the Blind Beggar of Bednal Green; With the Comical Humours of Squire Sousecrown and his Man Gudgeon*. The actors were again from Drury Lane. Miller played the foolish country squire and Norris his diminutive servant, while Penkethman was an undertaker. Mrs Wetherilt and Mrs Ratcliffe were newcomers to the fair.

At Lee's Great Booth over against the Hospital Gate was given the entertainment 'which gave such Satisfaction to all the Quality and Gentry that saw it, call'd *The Siege of Bethulia*; containing the History of Judith and Holofernes; together with the humours of Rustego and his man Terrible'. In this piece three actors who were to make their names first appeared at Smithfield: Anthony Boheme as Holofernes, Jack Harper as Rustego and Thomas Walker as Achior.[3] Thus started the

---

[1] *Ibid.*
[2] *Daily Courant*, 23 August 1721; *Daily Journal*, 24 August 1721.
[3] For their previous appearances at Southwark see below, pp. 77, 80.

connection of Lee and Harper, one of the most famous of booth partnerships.

An aquatint of a fan picture published by J. F. Setchel purports to depict Bartholomew Fair in 1721. It includes Lee and Harper's show cloth of *Judith and Holofernes* which, as we have seen, was the actual droll performed. On the balcony are Judith seated, Holofernes in Roman attire with plumed helmet and train, a trumpeter, a harlequin in a mask and a Merry Andrew. The audience is entering by a door below. Adjacent is a rope-dancing booth with a trumpeter on the balcony, and in another section the conjuror Fawkes or Faux is depicted on a show cloth in front of which a trumpeter and harlequin appear on a parade. Morley, however, queried the date on account of the peep-show of the Siege of Gibraltar, an event which did not occur until 1727.[1] The aquatint is said to have been executed in 1824.[2] A water-colour, which is probably the original, is in the British Museum. It is there tentatively attributed to Thomas Loggan, the dwarf fan painter, with a queried date 1740. Mr Croft-Murray and Mr Laver agree that the costumes would accord more with a date in the 'forties than in the 'twenties. This means that no reliance can be placed on the claim that the view was taken in 1721, and its value as evidence of what the fair looked like at that date must be suspect. Nevertheless, the artist, whether Thomas Loggan or another, presumably had some information about the performances that year as he has portrayed the correct droll for Lee and Harper. Was there perhaps an earlier sketch on which he based his fan design?

1722

Lee and Harper were joined by the low comedian James Spiller. They changed their booth to the Harts Horn Inn Yard where Penkethman had previously been. They presented a version of the droll which Lee had given the year before at Southwark[3] with

[1] *Op. cit.* p. 304. Morley was, however, mistaken in believing that *The Siege of Bethulia* was not given before 1732, p. 305.

[2] R. Chambers, *The Book of Days* (1888), vol. ii, p. 264. He says 're-engraved and printed' but there is no evidence of an earlier engraving.

[3] Below, p. 82.

I. Bartholomew Fair in 1721

its title changed to *Darius, King of Persia, with the Downfall of Babylon; or Innocence Preserved by the Noble Englishman. With the Comical Humours of Capt. Fearful and his Man Ninepence.* The two comics were played by Harper and Morgan, other characters by Smith, Hulett, Orfeur, Mrs Spiller and Mrs Morgan. Charles Hulett, who like Harper was corpulent, was an excellent mimic who had just started his ten years' career at Lincoln's Inn Fields.[1]

Penkethman and Miller had replaced Norris as a partner by Boheme and, at their booth in the Rounds, they presented a new dramatic interlude, *The Distressed Beauty or the London Prentice.* Penkethman was the Prentice, Miller his comical man Wantbrains, whilst the romantic roles were played by Boheme as Amurath, Oates as Achmet, Parker as Haly, Mrs Parker as Selima and Mrs Middleton as Zara. Dancing was provided by Newhouse, Mrs Willis, Mrs Middleton and Miss Francis and singing by Mrs Bowman and Mrs Willis. This piece had been brought out on 20 August at Penkethman's Theatre at Richmond[2] and was subsequently taken on to Southwark Fair.

1723

Jubilee Dicky was back with Penkethman at their old booth at the Horn Inn where they revived *The Blind Beggar of Bethnal Green or the Woman never Vexed* which they had presented two years previously as *The Injur'd General.* Norris was now Squire Sousecrown and Egleton his man Gudgeon; Huddy was the King; Orfeur, Montfort; Oates, Rakish; and other parts were played by Mrs Orfeur, Mrs Egleton and Mrs Middleton. Egleton was good in fops' parts. He adopted the title of Baron Egleton when squandering his small patrimony in France, and was to die, worn out by his wild life, in his twenty-ninth year. He married Mrs Giffard, an admired comic actress who was addicted to the bottle and who died in 1734.[3] The Orfeurs were from the Little Haymarket Theatre which had opened in 1720

---

[1] T. Davies, *Dramatic Miscellanies* (1784), vol. III, p. 274; *D.N.B.*

[2] S. Rosenfeld, *op. cit.* p. 283.

[3] J. Genest, *Some Account of the English Stage* (1832), vol. III, p. 396; Davies, *op. cit.* vol. III, p. 374.

and was thenceforth another recruiting ground for the fair
comedians. Dancing was supplied by the curiously named M. de
Long Dens and two children from Paris. At the back of the
booth Penkethman again showed his musical picture of the Royal
Family. He brought on both this and the droll from his Richmond Theatre.

1724–1725

Penkethman repeated the droll at his booth in the fair in 1724
with Bridgewater as Sousecrown, Butcher as Gudgeon, and
other parts by Huddy, Williams, Roberts, Mrs Willis, Mrs
Morgan and Mrs Roberts.[1] English and Italian rope dancers
and tumblers, whose feats caused general astonishment,[2] were
an added attraction, and the musical picture was shown every
quarter of an hour for 2s. 6d., 1s. 6d., 1s. and 6d.

At Lee's booth a dramatic 'opera' on the old puppet play
theme, *The Prodigal Son: or the Libertine Reclaimed. With the
Comical Humours of his Man Roger*, showed 'his Vicious Life, and
the Devil appearing to him, tempting him to go on in his
Wickedness; and the miserable State he was brought to by his
Extravagance; being reduced to that Extremity, that he was
forced to eat Husks with the Swine to satisfy his Hunger: Also
an Angel descending, exhorting him to Repent, and Return to
his Father, who receives him with great Joy'. Hulett played the
Prodigal and Harper his man; Aston, a country farmer; and
Mrs Spiller, Lucia. The afterpiece was the first pantomime
known in the fair, *The Loves of Harlequin and Columbine*. Lee
had intended to revive *The Siege of Troy* but the clothes and
scenes were not ready in time and the performance was postponed until Southwark Fair.[3] He found it necessary to warn
patrons that any droll so called was not the true one, which
could not be performed in a booth with less room than his
great one.

At the Greyhound Inn Yard Bullock and Spiller presented a
new droll, *The Jealous Husband: Or Suspected Innocence Cleared*,
'in which these two Arch Rogues are resolved to exert their

---

[1] *Weekly Journal*, 21 August 1724.   [2] *Daily Post*, 24 August 1724.
[3] *Ibid*. 25 August.

merry Pranks, and hope to give their Audience the Satisfaction they have been accustomed to'.[1]

Penkethman and Norris were in the George Inn Yard on the Pavement in 1725 with a new droll, *The True and Famous History of Semiramis Queen of Babylon: or the Woman wears the Breeches: Containing the Distressful Loves of the Prince Alexis and the Princess Ulamia; the Pleasant Adventures of Sir Solomon Grundy and his Man Spider, and the Comical Humours of Alderman Doodle, his Wife and Daughter Hoyden.*[2] This shows a considerable increase in the comic element, for not only were there the customary master and man, but also a comic sub-plot involving women. Theophilus Cibber made his first appearance in the fair as Alexis to the Semiramis of Mrs Plomer, the King Ninus of Huddy and the Ulamia of Mrs Haughton. The comic parts were taken as follows: Doodle, Williams; Sir Solomon Grundy, Bridgewater; Spider, Norris; Madam Doodle, Mrs Cook; Miss Hoyden Doodle, Mrs Willis. Penkethman himself did not act. He had moved in order to obtain a larger booth and a more commodious passage for the quality, which suggests that he was doing well and was drawing a superior audience. The Prince of Wales again visited the fair this year incognito, coming by the river from Richmond,[3] but there is no record of his having patronised Penkethman's show.

Penkethman does not seem to have attended Smithfield in 1726. He died on 20 September. He did well out of the fairs and is said to have gained more from them and the theatres in twelve years than those who had played for fifty.[4] Lee, Harper and Spiller revived *The Siege of Troy*.[5]

1727

We come upon a new combination in 1727 when Jo Miller, Hall and Milward shared a booth at Hosier Lane End.[6] They revived the droll of *Jane Shore* that had been given by Miller and Penkethman in 1719. Cory played King Edward; Smith, Richard

[1] *Original London Post*, 21 August 1724.
[2] *Weekly Journal*, 21 August 1725.   [3] *Daily Journal*, 30 August 1725
[4] Downes, *Roscius Anglicanus* (1708), p. 52.
[5] *Daily Journal*, 22 August 1726.   [6] *Ibid.* 24 August 1727.

the Protector; Milward, Shore; Oates, Brackenbury; Mrs Moffett, Jane Shore; and Miss Shireburn, Flora. Miller retained his old role of Noodle, with Ray as his man Weazle, and Hall as Blunderbuss. William Milward was a utility actor who had first appeared at the Little Haymarket Theatre in 1723. The scenes, machines, clothes and decorations of the droll were new. A dance in grotesque characters, that is from the *commedia dell'arte*, followed, entitled *The Wheel of Life or Harlequin's Death* in which Le Coudrière from Paris danced Harlequin. Lee and Harper revived *The Unnatural Parents or the Fair Maid of the West* which had originally been given by Doggett.[1] Mrs Spiller was the Fair Maid; Harper, Dame Strikefire the witch of Cornwall (an early Dame role); Morgan, the comic servant, Trusty; and other parts were filled by Spiller, Hulett, Mrs Bray and Mrs Morgan.

1728

Fair pieces were revolutionised this year as a result of the enormous success of *The Beggar's Opera* which had been produced at Lincoln's Inn Fields in January. Fair booth proprietors were quick to see the possibilities of the ballad opera for their patrons. Two newcomers, Timothy Fielding[2] and Richard Reynolds, brought a company from the Little Haymarket to the George Inn Yard with *The Beggar's Opera* itself.[3] It must have been a shortened version if the entertainment only lasted the usual hour.

The fair also produced its own ballad opera, *The Quaker's Opera, or the Escapes of Jack Sheppard*, based on the exploits of that notorious house- and gaol-breaker, by Thomas Walker, the original Macheath. It was put on by Lee, Harper and Spiller at special performances at 8 p.m., was taken on by them to Southwark Fair, and eventually, on 31 October, brought out at the Little Haymarket. It was printed in 1728 and sold at 1s. In the earlier part of the day, from 10 a.m. to 7 p.m., Lee and Harper gave the droll of *Hero and Leander with the Comical Humours of*

---

[1] *Daily Post*, 24 August 1727.

[2] For his identification see F. Latreille, 'Henry Fielding and Timothy Fielding', *Notes and Queries*, 5th series, vol. III, p. 502.

[3] *Mist's Weekly Journal*, 24 August 1728.

Otter and his Nurse.[1] The sea scene of Neptune, Tritons and floating Mermaids came in useful for the Hellespont where Leander was drowned. This was Spiller's last year at the fair; he died in 1730. Two other booths this season stuck to the customary drolls. Bullock showed *The Perjured Prince or the Married General, with the Comical Humours of Squire Calveshead, his Sister Hoyden and his Man Aminadab.* The Squire was taken by Bullock and Hoyden by Mrs Willis. Dancing was by Smith and Mrs Ogden. The clothes and scenes were new, and the latter are said to have been painted by an excellent artist, approved and commended by the best masters.

Bateman or the Unhappy Marriage. With the Comical Humours of Sparrow and his Man Pumpkin was revived at Hall and Miller's booth but was described as a dramatic opera, doubtless because of the rage for ballad opera.[2] Oates played Bateman; Mrs Cantrell, Queen Elizabeth; Miller, Sparrow; and Smith, Pumpkin. A big cast included the Wetherilts, Boucher, Pitt, Giffard, Clarke, Mrs Buchanan, Mrs Shireburn, Mrs Morgan and Mrs Mun. Henry Giffard, a newcomer, had recently arrived from Ireland; he was to take over Goodman's Fields Theatre in 1731.

The ballad opera craze stimulated fair performances and the fact that there were four booths this year and six the next is evidence of the impetus given to the actors by a form that well suited fairground audiences. These and the following years were the heyday of dramatic shows at Smithfield.

1729

This was a great season for ballad opera. *The Beggar's Opera* returned to the fair presented by Rayner and Pullen's company at the Black Boy, with Powell as Macheath, Mrs Rayner as Polly, and Mrs Pullen as Lucy.[3] This time performances took place from 11 a.m. to 11 p.m.

Reynolds and Fielding had separate booths but both gave versions of Coffey's *Beggar's Wedding*, a ballad opera which had been brought out that year, the music of which consisted of

---

[1] B.M. Add. MS. 32249 (Latreille).
[2] Above, p. 16. *Daily Journal*, 5 September 1728.
[3] *Daily Post*, 25 August 1729.

English, Scotch and Irish ballad tunes. There was trouble between the two about the players. Fielding announced that the best part of his company was from among those who performed the piece at the Haymarket with some others from Drury Lane, gave his list of performers, and added the following: 'Notwithstanding the ill advised Declaration of Richard Reynolds in this Paper of yesterday, to the contrary (whose wonderful Performances for the said Fair, so frequently and entertainingly express'd for the Diversion of the Publick, as well as his Advertisement, ought to be revis'd and alter'd) it is plainly to be prov'd that the People above mentioned are, and have been some considerable Time, legally engaged to Mr Fielding.'[1] The offending advertisement is missing, but from one on 9 August it is evident that both parties were claiming the services of Hulett, Charke and Mrs Palmer. In their final cast-lists Reynolds dropped Charke, and Fielding, Mrs Palmer, but both continued to include Hulett.

Fielding, who retained the George Inn Yard, advertised the piece as *Hunter: Or, The Beggar's Wedding* with Charke as Hunter, Mrs Roberts as Phebe, other parts by Hulett, Smith, Mountfort, R. and W. Williams, Boman, Mrs Egleton, Miss Shireburn, Mrs Goodshaw, Misses Fitzgerald and Francis.[2] The songs and entr'acte music were played by a band and dancing was supplied by M. St Luce from Paris, Fisher, Tench and Charke. Performances took place every hour from 2 to 11, this one-act ballad opera taking the same time to perform as a droll. The George Inn Yard had room for coaches and was provided with lights.

Reynolds's booth was between the Hospital Gate and Crown Tavern[3] and his version of *The Beggar's Wedding* was cast as follows: Hunter, Ray from Drury Lane; Chaunter (King of the Beggars), Hulett; Phebe, Mrs Mountfort; Tippet, Mrs Nokes; Mrs Chaunter, Mrs Thomas; other roles by Thomas, Wilcocks, Rosco, Pearce, Machen, Russell, Dove, Mrs Kilby, Mrs Palmer, Miss Mann, Mrs Clark, Mrs Jones and Mrs Barnett. From 8 p.m. to 11 p.m. Colley Cibber's ballad opera *Damon and Phillida* was substituted. This had been brought out only a week

---

[1] *Daily Post*, 7 August 1729.   [2] *Ibid.* 23 August.   [3] *Ibid.* 25 August.

before the fair at the Little Haymarket. In each case an entertainment of dancing in grotesque characters, *The Humours of
Harlequin*, was added as afterpiece with Reynolds, Davenport
and Miss Mann. The band, scenes, machines and decorations
were from the Little Haymarket.

Two other ballad operas were given as afterpieces to drolls
and this must have considerably increased the playing time of
each round of entertainment. At Bullock's booth[1] *Dorastus and
Fawnia; or the Royal Shepherdess* was revived with the following
cast:[2] Leontes, Ogden; Polixenes, Chapman; Dorastus, Houghton; Queen, Mrs Rice; Fawnia, Miss Chapman. This is the first
appearance at the fair of Thomas Chapman, a noted low
comedian, who built a new theatre in Richmond in 1730 in
succession to Penkethman's. The ballad opera was *Flora* altered
by the comedian John Hippisley from Colley Cibber's *Hob, or
the Country Wake*. It had 'new scenes, most curiously painted'
and was played by Bullock himself, Salway, Smith, Mrs Clark,
Mrs Rice and Mrs Ogden. The company was from Lincoln's
Inn Fields where *Flora* had been brought out the previous April.

At Hall and Oates's booth *Maudlin* was given with Mrs
Templer as Maudlin, Penkethman the younger as the comic
servant Roger, other parts by Giffard, Burnet, Hall, Downes,
Clark and Mrs Willis.[3] The ballad opera was *The Country
Wedding* with Hall as Roger, Mrs Willis as Joan, and Mrs
Cantrell as Shepherd.

At the sixth booth, that of Lee and Harper,[4] only a droll was
given, a revival of *The Siege of Bethulia*, with Mullart as Holofernes, Mrs Spiller as Judith, Harper in his old role of Rustego
and Morgan as his man. The droll was printed by G. Lee and
sold in the booth.

1730

Another ballad opera was specially written for the fair this year,
W. R. Chetwood's *The Generous Freemason; or, The Constant
Lady. With Humours of Squire Noodle and his Man Doodle*,[5]

[1] *Ibid.* 25 August 1729.   [2] Above, p. 16.
[3] *Daily Post*, 26 August.   [4] *Ibid.* 23 August; above, p. 25.
[5] *Ibid.* 21 August 1730; below, p. 145.

acted at Oates and Fielding's booth in the George Inn Yard and printed in 1731. The cast was: King of Tunis, Barcock; Mirza, Paget; Sebastian, Oates; Clerimont, Fielding; Queen, Mrs Kilby; Maria, Miss Oates; with Burnet, Berry, Smith, Excell, Brogden, Mrs Grace, Mrs Stevens and Mrs Roberts. All were newly dressed, and it is of interest to note that Neptune again rose with accompanying Tritons. The music was by Henry Carey, Richard Charke and John Shiels. Dancing was supplied by M. St Luce and Mlle DeLorme.

The younger Penkethman and William Giffard from Goodman's Fields had a booth opposite the Crown Tavern where they brought out a new droll, *Wat Tyler and Jack Straw*.[1] This had local interest as it showed how Straw 'stab'd the insolent Rebel, Wat Tyler, at the Head of his Rout, in Smithfield, for which Reason the Dagger, which he so loyally employ'd was added to the City Arms, and remains there still as a Memorial of the King's gratitude and the Lord Mayor's loyalty'. The actual dagger was lent for the show by Aldworth, a vintner of Islington. Penkethman was Wat Tyler; Collet, Straw; Bardin, the King; Huddy, Lancaster; Smith, Suffolk; W. Williams, Lord Mayor; Havard, Young Walworth; W. Giffard, Pease-Stack; Mrs Haughton, Aurelia; Mrs Palmer, Mrs Tyler; Mrs Thomas, Sukey Tyler; Burney, Goody Tyler; and Mrs Mountfort, Genius of England. The Lord Mayor's procession, with pageants as formerly used in honour of the city, was part of the show. Penkethman spoke an epilogue on an ass. The droll was printed and sold for 6d. On 24 August was substituted Doggett's *Mad Tom of Bedlam*,[2] which the Goodman's Fields company had just previously performed at Tottenham Court Fair.[3] The following day, *Wat Tyler* returned to the evening bill and on 27 August was followed by *The Tipplers: or the Dumb Philosophers or the Escapes of Harlequin*. This droll on London history was evidently popular since, from 31 August to 7 September, it also replaced *Mad Tom*, being followed by *Flora*.

At Reynolds's booth a new droll entitled *Scipio's Triumph; Or, The Siege of Carthage. With the Comical Humours of Noodle*

[1] *Daily Post*, 20 August 1730.
[2] *Ibid*. 20, 24, 25, 31 August, 1, 7 September.   [3] Below, p. 122.

Stitch, Puzzle &c., was given with Mullart as Scipio, Dulton as Stitch, Jones as Noodle, Hippisley as Puzzle, Mrs Mullart as Almeyda and other parts by Rosco, Stoppelaer, Mrs Williamson, and comedians from the Haymarket.[1] This was the first recorded appearance at the fair of the well-known comedian, John Hippisley. The droll was followed by a pantomime, *Harlequin's Contrivance; or, The Plague of a Wanton Wife*, with Knott as Harlequin, Mrs Forrester as Columbine, Reynolds as Forester, Dove as Clumsy his man; and Wathen, Hicks, Mrs Nokes, Mrs Clark and Miss Palms.

Lee and Harper repeated *The Siege of Bethulia* with Chapman as Holofernes in place of Mullart who had joined Reynolds.[2] This was played from 10 to 7, and at 8 was replaced by *Robin Hood and Little John*. This 'opera' with the music of its nineteen songs was printed and sold at the booth, the proprietors announcing that other versions were false. The piece must have been changed in the evening to entice patrons to two performances. The droll was followed by an entertainment in grotesque characters, *The Stratagems of Harlequin: or the Peasant Trick'd*, with new scenes, machines, flying and decorations. Playing continued until 3 September, except for 2 September which was a fast day for the fire of London.

At a fifth booth Bullock and Hall revived the *Whole History of Herod and Mariamne*, also followed by *Flora*.[3]

The popularity of ballad opera was on the wane and this year there were three ballad operas and three pantomime afterpieces.

1731

Chetwood again supplied the fair with a ballad opera, called a dramatic opera, *The Emperor of China Grand Vol-gi; Or, The Constant Couple and Virtue Rewarded. With the Comical Humours of 'Squire Shallow in his Treaties of Marriage &c. and his Man Robin Booby*, 'intermixt with Variety of Songs to old Ballad Tunes and Country dances'. It was given at Hippisley, Fielding

---

[1] *Daily Post*, 22 August 1730.   [2] *Ibid.* 31 August.
[3] *Grub-Street Journal*, 27 August 1730. I owe this reference to Leo Hughes, *A Century of English Farce* (1956), p. 221. The droll had been given at Southwark in 1723.

and Hall's booth in the George Inn Yard.[1] Hippisley played the Welsh squire Shallow; Hall, Robin Booby; Roberts, the Emperor of China; Mrs Templer, Fidelia; with other roles by Huddy, Rosco, Cross, Penkethman, Berry, Rainton senior, Excell, Mrs Grace and Mrs Egleton. The scenes were newly painted by 'a great Master', the habits were new and appropriate to the characters, and the final chorus from Handel's *Porus*[2] was accompanied by hautboys, trumpets and kettledrums.

Lee and Harper brought from Southwark Fair of 1730 *Guy, Earl of Warwick. Together with the Comical Distresses of Rogero, Guy's Servant*.[3] Hulett, Mr and Mrs Morgan and Harper played the same parts; others were: Jones, Old Warwick; Mullart, the Emperor; Aston junior, the Duke of Lorrain; Mrs Mullart, the Empress; and Mrs Taylor, Jilt. The book printed by G. Lee was sold in the booth. Bullock was at his Hosier Lane End booth with *The London Merchant*, an abridgement of Lillo's famous tragedy.[4] Chapman played George Barnwell; Ogden, Thorowgood; and other parts were played by Stoppelaer, Salway, Mrs Plomer, Mrs Bullock and Miss Chapman. Once again *Flora* was the afterpiece with Salway as Hob; Mrs Rice, Flora; and Bullock, Sir Thomas Trusty. Bullock claimed that the only rope dancing at the fair was shown at his booth before the droll.

As late as 3 September, Miller, Mills and Oates advertised their new opera, *The Banish'd General: or The Distrest Lovers. With the Comical Humours of Nicodemus Hobble-wallop Esq: and his Man Gudgeon*, with the following cast: Mountford the general, W. Mills; Wallup, Jo Miller; Gudgeon, Bencraft; other parts by Oates, Tenoe, R. Wetherilt, Adam Hallam, Evans, Bardin, Mrs Roberts, Mrs Wetherilt, Mrs Lacy, Mrs Phillpot, and Miss Oates.[5] Three days later, by desire of the masons, a new prologue and epilogue were spoken by Mills and Miss Oates. The masons extended their patronage of plays to those of the fair.

There were in all four theatrical booths. In addition, Yeates

[1] *Daily Post*, 21 August 1731.
[2] It had been brought out at the King's Theatre in February.
[3] *Daily Post*, 23 August. Below, p. 89.
[4] *Daily Advertiser*, 26 August 1731.
[5] *Daily Post*, 3 September 1731.

gave *The Generous Freemason* by puppets but with live singers,[1] as well as showing a clockwork from Italy with 300 figures. The conjuror Fawkes, one of the regular fair entertainers, had died on 25 May, and Yeates had hoped to succeed to his business, but Fawkes's son set up a rival show next to Lee and Harper's.[2]

1732

There were at least three booths in 1732.[3] Hippisley and Fielding continued in partnership at the George Inn Yard. They gave public rehearsals of their two offerings 'with the utmost Applause and Satisfaction'[4] on 16 and 21 August before the fair opened. The pieces were *The Envious Statesman or The Fall of Essex*, with Mrs Mullart as the Queen, and the *Humours of the Forced Physician*, taken from Molière's *Le Médecin Malgré Lui*, and intermixed with songs from old ballad tunes and country dances. Hippisley himself played the Physician, and others who took part were Huddy, A. Hallam, Mullart, Cole, Penkethman, Stoppelaer, R. Wetherilt, Leigh, Grey, Mrs Grace, Mrs Templer, Mrs Talbot, Mrs Palmer, Miss Atherton, Mrs Morse and Miss Mears. In addition to this large company of eleven men and seven women, there were at least three dancers: M. De Ferron Ville from Paris, Miss Brett and Miss Mears. The band, too, was becoming more elaborate and its instruments are henceforth frequently specified. On this occasion there was an extra band and one of the trumpets was sounded by Burk Thumoth. A new feature was the performance of postures by Phillips before the 'opera'. Such entertainments served to divert the audience whilst they waited for the booth to fill. The Prince of Wales and Princesses were among those who visited the booth and were so pleased that they stayed to see two performances. Special arrangements were again made to enable coaches to drive up the yard, whilst the passage thence to the booth was illuminated.[5]

Miller, Mills and Oates had their booth over against the Hospital Gate.[6] Their offering was *The History of King Henry*

---

[1] *Ibid.* 23 August 1731. [2] *Ibid.* 21 August.
[3] *Ibid.* 22 August 1732. [4] *Ibid.* 17 August.
[5] *Ibid.* 30 August, 7 September. [6] *Ibid.* 6 September.

the VIII and Anne Bullen, 'Containing, Her Marriage, Corona-
tion and Tragical Fall, by the Artful Insinuations of Cardinal
Wolsey; the Intercession of the young Princess Elizabeth; and
several other Historical Passages. Intermix'd with a Comic
Opera set to Old Ballad Tunes and Country Dances. With the
diverting humours of 'Squire Nump-Skull and his Man Lack-
Brains.' W. Mills played Henry VIII; Barcock, Wolsey; Tenoe,
Northumberland; Bardin, Percy; Cross, Rochfort; Mrs Clark,
Anne Bullen; Miss Anne Oates, Princess Elizabeth. The low
comedy was provided by Miller as Numpskull and Young Ben-
craft as Lackbrains. Mrs Charke made her first appearance at
the fair as Lucy in the comic opera, other parts being sustained
by Aston, Jones, Oates, Miss DeLorme, Miss Oates, and Mrs
Rogers. Dancing was by Davenport, Mr and Mrs Hind, Miss
DeLorme and Miss Price. Before the piece there was rope
dancing by Mlle de Reverant and two children, and tumbling by
Miss Derrum, a child of nine years.

The Duke of Dorset, accompanied by several foreign ministers,
patronised Bullock's booth, where they were playing *The Perjured Prince*, and ordered a company of tumblers to perform.[1]
He 'expressed an entire satisfaction with the Performance'.

1733

On 8 August 1733 the *Daily Post* reported that Fielding from
Drury Lane had begun to build his great booth at the George
Inn though he would not open until 23 August, the first day of
the fair. He announced that he had engaged some of the best
performers, and that 'several of the Gentlemen and Neighbours
in Bloomsbury (where he lives) intend to favour him with their
Company'. Hippisley was still his partner and they brought out
a new entertainment, *Love and Jealousy: Or the Downfall of
Alexander the Great*. The dramatis personae prove that this was
an adaptation of Lee's Restoration tragedy, *The Rival Queens*.[2]
A ballad opera, *A Cure for Covetousness or The Cheats of Scapin*,

[1] *Daily Post*, 1 September 1732.
[2] *Ibid*. 24 August 1733; Morley, *op. cit.* p. 332, reproduces the complete
advertisement.

taken from Otway's version of Molière, followed. It was notable for the appearance of Mrs Pritchard as Loveit, an extra character not in Otway. She made a sensation in a duet which she sang with Salway entitled 'Sweet if you love me, smiling turn', and was at once engaged for the Haymarket. She appeared there on 26 September and later went to Drury Lane, where she became the leading actress of her day, though it was said that her Bartholomew Fair origin was always evident.[1] To Otway's farce was added the diverting 'Humours of the Original Marquess en Chien' from the *Ridotto al' Fresco*, in which both Roman and modern characters were newly dressed. Theophilus Cibber's pantomime, *The Harlot's Progress; or, The Ridotto al' Fresco*, had been brought out at Drury Lane the previous March. Additional entertainments were dancing, Hippisley's Drunken Man scene as performed at Drury Lane, and a prelude by the posture master Phillips. The large band consisted of violins, hautboys, bassoons, kettledrums, trumpets and French horns. Indeed the entertainment did not fall far short of the variety at the patent theatres, except that the main piece was in an abridged version. The hours were from 1 to 11 p.m. and it would be interesting to know how many performances took place during that time. Fielding's success was such that he printed, by request, copies of Merliton and other songs from the droll. They were distributed free to occupants of pit and boxes, and copies of Mrs Pritchard's duet were also given out daily.[2] Timothy Fielding retired from Drury Lane in the autumn and opened the Buffalo Tavern at the corner of Bloomsbury Square.[3] Is it too much to surmise that this was made possible by his profits from the fair?

Theophilus Cibber shared a booth by Hosier Lane with Griffin, Bullock and Adam Hallam. This must still have been William Bullock senior, both of whose sons died this year. Here too an abridged tragedy, *Tamerlane the Great*, was the main dish. In the cast were Adam Hallam as Tamerlane; T. Cibber, Bajazet; his sister Mrs Charke, Haly; and Cross, Hale, W. Hallam and

[1] T. Campbell, *Life of Mrs Siddons* (1834), vol. i, p. 138.
[2] *A Dialogue between Sly and Lovett. Sung at Fielding's Booth at Bartholomew Fair.*
[3] *Daily Post*, 15, 20 October 1733.

H. Tench. It, too, was followed by an adaptation of Molière, Fielding's *The Miser*, with Griffin as Lovegold; Mrs Roberts as Lappet and other parts by Bullock, Stoppelaer, Leigh, Jones, Smith, Rainton, Miss Atherton, Miss Careless and Mrs Talbot. *Ridotto al' Fresco* as a pantomime dance and an epilogue spoken by Miss Cole, a child of four, in boy's clothes, wound up the entertainment. Italian rope dancers, posture masters and tumblers entertained the company before the droll started. The proprietors were at pains to deny rumours that, owing to the variety of entertainments and expensive decorations, the prices were to be raised.[1] They announced the common prices, customary at the fair, of boxes 2s. 6d., pit 1s. 6d., first gallery 1s., upper gallery 6d. The booth with its two galleries must have been quite a sizeable building. On 3 September, by desire, *The Comical Humours of Sir John Falstaff, Justice Shallow, Ancient Pistol and Others*, taken from Shakespeare, was added to the programme, with the following cast: Pistol, Cibber junior; Falstaff, Berry; Shallow, Griffin; Hostess, Mrs Roberts; Silence, Stoppelaer; Dol Common, Miss Atherton; King Henry, Cross; Prince John, Leigh; Lord Chief Justice, Hallam; Bardolph, Jones; Feeble, Bullock; Mouldy, W. Hallam; Shadow, Leigh; Ragged Wart, Smith.[2] Harper denied that he was to play his famous role of Falstaff at this booth.[3] As usual he had his own with Mrs Lee where *Jephtha's Rash Vow* was revived with Hulett as Jephtha; Hicks as Diddimo, and Harper himself as Bluster.[4] It was followed by the pantomimic opera, *The Fall of Phaeton*, with Aston as Phaeton, Hewet as Jupiter, and other roles by Nichols, Mrs Spiller, Mrs Williamson, Mrs Cantrell, Mrs Spelman and Mrs Fitzgerald. This was a spectacular piece according to the synopsis, 'Wherein is shewn the Rivalship of Phaeton and Epapus; their Quarrel about Lybia, Daughter to King Merops, which causes Phaeton to go to the Palace of the Sun, to know if Apollo is his Father, and for Proof of it requires the Guidance of his Father's Chariot, which obtain'd he ascends in the Chariot through the Air to light the World. In the Course the Horses prove unruly, go out of their Way, and set the World on Fire;

[1] *Daily Post*, 18 August 1733.   [2] *Ibid*. 3 September.
[3] *Ibid*. 4 September.   [4] *Country Journal*, 25 August.

Jupiter descends on an Eagle, and with his Thunderbolt strikes
Phaeton out of the Chariot into the River Po. The whole inter-
mixt with Comic Scenes between Punch, Harlequin, Scaramouch,
Pierrot and Columbine.' *Jephtha's Rash Vow* and *The Fall of
Phaeton* were printed this year by G. Lee, M. Deacon and
J. Bingham.[1] According to Morley, a fourth booth was erected
by Miller, Mills and Oates where they performed *Jane Shore* and
a dancing entertainment, *The Gardens of Venus or The Triumphs of
Love*.[2] Miss Oates was Jane Shore, and Mills replaced Milward
as Shore. The stroller, Tony Aston, and Paget from Drury Lane
were to have a booth together but, if they did, there are no
advertisements of their performances.[3]

1734

The tendency to adapt plays for performance in the fair, evident
in 1733 with abridgements of *The Rival Queens*, *Tamerlane*, and
Henry IV, was continued in 1734 with *The Libertine* and *Don
Carlos*. At Ryan, Legar (Laguerre), Chapman and Hall's booth
a version of Shadwell's comedy *The Libertine* was to be seen as
Don John or the Libertine Destroy'd with Ryan as Don John;
Chapman as his servant Jacomo; Miss Mann as his mistress
Leonora and Mrs Mullart as her maid Maria.[4] This was followed
by a ballad opera, *The Barren Island, or, The Petticoat Govern-
ment*, in which Aston, Hall, Mullart, Laguerre, Penkethman and
Mrs Roberts played, as well as by *The Farrier Nick'd: Or The
Exalted Cuckold*, an entertainment in grotesque characters, with
Clark as Harlequin and Miss Mann as Columbine. The advertisement refers to the expenses caused by this new entertainment.
A three-item bill was a long one for a fair booth, though the
dance may not have taken much more time than the customary
entr'acte dancing and singing. John Laguerre was the son of the
famous decorative painter, Louis Laguerre, and himself an artist
and scene painter.

Don Carlos, taken from Otway's tragedy, was presented by

1 Most of the pantomime is missing from the B.M. copy.
2 *Op. cit.* p. 322. I can find no trace of this in the advertisements.
3 Leo Hughes, *op. cit.* p. 225, n. 25, from *Daily Advertiser*, 18 August 1733.
4 *Daily Journal*, 2 September 1734.

Fielding and Oates at the George Inn Yard with Bardin as Don Carlos; Huddy, the King; Rosco, Rui Gomez; Mrs Lacy, the Queen; Mrs Talbot, Henrietta. It, too, was followed by a ballad opera, *The Constant Lovers with the Comical Humours of Mons. Ragout,* in which Mrs Pritchard made her second and last appearance at the fair as Cloe. Oates played Ragout, and others participating were the two Stoppelaers (senior and junior), Salway, Wetherilt, Lacy, Mrs Martin, Miss Oates and Binks. Large moons and lanthorns illuminated the passage to the booth.

The legend of Fair Rosamond, which had been used by fair puppeteers as early as 1655,[1] was given as a droll, *The True and Ancient History of Fair Rosamond,* by Hippisley, Bullock and Hallam, with Hale as King Henry; Mrs Forrester, Queen Eleanor; Winstone, Cardinal Aquinas; Ridout, Cardinal Columbus; Mrs Elmy, Rosamond. Mrs Elmy, who had appeared as Mrs Morse in 1732, was later to be a well-known actress at Drury Lane who played some of Shakespeare's heroines with Garrick. The afterpiece was *The Imposter, or the Biter Bit,* another version of the vintner in the suds farce, the cast of which included Hippisley as Vizard the Biter, Hulett as Mixum the Vintner, with other parts by Bullock, Berry, Este, Mrs Hale and Master Hallam. During the last week of the fair, Hippisley revived the medley of the Drunken Man. Both pieces were illuminated with glass lustres after the manner of the *Ridotto al' Fresco.*

1736–1737

The duration of the fair in 1735 was restricted to three days and all acting prohibited. But in 1736 the theatrical booths were functioning again.[2] Fielding and Hippisley repeated *Don Carlos,* with *The Cheats of Scapin* in which Hippisley played Scapin. Pritchard and Mrs Charke were also in the company, and the band played Neapolitan music.

Hallam, this year in partnership with Chapman, also repeated *Fair Rosamond* but with an entirely new cast: King Henry, Boman; Aquinas, Wallis; Columbus, Bambridge; Eleanor, Mrs

---

[1] G. Speaight, *op. cit.* p. 330; *Daily Advertiser,* 21 August 1734.
[2] *London Daily Post,* 16 August 1736.

Mullart; Rosamond, Mrs Bambridge. It was followed by a new ballad opera, *The Modern Pimp; or The Doctor Deceiv'd. With the Comical Humours of Crack the Pimp, Dr Grey-Goose and Sir Nehemiah Nestle-Cock*, these comics being taken respectively by Chapman, Mullart and Smith. The dancers were Livier, Mlle DeLorme, Janno and Mrs Woodward, and tumblers entertained while the booth was filling.

At Hallam's booth in 1737, *All Alive and Merry*, an 'opera' by Samuel Johnson which had been brought out the previous January at Lincoln's Inn Fields, was presented, with a ballet, *Le Badinage Champêtre*, foreign tumblers and posture masters, and the *Italian Shadows*, 'by the best Masters from Italy', which had not been seen for twenty years.[1]

The only other show advertised was of Yeates senior and junior's puppets.

[1] Morley, *op. cit.* p. 331.

CHAPTER III

BARTHOLOMEW FAIR
THE DECLINE

THE enforcement of the limitation of the fair to three or four days after 1735 was followed by a second blow to theatrical entertainments in 1737. This was the passing of the Licensing Act which restricted spoken drama to the patent theatres. These two factors resulted in the gradual decline of the theatrical booths. After 1735 it was less worth while for companies of actors from the theatres to set up their booths for a short time; after 1737 dancers and singers rather than actors were required to fill the bills. Up till 1741 fair booths were confined to showing pantomimes and ballad operas as their main feature. It is, therefore, not surprising that the players from the patent theatres started to turn their attention to the provinces for work in the long vacation. A London company had first been seen in Canterbury as early as 1733 but generally terminated their stay by mid-August. London companies started to visit Bristol and Ipswich in 1741 and Birmingham in 1744. Their place at Smithfield was sometimes taken by players and entertainments from the various Wells theatres which started to function after 1737.

1738

The fair was held for four days from 28 to 31 August and only two theatrical booths were functioning.[1] Penkethman, over against the Hospital Gate, brought out a new entertainment, *The Man's Bewitch'd; Or, The Devil to do about Her*. This was a pantomime with Hays as Harlequin, Mrs Dove as Columbine, and several other dancers including MM. De La Grange, Le Brune, Bellgard and Mlles De La Grange and Le Brune. Penkethman's wife appeared in the piece with him and Bencraft. This was followed by a revival of *The Country Wedding*, last given by Hall and

---

[1] *London Daily Post*, 21 August 1738.

Oates in 1729, in which Ray was Clown; Board, the Roving Shepherd; and Mrs Hale, Joan. The dance of bridesmen and maids from the droll at Tottenham Court Fair concluded the entertainments. Hallam provided a novel attraction at his booth, the Lilliputian Company from Drury Lane in Carey's burlesque opera, *The Dragon of Wantley*, which had first been brought out at the Haymarket in 1737. It was followed by a ballet danced by the Lilliputians in the characters of Pierrot, Punch, Scaramouch and their wives. Among the children were Masters W. and J. Hamilton and Ferg, and Misses Cole and Edwards. M. Rapinière entertained with postures while the booth was filling.

1739

The booths increased to four in 1739, though the fair was still limited to four days.[1]

At William Hallam's booth was the pantomime, *Harlequin Turn'd Philosopher; or The Country Squire Outwitted*, with Hays and Mrs Dove as Harlequin and Columbine. The afterpiece was a ballad opera, *The Sailor's Wedding; or the Wapping Landlady*, with Dove, Nichols, Granier, Osbaldiston, Littleton and Mrs Coker. It concluded once again with a scene of Neptune's Palace with Tritons and Sea Nymphs.

Bullock from Covent Garden advertised the largest booth in the fair.[2] His pantomime was entitled *The Escapes of Harlequin by Sea and Land; Or Columbine Made Happy at Last* in which Mr and Mrs Waters were Harlequin and Columbine, and Bullock was Justice Ballance. Signor Balducci's mathematical statues were shown before this entertainment.

Hippisley, Chapman and Laguerre at the George Inn Yard presented *The Top of the Tree; Or, A Tit Bit for a Nice Palate* in which the famous dog scene from *Perseus and Andromeda* and the skeleton scene from *The Royal Chace or Merlin's Cave* were introduced. Harlequin was taken by Yates as Signor Yaterini, Columbine by Mrs Talbot, and Pierrot by Arthur as Signor Arthurini 'who has a most surprizing talent at Grimace and will in this Occasion introduce upwards of 50 Whimsical, Sorrowful,

---

[1] *Ibid.* 22 August 1739.   [2] *Ibid.* 23 August.

Comical and Diverting Faces'. Hippisley was the Clown; Hale, Laguerre and Chapman also took part.

The old firm of Lee and Harper was replaced by Lee and Phillips whose booth was at the corner of Hosier Lane.[1] Phillips, who became such a famous harlequin at Drury Lane that he was known as Harlequin Phillips, is not to be confused with the earlier Merry Andrew, William Phillips.[2] Chetwood says that he was a pupil of the conjuror Fawkes, whom he could surpass in many tricks.[3] He appears to have started his managerial career with Mrs Lee. Their entertainments were a medley consisting of a 'Grand Scene of Cupid and Psyche', a Scaramouch dance, the 'Drunken Peasant' by Phillips, and a dialogue between Punch and Columbine; the last three had been performed at Tottenham Court Fair just previously.[4] The dramatic pantomime was *Colombine Courtezan*, in which Phillips danced Harlequin; Mrs Phillips, Colombine; Hemskirk, the Spaniard; and Scot-borough was Clown. Both the scene and the pantomime were taken from *Cupid and Psyche; or, Colombine-Courtezan*, which had been given at Drury Lane and printed in 1734. The mixed character of the audience at the time is testified to by a poem on Bartholomew Fair in *Farrago or Miscellanies in Verse and Prose*:

> Each wooden house then groans to bear
> The populace that croud the Fair. . . .
> The chambermaid and Countess sit
> Alike admirers of the wit:
> The Earl and footman *tête-à-tête*
> Sit down contented in one Seat.
> The Musick plays, the Curtain draws
> The Peer and 'prentice clap applause.
> The house is fill'd with roaring laughter
> From lowest pit, to highest rafter.

1740

It is noteworthy that in 1740 royalty was still visiting the fair, though it was limited to four days. The Princesses Amelia,

---

[1] *London Daily Post*, 27 August 1739.
[2] E. R. Rimbault, 'Gleanings for the History of Bartholomew Fair', *Notes and Queries*, 2nd series (1859), vol. VIII, p. 162, has confused the two.
[3] *A General History of the Stage* (1749), p. 209.   [4] Below, p. 126.

Caroline and Louisa, attended by the Duke of Grafton, visited William Hallam's booth on 25 August.[1] They must have witnessed his new entertainment, *The Rambling Lovers, Or a New Way to play an Old Game. With the Comical Humours of Squire Softhead, and his Man Bullcalf, and the Whimsical Distresses of Mother Catterwawl*, in which Hays and Mrs Dove were again Harlequin and Columbine; Pelling was Softhead; Dove, his man, and Mrs Hill, Mother Catterwawl. There was tumbling by M. Janno, dancing, including a grand dance *The Amorous Contention, or The Politic Maid*, and the scene of Neptune's Palace. The whole company was from Goodman's Fields New Wells which Hallam had opened in 1739; and at the end of the fair he thanked his patrons and invited them to the Wells.[2]

Hippisley and Chapman presented *Harlequin Scapin, or the Old One Caught in a Sack. With the Comical Tricks, Cheats, and Shifts of Scapin's two Companions, Trim the Barber and Bounce-about the Bully*. Hippisley was the mercurial Scapin, Chapman and Arthur his companions; other parts being played by Paget, Marr, Yates, Cross, Mrs Haughton, and Mrs Talbot, whilst the singing and dancing were provided by Oates, Bencraft, Yates, Gray, Julian, Mrs Villeneuve and Mrs Phillips. The new musical entertainment which followed was Carey's *The Parting Lovers: or, The Press Gang* which had come out at Covent Garden the previous December.[3]

Yeates transferred from puppets to living actors in *The History of Orpheus and the Death of Eurydice*, to which was added a pantomime, *The Metamorphosis of Harlequin*. The cast was: Orpheus, Cartwright; Eurydice, Mrs Jinghall; Harlequin, Rosoman; Pantaloon, Price; Squire Gawky, Yeates; Clown, Warner; Columbine, Mrs Warner. Rosoman later achieved fame as the owner of Sadler's Wells, and Warner was one of its best-known clowns. Yeates announced that he had put himself to great expense 'in getting the Machinery made to the neatest perfection'. His performances lasted from 10 a.m. to 10 p.m.

---

[1] *Daily Post*, 26 August 1740; *London Daily Post*, 21 August 1740.
[2] *London Daily Post*, 28 August. For Goodman's Fields New Wells see article by C. B. Hogan, *Theatre Notebook* (1949), vol. III, p. 67.
[3] Cast in Morley, *op. cit.* p. 333.

1741

This year saw the revival of the drolls and the abandonment of the restriction to pantomime and musical pieces.[1] The booth proprietors evidently found that they could defy the Licensing Act with impunity. There were four theatrical booths this year which offered full programmes. Two new proprietors were Turbutt from Drury Lane and Richard Yates from Goodman's Fields who had already been at the fair in 1739, and who must be distinguished from the puppet master, Yeates. Their booth was opposite the King's Head and Greyhound Inns. They kept on the safe side by announcing a dramatical, pantomimical piece, *Thamas Kouli Kan, the Persian Hero; Or, the Distress'd Princess. Interspers'd with The Descent of Harlequin from the Sun and his Adventures on Earth.* The tragedy contained 'the Banishment of Kouli Kan; his Love for the Princess Karanza; the famous Battle on the Golden Bridge; his Imprisonment, Sentence, surprising Deliverance from the Funeral Pile; and lastly, his happy Nuptials with the Princess'. Thamas was played by Crofts; Albufazan, Emperor of Persia by Marten; and the Princess by Mrs Dunstall; others who took part were Harrington, Julian, Marr, Taylor, Miss Bennet and Master Nanfan. The comedy contained the whimsical exploits of M. Gasconnade and Corporal Bounce with the humours of Joculo, Taffy and Welshman, Bog the Irishman, and Forge; likewise the comical death and revival of Joseph Snip, the Taylor. This last sounds to have affinities with the ritual of the mummers' play. Yates was Harlequin; Turbutt, Joculo; Dunstall, Bounce; Blakes, Gasconnade; and Vaughan the drunken blacksmith, Forge; whilst Adams, Lowder, Mackenzie, Arthur and Mrs Yates also participated. Yates spoke a drunken epilogue in the character of an English sailor. The entertainment was well received, for we read in *The Daily Post* of 24 August: 'On Saturday last (notwithstanding the excessive Rain) a considerable Number of eminent Citizens adjourn'd in about twenty Coaches from the King's-Arms Tavern in Lombard-street to Turbutt and Yates's Booth in Bartholomew Fair, and were so well satisfied with the Performances of *Thamas Kouli Kan*, that

[1] *London Daily Post*, 19, 20 August 1741.

they engag'd to meet again this Afternoon at Five o'clock at the
Sun Tavern in St Paul's Church-Yard, and proceed in the same
Manner to see the Droll a second Time.'

William Hallam had only tumbling and rope dancing this
season but was visited by the Duke of Cumberland.[1] Adam
Hallam brought a company from Covent Garden which revived
Fair Rosamond, last seen in the fair in 1736. This time the cast
was entirely different. Mrs Mullart exchanged the role of
Eleanor for that of Rosamond; Eleanor was taken by Mrs Steel;
and King Henry by Roberts. It was followed by the same after-
piece as in 1736, *The Modern Pimp*, with James as Crack, and
Mullart and Smith in their original parts.[2] Dancing was pro-
vided by the French children Master and Miss Granier from
Goodman's Fields, and a dance entitled *The Triumph of Britannia
Over the Four Parts of the World* had as many as four men and
five women performers. Hippisley and Chapman gave a droll,
*The Devil of a Duke; Or the Conjuror's Bastard. With the Comical
Humours of Captain Tipple.* It was probably taken from Drury's
Devil of a Duke; or Trapolin's Vagaries in which Trapolin was
the supposed son of a conjuror. The Conjuror's Bastard was
played by Chapman and the Drunken Captain by Hippisley;
other parts by Winstone, Mr and Mrs Cross, Ware, Bambridge,
Richards, Spackman, Gray, Clough, Mrs Taylor, Mrs Powell,
Mrs Booth and the Misses Ferguson and Dodson. The droll was
printed for the author and sold in the booth.[3] Intermixed with
it was a grand ballet, *The Infernals*, and the entertainments
concluded with a new comic interlude, *The Matrimonial Squabble,
Or a Cure for Jealousy.* This proved popular, especially a Jockey
Dance to the tune of 'Horse to Newmarket' which was acclaimed
the best performance of its kind.[4]

Mrs Lee was in partnership with Woodward, their droll
being *Darius, King of Persia; Or, The Noble Englishman. With
the Comical Humours of Sir Andrew Ague-Cheek at the Siege of
Babylon.* Redman from Dublin was Darius; Taswell from Drury
Lane, Antipates; Stephens from Covent Garden, Anglicanus

---

[1] *Ibid.* 25 August 1741.   [2] Above, pp. 42–3.
[3] See Peter Murray Hill, Catalogue 55, no. 266.
[4] *London Daily Post*, 25 August 1741.

4   R T

(presumably the noble Englishman); Vaughan, Fearful; Mrs Purden, Eudocia; Mrs Egerton, Queen; Mrs Wright, Mrs Pert; and Woodward, Aguecheek. This may have been the great Henry Woodward who had been at Drury Lane since 1738 but, as there was another player named Woodward active at the time, it is not possible to be certain. The droll was followed by singing, and dancing by M. Nivelon, and finally by a new entertainment, *The Wrangling Deities; Or Venus upon Earth*, in which Miss Williams made her first appearance on any stage as Venus-Columbine; Woodward was Harlequin; and Warner, Vulcan.

1742

In 1742 Turbutt and Yates took over Hallam's booth opposite Hospital Gate with a mixed company from Drury Lane, Covent Garden and Goodman's Fields.[1] They showed *The True and Ancient History of the Loves of King Edward the 4th, and his Famous Concubine, Jane Shore* — 'containing the reign and death of King Edward — the distresses and death of Jane Shore in Shoreditch, the acquisition of the crown by King Richard the 3d (commonly call'd crook-back'd Richard) and many other true historical passages—interspers'd with the comical and diverting humours of Sir Anthony Lackbrains, his man Weazel, and Capt. Blunderbuss'. This was the old droll that had been at the fair in 1719, 1727 and 1733, except that Lackbrains had replaced Noodle. This role was taken by Yates, his man Weazel by Green, and Blunderbuss by Turbutt. The serious characters were cast: K. Edward, Dighton; K. Richard, Taswell; Jane Shore, Mrs Lamball; Shore, Taylor; Capt. Ayres, Naylor; Flora, Mrs Yates; other parts were played by Holtham, Ray and Spackman.

Hippisley and Chapman presented a 'droll' version of the *Cheats of Scapin* which they had given as *Harlequin Scapin* in 1740.[2] It was entitled *Scaramouch Scapin, or the Old Miser Caught in a Sack. With the Comical Tricks, Shifts and Cheats of Scapin's Three Companions.* Sly had been added as third companion to Trim and Bounce-about. Hippisley was once again Scapin; and Chapman, Trim; with Mullart as Bounce-about, Paget as Gripe

---

[1] Genest, *op. cit.* vol. x, p. 164.   [2] Above, p. 47.

the Miser, Gray as Solomon Smack, Mrs Vallois as Medlar, Mrs Mullart as Loveit[1] and Miss Thynne as Lucia.

At Fawkes and Pinchbeck's booth Punch's celebrated company of comical tragedians from the Haymarket[2] gave *The Tragedy of Tragedies...called The Humours of Covent Garden, or the Covent Garden Tragedy.*[3] This mixture of two of Fielding's burlesques included live actors, since Mrs Charke was Lovegirlo and Page, Mother Punch-bowl in the *Covent Garden Tragedy.* The charges were: boxes 2s., pit 1s., gallery 6d.

At Phillips and Yeates's booth there was a two-act comedy, *The Indian Merchant: Or, the Happy Pair, Interspers'd with the Comical Humours of the Intriguing Chambermaid, Sir John Oldcastle, and the Drunken Colonel.* Those who took part were the two proprietors, Dove, Wallis, Powell, Davis, Johnson, Evenel, Wood, Archer, Mrs Tucker, Mrs Habito, Miss Ferguson, Mrs Simmons and Mrs Phillips. In the new pantomime entertainment, *The Miser Bit; or Harlequin Reveller*, Phillips was the Harlequin; Dove, the Clown; and Mrs Dove, Columbine.

Lastly at Godwin's opposite The White Hart near Cow Lane a comedy of three acts was given entitled *The Intriguing Footman: Or, The Spaniard Outwitted*, followed by a pantomime.

1743

There were five theatrical booths in 1743.[4] Dove replaced Yates as Turbutt's partner. The recent battle of Dettingen inspired their droll, *The Glorious Queen of Hungary; Or, The British Troops Triumphant. With the Comical Humours of Paddy the Irishman, Tom Thimble the Taylor, Tom Guzzle the Cobler and Mrs Doublescore the Landlady.* Mrs Bambridge played the Queen, and in the company were also Woodward, Malone, Dove and Mrs Hill. A new pantomime followed entitled *Harlequin Dissaffected; or, the Biter Bit* in which M. de Broke danced

[1] This character and that of Sly were also in the ballad opera based on *The Cheats of Scapin*, above, p. 39.
[2] Fawkes had probably bought Mrs Charke's puppets which used to perform at the Tennis Court, James Street, Haymarket. G. Speaight, *op. cit.* p. 106.
[3] Guildhall Library, a collection of cuttings...in connection with the metropolitan fairs.
[4] *London Daily Post*, 23 August 1743; *Daily Advertiser*, 22 August 1743.

Harlequin and Mrs Dove was again the Columbine. An equilibrist from Paris entertained the company while it was assembling.

An abridgement of the *Comedy of Errors* was to be seen at
Fawkes and Pinchbeck's booth as *The Ephesian Duke; Or Blunder
upon Blunder, Yet, All's Right At Last*. The parts were advertised
as by the best actors, singers and dancers from the Theatres
Royal. They too cashed in on Dettingen with an exact representation of the battle, the bridge of boats, towns and batteries.

Yeates, Warner and Rosoman had a booth opposite the
Greyhound where they presented 'a Pompous Tragedy', *The
Cruel Uncle; Or Usurping Monarch*, in which was introduced
'An Heroic Scene of Fighting Battle upon Battle, to the End of
the Chapter. Interspers'd with several prime scenes of Wit and
Humour.' Here also appeared the Bath morris dancers. In the
pantomime, *Trick upon Trick*, Rosoman was Harlequin; Warner,
Clown; and Mrs Rosoman, Columbine. A song on the victory
was rendered by Johnson.

Hippisley and Chapman's droll in the George Inn Yard was
*The French Doctor Outwitted; Or, The Old One in Danger of being
Dissected. With the Comical Humours of Sly Boot the Sham Physician*
who was taken by Chapman. Hippisley, Blakes, Bencraft, Berry,
Morgan, Mrs Dodson, Mrs Lamball and Mrs Bland were also
in the company, and Bencraft sang a new ballad in the character
of the valiant dragoon who retook a standard at Dettingen.

At Godwin and Adams's booth opposite the Hospital Gate
a new droll was performed entitled *The Triumphant Queen of
Hungary: Or, The French Defeated* with Miss Clarke as the
Queen and Freeman as the King of France. A representation of
Dettingen was included. The farcical afterpiece was *The Wanton
Maid; or, The Lover Outwitted* which was succeeded by a dramatic
scene *The Tricks of Harlequin*. Thus the famous victory was
celebrated in all five booths.

1746

Interludes and plays were forbidden in 1744 and no booths were
erected. The result was 'that the Fair terminated in a more
peaceable Manner than it had done in the Memory of Man'.[1]

---

[1] *Gentleman's Magazine*, August 1744, p. 451.

By 1746 the booths reappeared. Warner and Fawkes this season joined forces at a booth at the corner of Smithfield Rounds which they claimed was the largest and most commodious in the fair and which was illuminated and ornamented with a variety of decorations.[1] Their piece was *The Happy Hero. Interspers'd with the Humorous Scenes of All Alive and Merry*. This was the year of Culloden so the musical entertainment was *Harlequin Incendiary, or Colombine Cameron* with Mr and Mrs Cushing as Harlequin and Colombine and Warner as the Clown. It concluded with a song in praise of the victorious Duke of Cumberland.

A similar entertainment was given at Lee and Yeates junior's booth entitled *Harlequin Invader; or Colombine Cameron*.[2] This followed *Love in a Labyrinth; Or, A School for a Wife*. Lee (or was it still Mrs Lee?) thus returned to the fair after an absence of four years. There was a good band and the booth was large and properly decorated. Hussey took over Hippisley and Chapman's site in the George Inn Yard. He was careful to evade the letter of the Licensing Act by advertising a concert in two parts between which an historical piece by Shakespeare was given. This was followed by *The Schemes of Harlequin; Or, Mons. Le Saxe's Disappointment* in which Rayner danced Harlequin; Mlle Boneway, Columbine; Davis was the Clown, and Bennet, Le Saxe. This evidently had reference to the Marshal Saxe's projected expedition to England in support of the Pretender. Here, too, there was a chorus in praise of the Duke of Cumberland, and also rope dancing by Miss Rayner. Hussey advertised that his booth had 'for several years been honour'd with the Company of several persons of distinction, on account of the performances exhibited there'. Hughes and Scouten record a performance of Thomas Sheridan's *The Brave Irishman* at the fair this year.[3]

[1] *General Advertiser*, 25 August 1746.   [2] *Ibid*. 26 August.
[3] *Ten English Farces* (1948), p. 222.

1747

Hussey was back in 1747[1] with *Tamerlane the Great; with the Fall of Bajazet, Emperor of the Turks. Interspersed with Humorous Scenes of A Wife Well Manag'd, Or, A Cure against Cuckoldom.*[2] There was slack-rope dancing by a Turk, Mahomet Achmed Vizaro Mussulmo. Warner this year joined Lee and Yeates with a revival of *The Siege of Troy* for which the clothes, scenes, machinery and decorations were new 'and finish'd according to the Taste of the Antient Greeks'.

A third booth opposite the Greyhound Inn was owned by Chettle, who gave Garrick's *Miss in her Teens* followed by a new pantomime, *The Frolicksome Lasses; or Harlequin Fortune-Teller*, with Chettle as Harlequin, Miss Moreau as Columbine, and Smith as the Clown, Clodpole. The entertainments ended with a grand piece of Italian fireworks, as at the Opera House.

1748

The year saw a fresh combination in the George Inn Yard, to wit Bridges, Cross, Burton and Vaughan.[3] They gave a new droll founded on events in 1709 entitled *The Northern Heroes;* 'Or, the Bloody Contest between *Charles* the Twelfth, King of *Sweden*, and Peter the Great, Czar of *Muscovy*. With the loves of Count Gillensternia a Swedish General, and the Fair Elimira a Russian Princess. Containing the most remarkable Events of that Time; and concluding with the memorable Battle of Pultowa, and Charles's Retreat into the Turkish Dominions. Interspers'd with a comic interlude (never perform'd before) The Volunteers: Or, the Adventures of Roderick Random and his Friend Strap. Also the Comical Humours and Amours of Corporal Garbage and Serjeant Slim with Mrs Vanspriggen the Swedish Sutler's Widow; the merry Pranks of her foolish son Jonny', etc. Usher was Charles XII; Mrs Cross, Elimira; Cross, Roderick Random; Bridges, Garbage; Storer, Slim; Vaughan, Jonny; and Mrs Bridges, the widow Vanspriggen. Smollett's *Roderick Ran-*

[1] *General Advertiser*, 21 August 1747.
[2] Cf. Tottenham Court Fair, 1732, below, p. 124.
[3] *General Advertiser*, 20 August 1748.

dom had been published that year and had immediately been seized upon to provide the comic interlude.

Richard Yates, who had graduated to Drury Lane, had a booth facing the Hospital Gate and produced a droll inspired by Hogarth called *The Consequence of Industry and Idleness: or The Apprentice's Guide. And the Humours of the Irish Haymaker, Welsh Thief and Scotch Boatswain.* This was an early instance of Hogarth's influence on the drama, which was to become more widespread in the early nineteenth century. Yates himself was Patrick Macmurder; and Peterson, the apprentice Francis Goodchild; others who participated were Costollo, Lowder, Mills, Taswell, Dogget, Miss Jones, Mrs Graham and Miss Hippisley. Lee and Yeates senior and junior revived the old droll *The Unnatural Parents*, which was announced as the same performed by Mrs Lee fifteen years previously, though no record of its appearance is known after 1727.[1] Mrs Daniel was the Fair Maid, and Warner the servant Trusty. Others in the cast were Brassey, Mackarnea, George, Allen, Phoenix, Sturgess, Mrs Ingall, Mrs Field and Mrs Hickson. Hussey, who had a booth facing the Hospital Gate, brought out a new droll, *The Constant Quaker, or the Humours of Wapping*, and a pantomime, *Harlequin's Frolics or the Rambles of Covent Garden*, concluding with fireworks in honour of the approaching peace.

1749

This year was one of the most active for theatrical booths, there being no less than six, though the fair was still limited to four days.[2] Never again was there to be so large a number. Lee, Yeates and Warner revived *Whittington* in the same manner as Mrs Lee fifteen years previously, though there is no record of it at Bartholomew Fair after 1708. The scenery, clothes and decorations were new.

Another Yeates (one must have been the senior and the other the junior) was opposite the George Inn with *The Blind Beggar of Bethnal Green* and *The Amours of Harlequin; or The Bottle*

---

[1] *Jephtha's Rash Vow* was played at Lee and Harper's in 1733.
[2] *General Advertiser*, 19, 21 August 1749.

Conjuror Out-done. With the Escape of Harlequin into a Quart-Bottle. Phillips was opposite Cow Lane with a droll taken from Shakespeare entitled *The Tempest; or, The Inchanted Island* with Prospero, Bruodin; Duke, Platt; Anthonio, Reynolds; Ferdinand, Walker; Gonsalo, Hall; Ventoso, Smith; Stephano, Massey; Mustachio, Green; Monster Caliban, Machen; Sycorax, Mrs Miller; and Dorinda, Mrs Phillips from Covent Garden. The pantomime was *The Harlot's Progress with the Escape of Harlequin into a Quart-Bottle* and the additional scene of 'Sig. Jumpedo's Jumping Down his Own Throat'. Phillips and his wife were Harlequin and Columbine. The notorious bottle conjuror hoax had been perpetrated at the Haymarket this year and had been seized on as material for these two fair pantomimes. Phillips also engaged an English slack-rope walker and equilibrist who performed all the balances done before by the Turk 'to convince the World, that our Nation need have no Recourse to Foreigners for their Public Diversion'.

The Life and Death of King John, given by Cushing from Covent Garden at a booth facing the King's Head was the second Shakespearian droll this season. The synopsis[1] covers the Hubert–Arthur episode and the death of the king 'who is poisoned in the Midst of all his Glory, and in terrible Anguish and Distraction, pays his Nephew's Blood with the Price of his own'. It was interspersed with 'The Adventures of Sir Lubberly Lackbrains and His Man Blunderbuss'[2] which included their drolleries on a journey from Cumberland and exploits in London. The cast was: King John, Redman; Hubert, Simpson; Bastard, Pinner; Chatillion, Walker; Pembroke, Johnson; Pandulph, White; Lady Constance, Mrs Cushing; Prince Arthur, Miss Yates from Drury Lane. Cushing was Sir Lubberly Lackbrains.

Yates was at the George Inn where he brought out a new droll *The Descent of the Heathen Gods, With the Loves of Jupiter and Alcmena; or Cuckoldom No Scandal.* The usual comical scenes are quoted at length by Morley.[3] Jupiter was played by Oates; Yates took the part of a Hungarian footman and Miss Hippisley that of a wanton chambermaid. There were French and English

---

[1] Quoted in part by Morley, *op. cit.* p. 338.
[2] Cf. above, p. 50.   [3] *Op. cit.* p. 337.

dancers. Transparencies as well as the usual machines and flyings were advertised.

Cross and Bridges's booth was opposite the Hospital Gate and their new droll was *The Fair Lunatick; Or, The Generous Sailor*, which was founded on a story from real life as related in the *Memoirs* of Mrs Constantia Phillips. Into it was introduced a new scene of Bedlam called *Modern Madness; Or, A Touch at the Times* and it was also interspersed with an interlude, *The Jovial Jack Tars; Or, All Well Match'd*. 'With the Comical Humours of Nurse Prate and Will Bowling, the Jovial Tar; as also of Jack Handspike, Nick Hatchway and Simon Bucket, Sailors; with Mary the Chambermaid, Susan of the Dairy, Kate of the Kitchen, and Nan the Spinner.' The whole concluded with a Grand Scene of the Jubilee Ball. Hughes and Scouten mention a performance of *Trick upon Trick* which may have been the pantomime of 1743 revived or Yarrow's farce on the vintner outwitted theme.[1]

The anecdote of Garrick's visit to the fair may belong to this year, since it is said to have occurred shortly after his marriage in June. J. T. Smith was told it by Thomas Batrich, a Drury Lane barber.[2] Garrick conducted his wife to a booth, stated to have been Yates and Shuter's, though this combination is not recorded before 1757. Being rudely jostled, the actor called on his bill-sticker, old Palmer, who was taking money at the entrance, for protection. But Palmer regretted he could not help him as few Smithfield patrons knew Garrick off the stage.

On 23 August a gallery at Phillips's booth collapsed with a number of occupants, of whom two were killed and many others injured.[3] The accident may have caused the prohibition of show booths in 1750.[4] This marked a turning point, and henceforth companies from the theatres rarely appeared at the fairs. For the next four years medleys and olios replaced drolls.

[1] *Op. cit.* p. 205.   [2] *Antient Topography of London* (1815), p. 60.
[3] *An Historical Account of Bartholomew Fair* [1810], p. 24; *General Advertiser*, 24 August, says several people were hurt, some dangerously.
[4] Above, p. 3.

1751–1754

Yeates was reduced to conjuring, wire dancing and his machine 'The Temple of Apollo' at the King's Head in 1751,[1] and the following year he reverted to the old puppet show, *The Creation of the World*, by the 'Richest and largest Figures ever seen in England'.[2] His new machine represented the royal family and contained scenes, transparencies and decorations finished after the Italian manner; it was so large that a special place had to be fitted up for it.

The change of calendar affected the date of the fair, which from 1753 onwards was proclaimed on 3 September.[3]

'Mrs Midnight' from the Haymarket made her first appearance at the fair in a room at the bottom of Swan Inn Yard in 1753 with her 'Jubilee Concert, after the Venetian Manner'.[4] To this was added, gratis, *La Je Ne Sca Quoi, or, Wooden Spoons à la Mode* in which a new ballet was introduced entitled 'La Broomstickado', 'Likewise Variety of Trumpeters, Dancers, Fidlers, Pipers, and Merry Andrews, collected from all Parts of the World, at a great Expense...The Whole to conclude with a Dance in the British Taste, called, Lady Pentweazle's Vagaries'. She entreated 'the Nobility and Gentry not to encore any of her Performers on account of the Shortness of the Fair'. A back door in Hosier Lane led to the room which was illuminated with wax lights, and a flag was hoisted over the passage to show the way. Charges were 3s., 2s. and 1s. 'Mrs Midnight', originally the pseudonym chosen by Christopher Smart for his journal *The Midwife*, had been on the stage in a medley entertainment since 1751. It is uncertain what Smart's connection with the company was.[5]

At the lower booth in the George Inn Yard *The Distressed Sailor, or, The Merry Humours of the Ladies of Pleasure* was presented with wire dancing.[6]

---

[1] *General Advertiser*, 23 August 1751.   [2] *Ibid.* 24 August 1752.
[3] *Public Advertiser*, 3 September 1753.
[4] *Daily Advertiser*, 3, 5, 6 September; references supplied by Professor A. H. Scouten.
[5] See B. Bolting, 'Christopher Smart in London', *Research Studies of the State College of Washington* (March 1939), pp. 24 ff.
[6] *Daily Advertiser*, 3, 4, 5 September 1753.

'Mrs Midnight' returned to the Swan Inn Yard in 1754 but reduced her prices to pit 2s., first gallery 1s., upper gallery 6d. She advertised a concert with a free performance of *Gli Amanti Gelosi; or the Birth of Harlequin* by a company of Lilliputians from the Haymarket.[1] The entertainments concluded with *The Triumph of Love in the Temple of Apollo*.

1755–1758

It was not until 1755 that drolls were revived at Smithfield.[2] Yeates was dead but his widow carried on at the Swan Inn to support her family of small children. She showed a comic droll, *The Virgin's Wish. With the Humours of Squire Spoilal and Peter Shackle*, and a new pantomime, *The Inchanted Island, or Harlequin Fortune-teller*.

In Bence's room in the Swan Yard, 'Mrs Midnight' played Lady Laycock in *The Happy Gallant; or, The Modern Wife*, a droll taken from Betterton's *Amorous Widow*, with Sir Barnaby Brittle, Allen; Sir Anthony Laycock, Harper; Clodpole, Moore; Mrs Brittle, Mrs Harper; Damaris, Mrs Fell. The new pantomime was *The Fairy, or Harlequin in the Shades* with the Walkers as Harlequin and Columbine.

In 1756 Hallam's company presented at the Swan Inn *Adventures of Half an Hour* with Roebuck, Harman, Walters, Jones, Pack, Platt, Frisby, Mrs Harman, Miss Jones, Mrs Frimble.[3]

Mrs Charke and the King's Company of Comedians were at the Great Room, George Inn Yard where they put on a new droll *England Triumphant, or, The British General* to which was added *The Merry Beggars, with the Comical Humours of the Royal Consort Queen Tatter*, with singing, dancing, rope dancing and tumbling by performers recently come from Italy.

Ned Shuter, from Covent Garden, is first definitely recorded at Smithfield in partnership with Yates of Drury Lane in 1757.

[1] *General Advertiser*, 31 August 1754. Cocchi's comic opera of that name had appeared at Covent Garden, December 1753.

[2] *Public Advertiser*, 2 September 1755.

[3] *Daily Advertiser*, 3–6 September 1756. Information kindly supplied by Professor A. H. Scouten from files in the Folger Shakespeare Library.

They hired a newly erected Great Concert Hall in the Grey-hound Inn and gave a variety of unspecified entertainments there.[1] They returned in 1758 with the *Woman Turn'd Bully; or the Lover's Triumph with the Comical Humours of Squire Noodle and his Man Doodle*.[2] This was followed by a representation of the capture of Louisburg and Cape Breton by Admiral Boscawen and General Amherst which 'was allowed by all Judges a nice Representation, and what made the Entertainment more agree-able was that you may go to it by a large Passage into Cow lane, without the least Crowd or Interruption'; a guard was even provided to keep the passage clear. Thomas Weston was engaged at Shuter and Yates's booth, probably this year: 'Here he paraded, that is, shew'd himself between every performance to the mob in his stage dress, in a gallery erected before the booth and played nine times a day for a guinea.'[3] This may be com-pared with the sum of 15s. to £1 a day mentioned by Ned Ward in 1699. Evidently by mid-century actors at the fair were salaried and no longer on shares. It was extremely good pay, since even in the superior provincial companies an actor could not expect to make more than 25s. a week. No wonder that Weston, who had been receiving only 5s. a week on shares, was set up financially by his Smithfield engagement.

Dunstall, Vaughan and Warner had a booth in the George Inn Yard where a company from the Theatres Royal acted *The Old Widow Bewitch'd; or the Devil to do about Her. With the Droll Humours of Captain Fluellin, Capt. Culverin, Loadham, Pinchgut, Meagre, Capt. Bellair, Old Widow Rich, Belinda and Jenny*.[4] A representation of 'The Joyous Return of the Brave British Tars from the Conquest of Cape Breton' was also shown.

---

[1] *Public Advertiser*, 30 August, 3 September 1757.

[2] *Ibid*. 4, 5 August 1758.

[3] *Memoirs of that Celebrated Comedian...Thomas Weston* (1776), p. 21.

[4] Cf. *The Man's Bewitch'd; or the Devil to do about Her* given by Penkethman in 1738. The 'humours' are from Charles Molloy's *The Half-Pay Officers* (L.I.F., 1720).

1759–1760

In 1759 Shuter had a new booth at the George Inn Yard,[1] where he presented *The French Flogg'd; or the English Sailors in America*, a piece on the same theme as the old droll of *The Tempest*.[2] The conservatism of the fair is well illustrated by the revival of this droll after forty years.

Shuter specialised in comic advertisements. He announced that 'On the Grand Parade, immediately after the Fair is proclaimed the bold Shuter will review his Troop; and the Public are earnestly requested critically and optically to observe, that the full Figure, which will appear in the Middle of the Platform, is the Chief of the Cherokeese, Shawanese, Tyconderageese, Catabawa and Catawawa or Sachem of the Five Nations. He will be attended with Mamamawks, Papapawks, and Tomahawks.' The way to beat the French was to outweigh them: 'Therefore while they fret themselves, till they fall away in Flesh, let us laugh and be fat. The Particulars how are to be seen this Day in the George-Inn-Yard, There the Lords may laugh, and the Ladies may laugh, and the Commons may laugh, and that will make me laugh. Edward Shuter.'

Yates had his own booth in the Greyhound Inn Concert Hall where his offering was much of a piece with Shuter's. It was entitled *The Ship-Wreck'd Lovers; or, French Perfidy Punished*, 'Interspersed with the comical and diverting Humours and Adventures of Lieutenant Fireball, a true English Tar; Noddy Nestlecock, a distress'd Beau; Snivel Thimble, a Taylor; Split-farthing, an old Usurer; and Glisterpipe, a Finical Surgeon.'[3] It is noticeable that the low comic characters had increased in number from two or three to five. Both booths opened at midday.

The next year, 1760, Yates took a leaf out of Shuter's book and issued a comic, and culinary, advertisement.[4] He would, he announced, 'dress his Dramatic Turtle for the Entertainment of the Town. This most exquisite Dish will comprize the Essence of

[1] *Public Advertiser*, 3 September 1759.
[2] Above, p. 16; for description see below, p. 142.
[3] For description of droll see below, p. 143. *Public Advertiser*, 3 September 1759.
[4] *Public Advertiser*, 1, 2, 5 September 1760.

every Theatrical Rarity, In the Calipash will be found the most extraordinary Adventures of Timur Coran; or, The Favourite of the Sun. In the Calipee will be the Eighth Wonder of the World; or, The Heroic Taylors. With the Humours of General Trinculo and his pleasant Companion Humpkinn Buzz, The Blew Fat and Finns—the whole to be seasoned by Way of Chian Butter, With a most extraordinary Band of Music.' To this feast one entered the boxes and pit by a way next to the sheep pens. Timur Koran was but another name for the droll *Thamas Kouli Kan*; the adventures were the same and included the procession of the Princess Karanza and Timur to the funeral pile and their strange deliverance from death by the spirit Seraphel. Yates continued his culinary metaphor by stating that his friends were pleased with the feast and that the table was crowded. On 5 September he announced that he had received a fresh cargo from the Indies which would be available at his theatrical ordinary for the next two days.

Shuter went floral and advertised his *English Mirror* 'ornamented with a Festoon of Flowers, gathered by an admired Genius on the Banks of the Avon' together with a 'new Exhilaration of Mirth'.[1]

1761–1762

In 1761 Shuter's announcement took a medical turn: 'For the certain Cure of the Spleen, Essence of Comicality, prepared by the Directions of Dr Shuter in the "Warehouse" in George Inn Yard, as lately performed in Ireland.' Among the pieces was Wignell's masque *The Triumph of Hymen*,[2] written in honour of George III's forthcoming marriage with Princess Charlotte of Mecklenburg and showing the landing of the Queen.

The marriage was also reflected in the title of Yates's droll at the Greyhound Inn: *The Fair Bride: or, The Unexpected Event. With the British Tar's Triumph over Mons. Soup-Maigre*: 'Containing many surprising Occurrences at Sea, which could not possibly happen at Land. The Performance will be highly en-

---

[1] Bartholomew Fair is not actually mentioned, but as the advertisement appeared on 2 September it undoubtedly refers to performances there.

[2] Wignell, *Poems* (1762). I have not traced a copy of this, but see Morley, *op. cit.* p. 351.

livened with several entertaining Scenes between England, France, Ireland, and Scotland, in the diverting Personages of Ben Bowling, an English Sailor; Mons. Soup-Maigre, a French Captain; O'Flannaghan, an Irish Officer; M'Pherson, a Scotch Officer. Through which the manners of each Nation will be characteristically and humorously depicted. In which will be introduced as singular and curious a Procession as was ever exhibited in this Nation. The Objects that compose the Pageantry are both Exotic and British. The principal Figure is the Glory and Delight of Old England, and Envy of our Enemies.'[1] To this was added a loyal song on the king's approaching marriage. Three days later Yates announced that he had engaged a 'Theatrical Phaenomenon or Lilliputian Squintum',[2] a child of four who spoke the epilogue to Foote's *Minor* 'with such amazing Excellency as to *baffle* all Description'. Churchill in his *Rosciad* this year referred to the rival comedians in the following couplets:

> S[hute]r keeps open house at Southwark Fair
> And hopes the friends of humour will be there.
> In Smithfield Y[ate]s prepares the rival treat,
> For those who laughter love instead of meat.

Shuter and Yates were said, twenty-one years later, to have 'made more money in ten days, than their engagements came to at the Theatres Royal (exclusive of their benefits for the winter season)'.[3]

The attempt of the City Council in 1760–1 to suppress the fair, along with that of Southwark, failed, but Sir Samuel Fluyder, when he was Lord Mayor in 1762, again prohibited plays. The City Marshal and his officers obliged several players who were preparing booths in the inns to take down their show cloths and decamp.[4] It is related that 'the populace enraged at this circumstance, broke the windows of almost every inhabitant of Smithfield',[5] thus bearing witness to the popularity of the

---

[1] *Public Advertiser*, 2 September 1761.   [2] A character in *The Minor*.
[3] *Morning Chronicle*, 7 September 1782.
[4] Undated newspaper clipping; Harvard Theatre Collection, for which I am indebted to Professor A. H. Scouten.
[5] *An Historical Account of Bartholomew Fair* [1810]; *Annual Register* (1762), p. [90].

theatrical entertainments. As a result of these riots, the Lord
Mayor had the fair stopped.[1]

After that no further advertisements appeared in the newspapers and one has to rely on news paragraphs.

1774–1782

A large undated playbill in the Harvard Theatre Collection
announces Mrs Baker[2] and her Sadler's Wells company at the
Greyhound Yard Theatre.[3] The pieces were C. Dibdin's ballad
opera, *The Waterman, or the First of August*, with Rugg as the
Waterman, Connell as Bundle, Lewy Owen as Robin, Miss
Heydon as Mrs Bundle, and Miss Wakelin as Wilhelmina;
followed by *Harlequin's Whim or, The Merry Medley* with
Douglas as Harlequin, Rugg as the Lover, Owen as Clown and
Mrs Baker herself as Columbine. Mrs Baker took precautions
to evade the Licensing Act by announcing a concert between the
parts of which would be given 'a medley Entertainment; consisting of a usual Diversion of Sadler's Wells, a new Ballad
Opera, as it was performed 24 Nights[4] with Universal Applause
at the Theatres Royal in the Haymarket last season'. If this, as
seems likely, refers to *The Waterman* which was brought out in
July 1774, the bill must date from 1775, in which case it records
the earliest appearance of Mrs Baker at the fair. The performance
started at 12 o'clock and the prices were: pit 1s., gallery 6d.

An undated clipping in the Harvard Theatre Collection
announces that 'Mr Wacklin's Company of flesh and blood
substitutes, for the staple wood and wire comedians of Smithfield, struck with martial ardour gave out that they should
perform the Camp, and add Neck or Nothing for the farce'.[5]
This may have been a relative of Mrs Wakelin or Wakelyn, the
mother of Mrs Baker, who attended Stourbridge Fair up to
1776.[6] Harvard dates the clipping 1779, the year after *The Camp*
had been brought out at Drury Lane. The same cutting mentions

---

[1] Undated clipping, Harvard Theatre Collection. From Professor A. H. Scouten.
[2] For Mrs Baker see Norma Hodgson, 'Sarah Baker', *Studies in English Theatre
History* (Society for Theatre Research, 1952), pp. 65–83.
[3] Information from Professor Scouten.   [4] Genest, *op. cit.* records only thirteen.
[5] Information from Professor Scouten.
[6] *Studies in English Theatre History*, pp. 29–33.

Flockton's puppets in *Julius Caesar* and Jobson's Grand Medley. Evidently, at this time, puppets pretty well held the field. Flockton and Jobson attended Smithfield regularly for several years and, in addition, George Yates brought Italian fantoccini, 1779–80.

According to Chambers,[1] the last royal visit to the fair took place in 1778 when the Duke and Duchess of Gloucester rode through it.

At the fair of 1780, Mrs Baker brought her company to the Greyhound Theatre, where they appeared in *The Quaker*, followed by a pantomime, *Harlequin Wanderer; or, the Great Turk Outwitted*. In the cast were Miss Wakelyn as Columbine, Lewy Owen as Clown and Miss S. Baker as a maid.[2]

She returned from Rochester to Smithfield in 1782,[3] when she presented *The Lover's Mistake* and *Harlequin's Frolic*. The same year the Norwich Company of Comedians took a commodious room at the Paper Manufactory between Hosier Lane and Pye Corner, where they showed two otherwise unknown pieces: *Amorous Parley or The Lady's Conquest* and a pantomime, *Everything in Season, or Harlequin at Ease*. In a third room, at the Swan Inn, *The Old Bachelor* was given, with a view of Coxheath Camp.

The fair had lost its middle-class patrons and was now purely devoted to the entertainment of the populace and the diversions of children.[4] After Mrs Baker 'no comedian of respectability attended the Fair'.[5] Her company, 'which was always reckoned the best',[6] was missed at the fair in 1785. A few itinerant companies may have continued to come but the satirical descriptions of the fair in the newspapers give little information. Thus, in 1783, we hear that there were 'several new adventurers in the line of *low* comedy; two companies of comedians who asserted that they were really alive'.[7] But it was the puppet showmen, Jobson and Flockton, who were the main attractions until 1789.

---

[1] *The Book of Days* (1888), vol. I, p. 266.
[2] Guildhall Library, a collection of handbills relating to Bartholomew Fair, Granger 2. 1. 7, cutting dated 2 September 1780.
[3] *Morning Chronicle*, 5 September 1782.   [4] *Ibid.*
[5] *History and Origin of Bartholomew Fair* (1808).
[6] *Morning Chronicle*, 5 September 1785.
[7] *London Chronicle*, 2–4 September 1783.

1789–1793

In 1789, at a theatre at the first gateway from Hosier Lane, the musical interlude, *The Recruiting Serjeant*, was presented with Griffen, Roberts, Jones, Walton, Mrs Bolton and Mrs Slater.[1] It was followed by a pantomime *The Enchanted Urn, or, Harlequin's Release* with Roberts as Harlequin, Robinson as Pantaloon, Walton as Clown and Mrs Slater as Columbine. One of the attractions of the pantomime was a stone eater. There was a daily change of programme, and the announcement stated that expense had not been spared in fitting the place up, in engaging an able company, and in rendering the entertainments respectable. The following year, 1790, the old puppeteer Flockton was giving a live performance in his booth in the George Yard.[2] The farce of *Miss in her Teens; or, The Medley of Lovers* was performed by Hicken, Jones, Potter, Nevit, Scowton and Mrs and Miss Flint, followed by tumblers from the Royal Circus, a Prussian strong man and his children's ballet. At Yates and Shuter's old booth up the Greyhound Yard, 'the only real and commodious Place for Theatrical Performances', a new piece, *The Spaniard well Drub'd, or The British Tar Victorious*, was performed by a company collected from theatres in England, Scotland and Ireland. It concluded with a grand procession of the French court and soldiers to the Champ de Mars, to swear to the Revolutionary Laws, a piece of highly topical interest.[3] Other entertainments were singing, dancing, recitations, and 'warbling' by a Mrs Billington from Norwich.

The Pie Powder Court Book in the Guildhall Library[4] for 1790 and ensuing years of the century provides us with the names of the various entertainments of the decade. The charges for licences to play are entered as:

	s.	d.
For every Shew under the Master of the Revels 3s. 4d.		
Whereof the Judges have 2s. and the Clerk of the Papers 1s. 4d.	3	4
If under the Great Seal 6s. 8d. whereof the Judges have 4s. and the Clerk of the Papers the Rest	6	8
If a Foreigner he is to pay double for his Licence	6	8

[1] Guildhall, Granger, 2. 1. 7, clipping dated 3 September 1789.
[2] *Ibid.* clipping dated 4 September 1790.   [3] Below, p. 144.
[4] Smithfield Court Book, MS. 95.

The actual payments added 8*d*. and 1*s*. 4*d*. respectively to the amounts given above. On 4 September 1790 the following were made:

s.	*d.*		
8	0	Jobson and Hart	Drollery
8	0	Flockton	Medley
8	0	Jobson	Puppets
4	0	Clark	Pantomime
8	0	Jonas	Puppets

On the 6th, 'A very fine day', the following were added:

8	0	Masena	Puppets
8	0	Morella [*sic*]	Puppets
8	0	Bannister	Medley
8	0	Charles Morella [*sic*]	Puppets
8	0	Blackmore	Puppets
8	0	White	Puppets
8	0	Bannister	Puppets
4	0	Aldridge	Medley

The list gives thirteen entertainments, of which eight were puppet shows. 'Not all the wars, nor rumours of war . . . thinned the ranks of shew men' nor interfered with the attendance of the old regulars.[1] In 1791 puppets were shown by Jonas, Jobson, Blower, Morello, Wilson; exhibitions by Flockton, Johnson, Perknelly and Brown, whilst Jonas also appeared as a comedian and Lawrence had a pantomime. In 1792 there were ten puppet shows by Powell, Wells, Morello, Appleby, Wilson, Logee, Portinary, Jonas, Davidge and Jobson, a medley by Flockton and a pantomime by Simes. Jonas reappeared as a comedian in 1793; puppets were provided by Jobson, Wilson, Blower and Samuel, an unspecified show by Flockton, an entertainment entered as 'Tipoo' by Scowton and 'The Siege of Valenciennes' by Abraham as well as conjuring, wire and rope dancing.

In this year Pennant remarked of Smithfield that 'theatrical performances by the better actors were exhibited here, and it was frequented by a great deal of good company; but, becoming

---

[1] *London Chronicle*, 2–4 September 1790.

the resort of the debauched of all denominations, certain regula-
tions took place, which in later days have spoiled the mirth, but
produced the desired decency'.[1]

1794–1800

In 1794 Flockton was dead but his daughter, Mrs Sturmer, had
a company at the fair at a New Theatre in Swan Yard.[2] They
performed Cross's *The Purse*, a musical drama which had been
brought out at the Haymarket in February. Her husband and two
children were in the cast. *The Life and Death of Harlequin*
followed, with Humphries as Harlequin, Miss Fowler as Columbine, Bowman as Pantaloon and Johnson as Clown. There were
only two prices, pit 1*s.* and gallery 6*d.*, and children were
admitted at half price. Sturmer is listed as a puppet showman in
the Pie Powder Court Book this year. The widow Flint and the
conjuror Gyngell had taken over Flockton's puppets and his
booth in the Greyhound Yard. Jonas's company was at the
George Inn Yard. They presented Oulton's *All in Good Humour*
and a pantomime *The Whim, or Harlequin's Last Shift* with
Penley as Harlequin and Mrs W. Penley as Columbine. Penley
was for many years to come in partnership with Jonas in a
travelling company which toured Windsor, Henley, Folkestone,
and even crossed to Boulogne.

Other shows entered in the Pie Powder Court Book in 1794
were puppets by White, Morello, Diswell, Southby, Jobson,
a Medley by Samuel, and exhibitions by Johnson. In 1795 Jonas,
Ives and Wilson are listed as comedians; Sturmer, Flint,
Morello as puppeteers; Subbeys had a medley and Devonshire,
a transparency. These categories may not be altogether reliable
since in 1796 Flint and Gyngell, who, as we have seen, inherited
Flockton's puppets, are listed as comedians along with Jonas. It
is, of course, possible that, like Flockton, they had transferred
to a live show. Puppets were shown this year by Humphreys,
Bernal, Morello, Wilson, Howis and Seward. In 1797 Jonas
and Flint were again entered as comedians; Howis had a puppet

---

[1] *Some Account of London* (1793), p. 194.
[2] Granger 2. 1. 7, clipping dated 4 September 1794.

show, Scowton a theatre, and Wild a transparency. In 1798 the comedians were Jonas, Flint, Richardson and Morrell, the puppet shows Morello and Noland. This was the famous Richardson's first visit to the fair. The exhibitions, he says, were usually up inn yards or the upstairs of public houses and he mentions as examples 'Old Jobson, the great puppet-show man in one yard; Jones [sic] and Penley in the George Yard; the celebrated Mrs Baker had the Greyhound, in a room up one pair of stairs; O'Brian, the Irish Giant, in the King's Head'.[1] He described his own show. The scenery was painted by Tom Greenwood (probably the son, as the father died in 1798) and Thomas Banks, both of whom worked at Drury Lane. A dressmaker named Davis was employed 'to decorate' the company and among the actors were the two Southbys, who became celebrated clowns; Thwaites who played 'the first line of business'; Vaughan; Miss Sims, a pretty singer from Astley's; Mrs Hicks, and an old woman, Mrs Monk, well known in the theatrical world. Richardson continues: 'My band I selected out of the streets, which consisted of three blind Scotchmen, but noted as clarionet players. I had a great run of business; in fact, we were compelled to perform twenty-one times in a day, so numerous were the visitors. I cannot say much in favour of the pieces, as each audience did not fail to abuse us as they left the house; poor old Mrs Monk generally got upon the garret stairs to cool herself, and, as the spectators had to pass her in going out, she was generally saluted with many "damns!" and "you old bitch, you have taken us in!" Mrs Monk was a good-natured creature, and her only reply was, "What can you expect, gentlemen, at a fair?" Upon the whole, our performances passed off tolerably quiet.'

Richardson is not listed in the Pie Powder Court Book for 1799, but for the rest of the fair's career his show was the 'grand magnet of attraction'.[2] Brown had a theatre this year, but Jonas is listed as a puppeteer along with Catchpole, Flint, Holinds, Jones, Scowton, Hall and Samuel.

The eighteenth century had seen the development of the fair

[1] Pierce Egan, *Life of an Actor* (1892), p. 195.
[2] *A Peep at Bartholomew Fair* [1837].

entertainments from puppet shows and political drolls given by strollers to performances of more elaborate drolls, ballad operas and pantomimes presented by some of the leading comedians of the day, whose earnings there far outstripped their salaries at the theatres. The itinerant booth holders still held their place side by side with these. Mrs Mynns, the Lees, Yeates, Fawkes, Pinchbeck and others had no connection with the London theatres. We have seen that after 1735 the limitation of the fair to three or four days was at last enforced, and play booths were frequently forbidden. Gradually the companies from the theatres ceased to visit it. With the change of calendar in 1752 and the consequent advancement of the fair to the beginning of September the date came too near the opening of the patent houses. A few regular comedians such as Shuter, Yates, Dunstall and Vaughan lingered on to share the declining dramatic entertainments with Mrs Yeates and 'Mrs Midnight'. Later, a few provincial companies such as those of Jonas and Penley, Mrs Baker, and the Norwich Company took the fair in their circuit, playing alongside the popular puppet shows and medleys. But a revival was at hand. Richardson was to infuse new dramatic life into the fair in the nineteenth century with his elaborate spectacles in melodrama and pantomime. It was the final break from the traditional drolls.

CHAPTER IV

SOUTHWARK FAIR
EARLY SHOWS TO 1735

THE FAIR AND THE LAW

Southwark or Lady Fair originated in 1462 with a charter granted by Edward IV to the City of London to hold a fair from 7 to 9 September. The king renewed the charter in 1550.[1] The fair was held in the fields of St Margaret's Hill, but later extended to the old mint of Henry VIII. It was also extended in time, the original limit of three days being expanded to two weeks and more. Gradually it became less a mart than an amusement fair and, in 1720, Strype described it as noted 'chiefly for shows, as drolls, puppet-shows, rope-dancing, music booths and tippling houses'.[2]

As at Bartholomew Fair continuous efforts were made to limit its duration to the statutory three days. An order had been issued in August 1690 but had been ignored, so that the Court of Aldermen which met on 29 August 1693 ordered those who rented ground and built booths which were opened for a longer period to be prosecuted with the utmost severity.[3] In spite of this, it was reported on 12 September that drolls and other shows were being continued beyond three days, and advertisements announcing that the fair would be held for a fortnight were flagrantly inserted in the newspapers by booth masters. The Court recommended justices to bind over offenders at the next Quarter Sessions or King's Bench, especially those who had been responsible for the defiant advertisements. Many further attempts in the eighteenth century to enforce limitation met with small success.

In 1710 the justices ordered warrants to apprehend offenders who refused to depart after that limit.[4] On 13 September 1717

---

[1] R. M. Wingent, *Historical Notes on the Borough* (1913), p. 21.
[2] *Survey of the Cities of London and Westminster* (1720).
[3] Repertory 97, ff. 410–11, 430; *London Gazette*, 31 August 1693.
[4] *Post Man*, 24–6 August 1710.

constables visited Penkethman's booth and arrested him and other members of his company just as they had finished performing a play in the presence of one hundred and fifty noblemen and gentlemen who were seated on the stage.[1] Bullock and Leigh were also taken from their booth upon information lodged against them but, after being carried before the Lord Mayor, were released on bail.[2] A week later *The Weekly Journal* reported: 'We hear that Mr Pinkethman will bring his Action against the informing Constables, for breaking open his Booth last Friday was 7-Night, and taking him off the Stage contrary to the King's Patent, under the Umbrage of which he acts, being sworn Servant to His Majesty; especially against such of them as were out of their Liberty, when they executed that Office'.[3] The case came before the Southwark Quarter Sessions on 2 October, when the recorder not only vindicated the actors but severely snubbed the constables and magistrate for their interference: 'Mr Pinkethman, Mr Leigh, and other Persons taken out of their Booths by the Informing Constables during the time of the Fair, appear'd upon their Recognizances, and were immediately Discharg'd, there being no Prosecution; upon which Occasion the Recorder severely reprimanded the Constables for presuming to molest such as Acted under a Lawful Patent, whilst they let others pass undisturb'd, who were really under the Censure of the Act against strolling, or Vagrant Players. Nor did the Conduct of the Worshipful Justice pass unobserv'd, for Binding over Persons after they had alledg'd to him they were the King's sworn Servants.'[4] This judgment makes it clear that the players from the patent theatres were protected by the patent, but the strolling players were always open to prosecution.

In 1718 another order limiting the fair to three days was made on the petition of the inhabitants. If the booths were not removed, the bailiff was instructed to pull them down with the

---

[1] George Daniel, *Merrie England in the Olden Time* (1842), vol. II, p. 119 n. 1. The aristocratic nature of the audience is confirmed in a letter signed Timothy Harlequin in *Mist's Weekly Journal*, 26 October 1717.

[2] *Weekly Journal*, 14 September 1717.

[3] *Ibid.* 21 September. I owe this and the next reference to Dr A. Mackenzie Taylor.

[4] *Ibid.* 5 October.

assistance of labourers and bridgehouse artificers, and to bring the occupants before the justices to be bound over to appear at the Quarter Sessions.[1] A similar order was made in 1721 and, so that no one could plead ignorance, copies were affixed to public places nearby.[2] Though the fair was supposed to close on 9 September an advertisement for a theatrical booth for the residue of the time was printed as late as 18 September in *The Daily Courant*. A further order, issued in 1735,[3] stated that for several years previously the fair had continued for fourteen days despite the orders of the court to the contrary. On 23 September that year the Court of Aldermen was informed that Mrs Lee had erected a booth and continued to act plays and interludes in defiance of the law.[4] The bailiff of the Borough was ordered to attend in a fortnight's time and present an account, but no further action is recorded.

At the Surrey Assizes in Lent 1741, James Seward, Richard Smith, Edward Pinchbeck and Thomas Yeates the elder were charged with 'Unlawfully exposing to publick shew diverse unlawful Games Sports & pantomimes in a Booth there [Southwark] whereby diverse dissolute & disorderly psons assembled and made great Noises and disturbances', to the annoyance of the inhabitants and of passers-by, between 11 and 16 September, that is after the fair had been open three days. Smith was fined 6s. 8d. and Pinchbeck 1s., which could hardly have been deterrent.[5]

In 1743 the inhabitants of the Borough determined to prosecute anyone who exhibited shows and drolls, 'in order to preserve the Morals of their Children and Servants from being Corrupted'.[6] The Southwark justices ordered the bellman to cry round the fairground that all persons offering interludes etc. would be taken up as vagrants and punished. An attempt to limit the fair to three days caused a riot. The booth keepers had for many years been accustomed to make a collection for the

[1] *Daily Courant*, 23 August 1718.   [2] *Ibid*. 9 September 1721.
[3] Order of the Common Council, 1735: Guildhall Library, Taylor Collection of Broadsides, no. 123.
[4] Repertory 139, p. 321.
[5] P.R.O. Assizes Books, 31/1, ff. 124v-125. *Daily Post*, 23 August 1743.
[6] *Daily Post*, 23 August 1743.

debtors in the Marshalsea Prison which abutted on the fair-ground. They decided that they could not afford to do this when the fair was held for only three days. The enraged debtors took their revenge by hurling stones over the wall on to the crowd outside, thereby killing a child and injuring several people.[1]

In 1750 the principal residents of Southwark petitioned the Lord Mayor to have the fair abolished, 'it tending only to the Destruction of Youth of both Sexes, and the Encouragement of Thieves and Strollers'.[2]

With the change of the calendar in 1752 the date of the fair was put forward to 18 September and the two following days. Anyone who kept a booth open beyond that was again threatened with prosecution.[3] Evidently the fair was still continued beyond the three days, and fresh orders were made the following year.[4]

Finally on 17 June 1762 the Court of Common Council ordered the dissolution of the fair. The bailiff of the Borough, Robert Henshaw, claimed compensation for the £20 a year he earned for licensing interludes and shows.[5] The following year the fair was suppressed by the high constable, supported by 100 officers, who forcibly prevented the showmen from erecting their booths.[6]

EARLY SHOWS TO 1714

We know little of the entertainments of the fair in the second half of the seventeenth century. There were both puppet shows and plays. Pepys saw a puppet show of *Whittington* in 1668 and remarked that it 'was pretty to see; and how the idle throng do work upon people that see it, and even my self too'.[7] Since Pepys was a sophisticated patron, used to entertainments of the patent theatres, the puppeteer was evidently skilled and the show far from crude. The first play of which we have record was *The Coronation of Queen Elizabeth*, which was acted both at

---

[1] *Gentleman's Magazine* (1743), vol. XIII, p. 495; R. M. Wingent, *op. cit.* p. 21.
[2] *Penny London Post*, 6–8 August 1750.
[3] *General Advertiser*, 18 September 1752.
[4] *Public Advertiser*, 19 September 1753.
[5] Corporation Records Office, Journal, 62, p. 180.
[6] *St James's Chronicle*, 17–20 September 1763.
[7] *Diary*, ed. Wheatley, 21 September 1668, vol. VIII, p. 110.

Bartholomew and Southwark Fairs in 1680.[1] Narcissus Luttrell, writing on Thursday, 15 September 1692, says: 'Last Teusday the lord mayor sent his officers to cry downe the faire, the actors of the drolls having presumed to act the earthquake in Jamaica with scenes, and to make a droll of it.'[2] Evelyn, disgusted that the recent disaster should be exploited, wrote in his *Diary* that the disaster was 'profanely and ludicrously represented in a puppet-play or some such lewd pastime...which caused the Queen to put down that idle and vicious mock show'.[3] Whether droll or puppet show (and Luttrell seems more sure of his facts than Evelyn) the contemporary event was seized upon by the showmen.

Two playbills which must date before the death of Queen Mary in December 1694, since they conclude with 'Vivant Rex & Regina', record the performance of two drolls.[4] One was given at the Queen's Arms Tavern during the fortnight of the fair and was called *The Exile of the Earl of Huntington, Commonly known by the Name of Robin Hood. With the Merry Conceits of Little John, And the Humours of the Jolly Pindar of Wakefield. With Variety of Singing and Dancing, New Scenes and Machines, the like was never seen in the Fair before* (Pl. II). The other was presented at Parker's booth near the King's Bench for twelve days and was called *A New Wonder, A Woman never Vex'd: or The Blind Beggar of Bednal Green. With the Humours of Tom Stroud, and his Man Gudgeon.* Again a variety of 'Scenes, Machines, Songs and Dances' was advertised. These are the earliest droll playbills so far recorded. Barnes and Appleby had a booth in Coachmakers' Yard for rope dancing in 1698,[5] and in the first years of the eighteenth century rope dancing and puppets appear to have been the main entertainments. Crawley, whom we met at Bartholomew Fair,[6] gave his puppet show of the *Old Creation of the World* with *Noah's Flood* at the Golden Lion near St George's Church, but the handbill does not include the elaborate scenes and machines of the Bartholomew Fair bill.[7]

[1] Above, p. 7.
[2] *A Brief Historical Relation of State Affairs* (1857), vol. ii, p. 565.
[3] *Diary*, ed. E. S. de Beer (1955), 15 September 1692, vol. v, p. 115.
[4] Corporation Records Office, P.D. 71. 18.
[5] *Post Man*, 13–15 September 1698.   [6] Above, p. 14.   [7] Harl. 5931.

Penkethman is first heard of at Southwark Fair in 1704 when he opened a booth in the Coachmakers' Yard,[1] formerly used by Barnes and Appleby, with a company of rope dancers and the famous Anglo-French couple of the Paris fairs, Sorine and Baxter, in Italian interludes of Scaramouch and Harlequin. The French rope dancers, Lady Isabella and her sister, together with vaulters and tumblers, appeared at a rope-dancing booth in 1705.[2]

We have no further information about the entertainments until 1714[3] when Penkethman had graduated from rope dancing to drolls. He presented *The Constant Lovers: or Sir Paul Slouch, alias Sir Timothy Little-Wit. With the Comical Humours of his Man Trip*. These two comics were played by Bullock and Dicky Norris, whilst Penkethman himself played Buzzard.

The beautiful Christiana Horton was seen acting in *Cupid and Psyche* by Barton Booth, who promptly engaged her for Drury Lane, where she came out the following season.[4]

In November, some time after the close of the fair, the King's Arms Tavern housed a performance of Benjamin Griffin's *Injur'd Virtue; or, The Virgin Martyr*.[5]

1715–1716

Mrs Mynns brought her spectacular droll, *The Siege of Troy*, to the Queen's Arms Tavern in 1715 'to the full Grandeur of what it appeared Eight Years since in Bartholomew Fair'. It was repeated in 1716 and was printed that year by S. Lee as 'Presented in Mrs Mynn's Great Booth in the Queens-Arms-Yard near the Marshalsea-Gate in Southwark, during the Time of the Fair'.[6] In the preface to the reader it is stated that the entertainment had made its entry nine years previously at Bartholomew Fair, and that this was the third year of its appearance. It was set forth 'with the Additions of several New

---

[1] *Daily Courant*, 18 September 1704.   [2] *Post Man*, 11–13 September 1705.
[3] *Daily Courant*, 31 August 1714.
[4] B. Victor, *Original Letters* (1776), p. 63.
[5] *Daily Courant*, 1 November 1714.
[6] A copy with dated title-page is in the Minet Library. The B.M. copy, which may belong to the previous year, is undated.

AT the *Queens-Arms* Tavern, in *Southwark*, during a
Fortnight, (the usual time of the Fair) will be presented an excellent Droll, call'd,

The Exile of the Earl of Huntington,

Commonly known by the Name of

ROBIN HOOD.

With the Merry Conceits of Little *John*,

And the Humours of the Jolly PINDAR of WAKEFIELD.

With Variety of Singing and Dancing, New Scenes and
Machine., the like was never seen in the Fair before.

VIVANT REX & REGINA.

II. Southwark Fair playbill of the late seventeenth century

III. Southwark Fair in 1700

Scenes but likewise the whole Paintings heightened with those New Enrichments and Gilding, as to make it very much Superior even to its first Original'. The managers claimed that 'much more able Performers from the Comedians of both Theatres' had been selected for its representation; 'Nor have they been wanting in their Care of the Musical and Dancing part of it, to exceed what the Hurry of the last Years hasty Preparation for it could not so well furnish'. The cast was Menelaus, W. Wilks; Ulysses, Tho. Rogers; Paris, T. Walker; Sinon, Tho. Penderey; Cassandra, Mrs Spiller; and the comic parts were played by Miller, Spiller and Morgan. Barton Booth is said to have seen Thomas Walker, the original Macheath, in his role of Paris, and afterwards to have engaged him for Drury Lane, where he first appeared that winter.[1] William Wilks was also taken on at Drury Lane, and Rogers, Morgan and Mrs Spiller at Lincoln's Inn Fields. Miller was already in the Drury Lane company and Spiller in that of Lincoln's Inn Fields, so that Mrs Mynns's troupe was indeed partly recruited from the London theatres.

There was a crowd of extras: in addition to the Trojan mob, 'Three Persons drest in Gold for Statues in Diana's Temple', nine priests and priestesses, ten persons richly dressed as the retinue of Paris and Helen, twenty-two officers, guards and trumpeters attendant on Menelaus, 'In the whole Fifty-three Persons drest, besides the Actors and Dancers in the Play'. This was a most unusual number of supers for a fair show.

The booth erected in the Queen's Arms Yard must have been a large one, for in the same house, on a smaller stage, Maddox presented the droll of *Bateman, or the Fair Vow-breaker* in 1715.[2] Norris, and Penkethman and Bullock, also had booths that year. They were visited on 15 September by Dudley Rider who relates that he saw there 'farces...made up out of several very comical parts of other plays which are collected together', as well as rope dancing and tumbling.[3]

---

[1] *Biographica Dramatica*, vol. I, p. 732.
[2] *Daily Courant*, 5 September 1715.
[3] *Diary of Dudley Rider, 1715–1716*, ed. W. Mathews (1939), p. 101. Reference supplied by Professor A. H. Scouten.

Penkethman had a benefit on 25 September 1716,[1] when he played his original part of Timothy Peascod in Gay's *What D'Ye Call It*, with Jubilee Dicky as Sir Roger. The performance, which was Penkethman's last in the fair that year, began at 6 p.m., and included singing, dancing and rope dancing.

1717

In 1717 Penkethman and Pack built a large, commodious booth, fitted for the reception of the quality, at the old place over against St George's Church, and there produced the quaintly named droll *Twice Married and a Maid Still or Bedding makes the Bargain Fast*.[2] In addition to the proprietors, the players were Quin, Ryan, Diggs, Shepard, Norris, Spiller, Mrs Spiller and Mrs Baxter. This is the only recorded appearance of James Quin at the fair. On 25 September *The Recruiting Officer* was given for the benefit of Penkethman, Pack and Spiller, followed by a Lancashire hornpipe, a mimic scene between Harlequin and a Peasant, vaulting on a horse by a gentleman lately arrived from France and the 'usual' epilogue on an ass, which Penkethman had taken over from Joseph Haines. For this occasion the boxes and pit were laid together, which meant that box prices of 2s. 6d. could be charged for the pit instead of the ordinary 1s. 6d. The next day the booth was pulled down.[3] It was during this season that Penkethman was arrested, as previously related.[4] He had not prepared for the quality in vain since, as we have seen, a hundred and fifty noblemen and gentlemen sat on his stage, which must have been of considerable size to accommodate them. His audience was, in part at any rate, one that was accustomed to the patent theatres and was not restricted to the rougher elements of the fair. His prices for the latter would have been high, since even a gallery seat cost 1s. Penkethman had a strong company with two first-class actors in James Quin and Lacy Ryan, and three excellent low comedians in Spiller, Norris and himself, which shows that the performances were of good standard.

[1] *Daily Courant*, 24 September 1716.   [2] *Weekly Journal*, 7 September 1717.
[3] *Daily Courant*, 25 September 1717.   [4] Above, p. 72.

Bullock and Francis Leigh had a booth in Angel Court near the King's Bench, with a large raffling room adjoining.[1] They presented a dramatic opera entitled *The Noble Soldier, or Love in Distress. With the Comical Adventures of Master Billy Softhead, his Mother, and his Sister Sally*.

1718

This year Bullock and Leigh removed from Angel Court to a new booth next to Penkethman's, where they gave a dramatic opera with music by Haydn entitled *Love's Triumph or the Happy Fair One. With the Comical and Pleasant Humours of Colin the Shepherd's Foolish Son and his Sister Mopsa*. In the bucolic sub-plot Bullock was Colin; Leigh, the Old Shepherd, and Mrs Willis, Mopsa. All the clothes and scenes were new.[2]

Penkethman and Norris came on from the former's Richmond Theatre to their booth, on the same site as the previous year, with a company from both the patent theatres.[3] They played *Jephtha's Rash Vow, or the Virgin Sacrifice*, with alterations and additions. The low comedy was sustained by Penkethman, Norris and Norris junior. A correspondent of *Mist's Weekly Journal* attacked the exploitation of a scriptural story 'by a Pack of strolling Buffoons'.[4] A great attraction was the dancing dogs which had recently arrived from France and had been shown at Hampton Court and Richmond: 'their dresses, as well as their dances, being entirely after the French mode particularly Miss Depingle in her Hoop petticoat and leading strings and only at the common prices of the droll'.[5]

Spiller and Pack split off from Penkethman and added Hall as a third partner in their booth on Leigh and Bullock's former site in Angel Court. They presented a new version of *The True and Ancient History of Sir Richard Whittington, thrice Lord Mayor of London. With the Pleasing Humours of Madge the Cook Maid and John the Butler*. Pack played Whittington; Hall, Madge; Spiller, John; Mrs Spiller, Alicia; Schoolding, Fitzwarren; and other parts were by Mr and Mrs Giffard and J. Leigh. Clothes, scenes

[1] *Daily Courant*, 9 September 1717.   [2] *Ibid.* 4 September 1718.
[3] *Ibid.* 5 September.   [4] 20 September 1718.
[5] *Daily Courant*, 6 September.

and decorations were advertised as new.[1] Three theatrical booths were the most there had yet been at the fair. In addition there must have been a revival of *The Siege of Troy*. Victor says that Anthony Boheme's first appearance on the stage 'was at a Booth in *Southwark* Fair, which in those Days, lasted two Weeks, and was much frequented by Persons of all Distinctions of both Sexes; he acted the part of Menelaus in the best droll I ever saw, called *The Siege of Troy*'.[2] On enquiring backstage, Victor was told that Boheme had been engaged at Lincoln's Inn Fields for the next season. As Boheme first appeared at that theatre in October 1718, Victor must have seen him in September. The droll was reprinted that year, which is confirmation that it was revived.

1719–1720

Francis Leigh was dead by the autumn of 1719, but his widow shared the booth in Bird Cage Alley with Bullock, where they revived *The Noble Soldier*. Jack Harper, who started his career at Southwark, was a member of the company. He mimicked a drunken man in a scene which had been admired at Lincoln's Inn Fields and, on 24 September, he was accorded a benefit at which *The Jew of Venice* was given.[3] Serious and comic dancing was performed by Newhouse, Pelling, Mrs Willis, Miss Francis and others. The fact that entertainments were being given as late as this shows that the order of 1718 limiting the fair to three days was simply ignored. Indeed, in 1720 Hall gave a performance of *The Old Bachelor* and *The Italian Shadows* as late as 28 November, long after the end of the fair.[4] The booth, which he shared with John Leigh, was formerly Penkethman's and adjoined Bullock's. This large booth was probably the one which Penkethman built in 1717, and it may have been a permanent structure not, as usual, taken down every year. Hall and Leigh gave there a dramatic opera, *The History of the Famous Friar Bacon. With the Comical Humours of Justice Wantbrains, Hopper*

---

[1] *Daily Journal*, 5 September 1718.
[2] *History of the Theatres of London and Dublin* (1761), vol. II, p. 74.
[3] *Daily Courant*, 5, 24 September 1719.
[4] B.M. Add. MS. 32249 (Latreille) for this year's performances.

the Miller and his Son Ralph, with new clothes, scenes, machines and decorations. The principal parts were taken by Leigh, Hall, Boheme, Williams, Oates, Egleton, Schoolding, Knapp, Mrs Giffard and Mrs Ratcliffe. *The Italian Shadows*, which followed, was the first pantomime to be seen at the fair; it had been brought out at Lincoln's Inn Fields in April. Leigh and Hall took their benefit after the fair was over, on 10 October, when *Henry IV* was given with Hall as Falstaff and Harper as Bardolph, with an afterpiece entitled *The Broken Stock-Jobbers, or Work for the Bailiffs*,[1] which satirised the gamblers of the South Sea Bubble.

During the fair, Harper had again been at Bullock's booth and, at his benefit on 23 September, had played Kite in *The Recruiting Officer* with Spiller as Brazen and Bullock as his namesake, the country clown Bullock.

A booth in the Queen's Arms Yard was also functioning as late as 10 October, when a benefit was given for Dr Thornhill, who spoke a comical dialogue with his old Merry Andrew. The play was *Love for Love* and it was performed by actors from both houses. No notice was taken of the limitation of the fair to three days.

1721–1722

After two years' absence, Penkethman returned to the fair in 1721, sharing with Miller and Norris a new booth in Blue Maid Alley adjoining the Half Moon Inn.[2] They brought from Bartholomew Fair their droll, *The Injur'd General, or, The Blind Beggar of Bethnal Green*, and also showed a representation of the waterworks at Versailles invented by Mr Brouard. A note, two weeks later, adds: 'There is a Passage thro' the Half Moon Inn for the Quality to the Boxes, and a handsome Long Room joining to the Booth, where will be Raffling and other Diversions.'[3] These passages are frequently advertised to inform the quality that they could walk from their carriages to the booth, unmolested by crowds and unsoiled by the dirt of the fairground.

---

[1] See below, p. 144.
[2] *Weekly Journal or British Gazetteer*, 2 September 1721.
[3] *Ibid.* 16 September.

They are evidence that the fair was frequented by the middle classes, who came to enjoy the comedians when the theatres were shut.

At the Queen's Arms Yard, Lee had a booth where he brought out a new entertainment, *The Noble Englishman or the History of Darius King of Persia and the Destruction of Babylon. With the Pleasant Humours of Captain Fearful and his Man Ninepence*.[1] Boheme was Darius; Rogers, Achmet; and Walker, the Englishman; with Mrs Gulick, Mrs Morgan and Mrs Elsam; the low comedy was sustained by Harper as Fearful and Morgan as Ninepence.

Hall and Leigh advertised themselves as from the New Playhouse, which must refer to the Little Haymarket, which had opened in 1720.[2] At their booth in Bird Cage Alley they presented one of the rare biblical drolls, *The True, Famous and Ancient History of King Saul, and the Witch of Endo*: 'Containing the Death of the Gyant Goliah, the Friendship of David and Jonathan, and the Defeat of King Saul and his Host, by the Philistine Army. With the Comical Humours of Dame Double-Dabber, Weazel her Son and Corporal Rowling-pin'. The performers were Leigh, Hall, Williams, Oates, Hulett, Mrs Willis and Mrs Cook; the singers Ray and Mrs Bowman.

Boheme had a booth with Penkethman in 1722,[3] and they brought on from Bartholomew Fair their droll, *The Distressed Beauty or the London Prentice*, with one change in cast, Wetherilt replacing Miller as the comical Wantbrains. Sandham's son and daughter made their first public appearance, other than in the theatre, as dancers.

Walker's booth adjoined Bullock's in Bird Cage Alley, and he gave a three-act entertainment, *Royal Revenge or the Princely Shepherd, containing the History of Valentine and Orson. With the Sad and Dismal Humours of Peter Pitiful*.[4] All the habits were new; select vocal and instrumental music was adapted to the entertainment, and there was dancing between the acts.

[1] B.M. Add. MS. 32250 (Latreille).
[2] B.M. J. H[aslewood], *Collections Relating to the Drama*, vol. ix, f. 60.
[3] *Daily Post*, 5 September 1722; above, p. 27.
[4] *Ibid*. 13 September.

Miller at the Angel Tavern presented a new droll, *The Faithful Couple or The Royal Shepherdess. With a very Pleasant Entertainment between Old Hob and his Wife and the Comical Humours of Mopsey and Colin.*[1] Old Hob and his wife were characters taken from Cibber's *Hob; or The Country Wake. Hob* itself seems also to have been given.[2]

Hall had a booth in Bird Cage Alley and took a benefit on 26 September when *The Recruiting Officer* was given by actors from the Theatre Royal.[3] As late as 3 October a benefit for one Coe took place at the Great Theatrical Booth in Bird Cage Alley, when *The Busy Body* was presented, with a new prologue and epilogue, by actors from the theatres, and tumbling by Fawkes's famous boy.[4] This booth was permanent as it was in use again in February for a performance of *Oroonoko*.[5] Lee and Spiller at the Queen's Arms Tavern had a company of Dutch rope dancers and tumblers this year.

1723–1724

In 1723 Penkethman revived *Jane Shore. With the Comical Humours of Sir Anthony Noodle and his Man Weazle,*[6] with the following cast: Noodle, Egleton; King, Huddy; Shore, Oates; Capt. Blunderbuss, Orfeur; Mrs Blake, Mrs Middleton; Mrs Aris, Mrs Egleton. The Prince of Wales with several people of quality of both sexes visited the booth and expressed satisfaction with the show, which also included the picture of the royal family, and tumblers.[7]

Bullock presented a new droll, *Herod and Mariamne* and, at the adjoining booth, Spiller and Hall performed *The True and Ancient History of Richard Whittington.*[8]

There were five theatrical booths in 1724. The famous partnership of Lee and Harper is first heard of at Southwark this year, though Harper had acted at Lee's booth in 1721. They

---

[1] B.M. Add. MS. 32250.

[2] *Daily Post*, 25 September 1722, quoted in L. Hughes and A. H. Scouten, *Ten English Farces* (1948), p. 126, where it is attributed to Doggett.

[3] B.M. Add. MS. 32250.   [4] *Ibid.*   [5] *Ibid.*

[6] *Daily Post*, 14 September 1723; *Weekly Journal or British Gazetteer*, 7 September.

[7] B.M. Add. MS. 32250.   [8] *Weekly Journal*, 7 September 1723.

revived *The Siege of Troy* and Mrs Lee claimed that she had spared no cost to surpass her mother's production: 'the Booth coming as near the perfection of the Theatre as possible, being adorned by the most ingenious Workmen: Her Head Characters are all Dress'd in real Gold and Silver beyond what was ever worn at any Fair before but by her own People'.[1] Decorations, paintings and machinery were said far to excel the original ones at Bartholomew Fair. So popular was the droll that rival booths designed to have imitations under the same name, and Mrs Lee was at pains to make clear that hers was the only true one. The fact that some of the scenes for the droll were gilded is confirmation of the story[2] that Hogarth and Oram[3] were employed by a famous woman booth keeper at Bartholomew Fair to paint a splendid set of scenes. The agreement specified that the scenes were to be gilt, but the painters covered them with Dutch metal instead of gold leaf. The mistress of the drolls thereupon declared the contract broken and refused to pay for the scenes. The anecdote is related of Bartholomew Fair[4] where, it will be recalled, *The Siege of Troy* was postponed because scenes and dresses were not ready; this may well have been because of the trouble over the gold leaf.

Lee and Harper's booth was at the Bowling Green, the lower end of Blue Maid Alley, and Mrs Lee had another booth down the Queen's Arms Tavern Yard where she had been in 1721. In this second booth she presented a droll, *The Adventures of Robin Hood, Earl of Huntington, and his Man Little John. With the Comical and Diverting Humours of the Pindar of Wakefield and his Wife; with Prim, a Usurer and Johnny Thump his Man.*[5]

At Penkethman's booth a company of comedians from both theatres performed the droll of *Valentine and Orson. With the Comical Whining Humours of Peter Pitiful*, which was evidently much the same as that given by Walker two years previously.[6] Valentine and Orson were played by Roberts and Bridgewater;

---

[1] *Original London Post*, 28 August 1724; *Daily Post*, 7 September.

[2] J. T. Smith, *Antient Topography of London* (1815), p. 60. See my note 'Was Hogarth a Scene Painter?' *Theatre Notebook*, vol. VIII, p. 18.

[3] Called Edward Oram senior, but probably William Oram. See *D.N.B.*

[4] Above, p. 28. [5] *Daily Post*, 7 September 1724.

[6] *Ibid.* 5 September 1724; above, p. 82.

Peter Pitiful by Butcher, and other parts by Huddy, Williams, Mrs Morgan, Mrs Butcher and Mrs Willis. Penkethman also brought on from Bartholomew Fair a company of rope dancers and tumblers due to leave the country after the fair. In the passage, opposite the door of his booth, Penkethman showed his moving picture of the royal family. Later on the droll was changed to *The Blind Beggar of Bednal Green; or The Woman never Vex'd*[1] which had been given at Bartholomew Fair this year. This was Penkethman's last appearance at Southwark; he died in September 1726.

Chetwood, a newcomer to the fair, shared a booth with Norris, Orfeur and Oates next to Bullock's in Bird Cage Alley.[2] Their new droll was *Merlin, the British Enchanter; or The Child has found his Father. With the Comical Humours of Sir Nicodemus Nothing, Simon Go To'at, and his Sister Joan,* 'with a Representation of the terrible Battles that were fought between the Saxons and the ancient Britains [*sic*], with a shower of Fire and the appearance of a Comet, with a fiery Dragon that prognosticated the Birth of King Arthur, the British Worthy'. The plot was derived from a play printed in 1662 and ascribed on the title-page to Rowley and Shakespeare. Jubilee Dicky was Sir Nicodemus Nothing, and his son played Merlin. Chetwood was Bufflehead; Oates, Simon; Chapman, Aurelius, King of Britain, and other roles were taken by Cory, Marshall, Walford, Harrison, Penkethman junior, Wilks junior, Orfeur and his wife, Mrs Sterling and Mrs Vincent.

The fifth booth was Bullock and Spiller's where, on 24 September,[3] Dryden and Lee's *Oedipus, King of Thebes* was given for the benefit of Ward and Mrs Haughton. The cast was: Oedipus, Ward; Creon, Ogden; Adrastus, Miller; Haemon, Buck; Tiresias, Browne; Diocles, Buchanan; Phorbas, Merrivale; Jocasta, Mrs Haughton; Eurydice, Mrs Plomer; Manto, Miss Edwards; with comic parts by Bullock, Spiller, Penkethman and Willcox, and dancing by the Haughtons, Ogden and James.

---

[1] *Ibid.* 14 September 1724; above, p. 28.   [2] *Ibid.* 5 September.
[3] *Daily Post*, 24 September.

1725–1727

Little is known about the drama at the fair of 1725 except that
a gallery fell at Lee's booth, killing one man on the iron spikes
and badly injuring the leg of another.[1] In 1726 at Lee and
Harper's Bowling Green booth *The Siege of Troy* was revived:
'The whole Entertainment having been justly Acknowledg'd by
all Spectators, to be infinitely superior to all Public Performances
of this kind ever seen in a Fair.'[2] Spiller and Baron Egleton's
booth down the Queen's Arms Yard was the only other dramatic
one advertised. There was played *The True and Ancient History
of the Unnatural Parents, or, The Fair Maid of the West*. Egleton
was the wicked witch of Cornwall; Mrs Haughton, the Fair
Maid; Mrs Morgan, her sister Betty Wealthy; Spiller and Mrs
Elsam, her cruel parents; Eaton, her lover Lord Lovewell; and
Morgan, the comic servant Trusty. Poor Egleton was given
a benefit at his booth on 27 September, as he had spent three
months under confinement, presumably for debt. He played
Marplot in *The Busy Body*.[3] The Moroccan ambassador attended
Gibbins and Violante's rope dancing performances,[4] and the
Prince of Wales also visited the fair incognito.[5]

No plays or drolls were advertised in 1727, but Mrs Lee must
have been at the fair as Yeates had a medley and puppet show in
a booth facing Mme Lee's, with a passage through the Half
Moon by which the quality could come to the pit door.[6]

A description of the entertainments of the fair at this time
is to be found in Gay's *Fables*.[7] He satirically describes the
visit of two monkeys:

> Brother, says Pug, and turn'd his head,
> The rabble's monstrously ill-bred.
> Now through the booth loud hisses ran
> Nor ended 'till the Show began.
> The tumbler whirls the flipflap round,
> With summersets he shakes the ground:

[1] *Daily Journal*, 11 September 1725.
[2] *Daily Post*, 10 September 1726.
[3] *Ibid.* 26 September.
[4] *Ibid.* 16 September.
[5] *Daily Journal*, 13 September.
[6] *Daily Post*, 13 September 1727.
[7] 1727, p. 135, Fable 40.

The cord beneath the dancer springs;
Aloft in air the vaulter swings,
Distorted now, now prone depends,
Now through his twisted arms ascends;
The croud in wonder and delight,
With clapping hands applaud the sight.

1728–1729

The fair offerings were transformed in 1728 by the resounding success of *The Beggar's Opera*. This was brought on from Bartholomew Fair by Fielding and Reynolds who had taken over Penkethman's booth. They advertised that the ballad opera was set to music as at Lincoln's Inn Fields.[1] Thomas Walker's imitation for the fairs, *The Quaker's Opera, with Jack Sheppard's Escapes out of Newgate and the Comical Humours of Blunder an Irishman*, was also brought on from Bartholomew Fair by Lee, Harper and Spiller, who had a booth in the Queen's Arms Yard. At Lee and Harper's second booth on the Bowling Green a dramatic entertainment, *The Royal Champion: Or, St George for England, With the Comical Humours of Rumbelo*, was presented. Coaches had a free passage through the Blue Maid Alley to the booth.[2]

For the next decade the fairs were at the height of their dramatic activity. The ballad opera craze continued in 1729. Coffey's *The Beggar's Wedding* was brought on from Bartholomew Fair[3] by Reynolds whose booth was in the Half Moon Inn. Newcomers in the cast were Giffard, Penkethman junior and Stoppelaer. Coffey also wrote a special ballad opera for Reynolds's booth entitled *Southwark Fair or the Sheep Shearing*, in which the chief attraction was Miss Mann's first appearance in boy's clothes. Leo Hughes writes of this piece that it is 'a match of wits between a heavy father and a clever pair of lovers. The setting does, of course, provide for certain items suggestive of the fair: a merry-andrew—more fashionably named Harlequin—a showcloth, and some trading in and shearing of sheep.'[4] To each opera was added *The Humours of Harlequin* in which Knott was Harlequin; Penkethman, a Miller; Miss Mann, the

---

[1] *Daily Post*, 12 September 1728.   [2] *Ibid.*   [3] Above, p. 31.
[4] *Op. cit.* p. 219. The Guildhall Library copy was destroyed in the war.

Miller's wife; and Giffard, his man. Mrs Nokes greeted the Lord Mayor, when he passed by the Half Moon Inn to proclaim the fair, with a song which she also sang in boy's clothes, accompanied by a band. That opening night, fireworks were sent off by the engineer who was responsible for those at the Royal Exchange.[1] At Mrs Nokes's benefit on 18 September *The Beggar's Wedding* and Colley Cibber's *Flora* were given. In the latter Mrs Nokes herself was Friendly; Ray, Hob; and Mrs Mountfort, Flora.[2] On 23 September it was Ray's turn for a benefit at which he played Plume in *The Recruiting Officer*, supported by: Giffard, Balance; R. Williams, Worthy; Gilbert, Brazen; Penkethman, Bullock; W. Williams, Kite; Miss Mann, Melinda; Mrs Thomas, Silvia; Miss Ward, Rose; Mrs Nokes, Lucy. This too was followed by *Flora*. The performance began at 6 p.m. and no one was admitted except by ticket.[3]

Lee also gave *The Beggar's Wedding or Rackall the Gaol Keeper outwitted*. The Rackall part does not appear in the original ballad opera and was tacked on for the fair. Hulett was Hunter; Mrs Spiller, Phebe; and Mullart, Chaunter. A new entertainment in grotesque characters followed, entitled *The Stratagems of Harlequin or the Peasant Tricked*, with new machines, scenes and flyings.

At Lee and Harper's booth, *The Siege of Bethulia, containing the Ancient History of Judith and Holofernes. Together with the Comical Humours of Rustego and his Man Terrible* was given with Mullart as Holofernes; Roberts, Achior; Harper, Rustego; Morgan, Terrible; Mrs Spiller, Judith; Mrs Purden, Dulcimenta. Mullart and Mrs Spiller appeared at both of Lee's booths. The droll was printed by George Lee.

After an interval of nine years since the first pantomime had been seen at Southwark two were shown in 1729.

1730

During the fair of 1730 at least six pieces and two pantomimes were to be seen.[4] Chetwood's ballad opera, *The Generous Freemason*, was brought on from Bartholomew Fair by Oates and

[1] B.M. Add. MS. 32250.   [2] *Ibid.*
[3] *Ibid.*   [4] *Daily Post*, 10 September 1730.

Fielding, with dancing by Smith, young Charke, and Miss Williams. The performances began daily at 2 p.m. instead of the more customary 10 or 11 a.m.

Lee and Harper presented at their Bowling Green booth a new droll, *Guy of Warwick. Together with the Comical Distresses of Rogero, Guy's Servant.* The cast was: Guy, Hulett; Phillis, Mrs Morgan; the comics Rogero and Boozall the Constable were played by Morgan and Harper; other parts by Rosco, Lacy and Mrs Egleton. The book of the droll was sold at the booth, others sold outside were not authentic. On the last day of the fair the booth was patronised by princes and generals who had recently arrived from South Carolina.

At their Great Booth in the Queen's Arms Yard, Lee and Harper revived *Robin Hood and Little John* with Hulett as Robin Hood, Ray as Little John, Harper as the Pindar, and Mrs Egleton as the Pindar's Wife, together with Chapman, Mrs Lacy and Mrs Morgan. It was followed by a pantomime, *The Stratagems of Harlequin ; or the Peasant Trick'd.* On 24 September *The Beaux Stratagem* was given for Ray's benefit with the following cast:[1] Archer, Chapman; Aimwell, Pitt; Boniface, Wilcocks; Sir Charles Freeman, Macklin; Gibbet, Ayres; Foigard, Eaton; Scrub, Ray; Mrs Sullen, Mrs Mills; Lady Bountiful, Mrs Elsam; Cherry, Mrs Careless; Dorina, a gentlewoman for her diversion. According to Kirkman,[2] Macklin was acting with a strolling company at Stratford-le-Bow which proceeded to Southwark Fair, where they reaped a rich harvest. If this is the case, Lee and Harper must have engaged a band of itinerants to support them in their second booth. Kirkman also states that the manager of Sadler's Wells engaged Macklin from the fair but, if so, it was not for long, as by December he was acting at Lincoln's Inn Fields. Macklin appeared at the fair 'in a fine laced coat and bag wig and cleared half a guinea a day', a tidy sum for an unknown stroller.

Mrs Lee continued to have shows at the Bowling Green booth after fair time. On 8 October *The Recruiting Officer* was performed by the comedians of both houses for Charles, the

---

[1] B.M. Add. MS. 32250.
[2] *Memoirs of Charles Macklin* (1799), vol. I, p. 166.

Merry Trumpeter of Oxford.[1] On 28 December and during the
Christmas vacation she presented there an 'opera', *Punch's Poli-
ticks: or the Nuns Conclave*, followed by a pantomime, *The Nuns
Turn'd Libertines: or, The Devil Turn'd Humourist* by William
Geast, who announced that he had suffered insupportable losses
through being misrepresented as a lunatic.[2] He claimed that
'Particular Care will be taken to have the Parts play'd perfect'.

Penkethman had a booth in Bird Cage Alley with comedians
from the Haymarket. He revived *The Distressed Beauty* from
1722[3] as *Amurath the Great, Emperor of the Turks, containing the
Distressed Loves of Achmet and Selima, or the London Prentice's
Glory—With the Comical Humours and Surprizing Adventures of
the London Prentice and Wantbrains his Man.* Penkethman took
over from his famous father the role of the Prentice. He was
supported by Reynolds as Wantbrains; Huddy, Amurath; Mullart, Achmet; Mrs Newstead, Selima; Mrs Dulton, Zara; Jones,
Haly; and Achurch, Selim. A new pantomime, *Harlequin's Contrivance or the Plague of a Wanton Wife* followed, in which
Davenport and Mrs Nokes were Harlequin and Columbine, and
other roles were filled by Reynolds, Dove, Jones, Arthur,
Achurch, Mr and Mrs Dulton, Mrs Clark and Miss Palms.[4]
Tom Thumb also found a place in the programme with Achurch
as Noodle; Walker, Boodle; Mrs Newstead, Queen Dollalolla;
Mrs Jones, Princess Huncamunca; Mullart, King Arthur; Jones,
Lord Grizzle; and Miss Jones, Tom Thumb.[5]

1731

There were five play booths in the fair of 1731. Lee and Harper
had their usual couple. At one, the *True and Ancient History of
Whittington* was revived but, as is evident from the dramatis
personae, in a different version from that of 1718, if not from
that of 1723 of which we know nothing. Morgan was the hero;
Harper, the Cholerick Cookmaid; Rosco, the Emperor; Jones,
the Merchant; Hulett, the Captain; Mullart, the Factor; Mrs

---

[1] *Daily Post*, 8 October 1730.   [2] *Ibid.* 15, 26 December.
[3] Above, pp. 27, 82.   [4] B.M. Add. MS. 32250.
[5] *Daily Post*, 14 September 1730.

Taylor, Mrs Fitzwarren; Mrs Mullart, Mrs Grace; Mrs Morgan, Gilflirt; Mrs Coker, Bawd; Mrs Spiller, Britannia. The book was sold in the booth, printed by G. Lee, other versions being false. Platt and Papillion were the singers.[1] At their other booth Lee and Harper presented Coffey's ballad opera, *The Devil to Pay, or the Wives Metamorphosed*, 'Intermixt with above thirty new songs made to old ballad tunes and country dances', with new clothes and scenes. It had first been brought out at Drury Lane on 8 August in a three-act version. At the fair it may have been reduced to one act as the part of the Parson, which had offended, and other parts, are not mentioned in the dramatis personae.[2] The book of the droll was sold at the booth, printed by G. Lee, but no copy has been traced. The cast was: Sir John Loverule, Mullart; Ranger, Taylor; Doctor, Ayres; Butler, Rosco; Cook, Eaton; Lady Loverule, Mrs Mullart; Nell Jobson, Miss Tollet; Lettice, Mrs Coker; Lucy, Mrs Hulett; Jobson, Hulett. It will be noticed that some of the players performed at both booths. Since this one was open from 10 a.m. to 9 p.m. they must have arranged to play at one booth whilst tumbling or an interval was in progress at the other—a strenuous schedule for so long a day. Mrs Lee engaged a company of tumblers at this second booth, one of whom threw himself from a twelve-foot scaffold.[3]

Fielding, Hippisley and Hall had the booth in Bird Cage Alley, this being Hippisley's first appearance at Southwark. They brought on from Bartholomew Fair Chetwood's dramatic opera, *The Emperor of China Grand Vol-gi*.[4] This show did not open until 1 p.m. On 28 September *A Bold Stroke for a Wife* was performed for the benefit of Charles the Merry Trumpeter.[5]

At a booth in the Half Moon Inn Yard, Lillo's tragedy, *The London Merchant*, originally performed at Drury Lane, was given with the following cast: Barnwell, Peterson; Thorowgood, Furnival; O. Barnwell, Symonds; Truman, Jenkins; Maria, Miss Price; Millwood, Miss Smith; Lucy, [Mrs] Furnival.

---

[1] *Daily Advertiser*, 8 September 1731.
[2] It was cut down to one act by T. Cibber at Drury Lane on 2 October. See Leo Hughes and A. H. Scouten, *Ten English Farces* (1948), pp. 176–7.
[3] *Daily Advertiser*, 14 September 1731.   [4] *Ibid.* 8 September; above, p. 35.
[5] *Ibid.* 27 September.

After it came an entertainment of dancing in burlesque characters entitled *Merlin: Or, The British Enchanter*. Collier was Merlin in the character of Harlequin, and Cross, Hicks, Wright, etc., the Demons and infernal Spirits; Miss Price, Columbine; Jenkins, Gardener; and Pigeon, his man Pumpkin. This was probably a strolling company, as the names are not known in the London theatres of the year. The show also opened at 1 p.m., and a company of tumblers entertained the company whilst the booth was filling.[1] Henceforth many such companies are advertised.

Miller, Mills and Oates's booth in Bird Cage Alley presented the new opera, *The Banish'd General*, which they had given in Bartholomew Fair.[2] The cast varied slightly from that at Smithfield: Barcock, Peckham, and Clark replacing R. Wetherilt, Adam Hallam and Evans. The opera concluded with a grand dance and chorus accompanied by kettledrums and trumpets which appear in the fair for the first time. Rope dancers from Italy entertained the audience between every show;[3] this was the third booth this year to engage a company for this purpose.

1732

Lee and Harper's two booths are the only theatrical ones of which we know in 1732. At one a new comedy, *Female Innocence; or, A School for a Wife*, was performed and was printed as 'Acted at Mrs Lee's Great Booth, on the Bowling Green'.[4] Postures and tumbling by Phillips preceded the droll, and it was followed by *The Stratagems of Harlequin or the Miser Trick'd*, a variant of the pantomime of 1730 in which a peasant was tricked. The Prince of Wales honoured the booth with a visit on 13 September.[5] Charles the Merry Trumpeter, who sounded before him, the Princesses, and several of the nobility, was accorded a benefit on 12 October, three weeks after the close of the fair. Cibber's *Love makes a Man* was put on by a cast from the theatres, 'but the principal part to be performed by Charles, the merry

[1] *Daily Post*, 8 September 1731.   [2] Above, p. 36.
[3] *Daily Post*, 11 September.
[4] Guildhall Library: A. B. Osborne. Bartholomew, frost and suburban fairs; A. Nicoll, *A History of English Drama* (1952), vol. II, p. 372.
[5] *Daily Journal*, 17 September 1732.

Trumpeter—that is, to take the Money'. The play was followed by a dance between Harlequin and a Countryman:

> The Countryman by Charles, and 'tis well if it takes,
> If not, the Trumpeter breaks;
> And they that are my friends, that come to see my Play
> If it happens to rain shall have a Coach to carry 'em away.[1]

For this performance the doors were opened at 5 p.m. and the curtain rose at 7 p.m.

A new company of comedians advertised on 26 December that they intended to play in the Bowling Green booth for the remainder of the winter.[2] The booth was evidently a permanent one and was made commodious and warm for mid-winter. At their other booth Lee and Harper revived *Whittington* from the previous year since it had given such 'a general Satisfaction to all Spectators that had seen it'.[3]

Fielding did not attend Southwark this year 'for that he received such continual insults from the Constables of that place in the time of the last Southwark Fair'.[4]

1733

Hogarth's picture of Southwark Fair was painted in 1733 and engraved two years later. As it has been described in detail elsewhere,[5] it suffices here to mention the theatrical booths that it illustrates (Pl. III). Before each one is the balcony on which the actors parade to attract patrons. Show cloths advertise what can be seen within. On the left in the engraving, Theophilus Cibber and Bullock show the *Fall of Bajazet* and the parade platform is breaking, hurling the players in confusion to the ground. This was the year in which Cibber and some of the chief Drury Lane players seceded from that theatre as a result of a quarrel with the chief patentee, Highmore. Hogarth depicts a show cloth hung from Cibber and Bullock's booth, the design of which closely follows Laguerre's engraving, 'Stage Mutiny',

---

[1] *Daily Post*, 12 October 1732.   [2] *Ibid.* 26 December.
[3] *Daily Post*, 18 September.   [4] *Ibid.* 4 September.
[5] *Catalogue of Prints and Drawings in the British Museum. Political and Personal Satires*, vol. II, p. 832.

which caricatured the situation. Whether in fact such a banner was hung out we do not know, but the play is correct. At Cibber, Griffin, Bullock and Hallam's booth *Tamerlane* was performed intermixed with *The Miser*.[1] This is the first example in the fair of two separate plays being mingled, presumably in alternate scenes of tragedy and comedy; but it was only an extension of the traditional custom of low comedy interludes in romantic drolls. Hogarth depicts Lee and Harper's booth with a show cloth of their famous *Siege of Troy*, which they had not actually played at Southwark Fair since 1726. In 1733 they repeated their Bartholomew Fair programme[2] of *Jephtha's Rash Vow*, with Hulett, Hicks and Harper in the same roles, Roberts as Elon; Hewet as Jethro; Morgan as Zekiel; Mrs Purden as Miriam, and Mrs Morgan as Nurse; followed by the same pantomimic opera, *The Fall of Phaeton*.

At their second booth, at the lower end of Mermaid Court, Lee and Harper brought, from Tottenham Court Fair, *Bateman: or, the Unhappy Marriage*, followed by Theophilus Cibber's pantomime *The Harlot's Progress or The Ridotto Al' Fresco*.[3]

The terrible press of the crowds caused a fatal accident. On 12 September the *Daily Journal* reported: 'On Monday night last a woman who delivered out Bills at Mrs Lee and Harper's in Borough Fair, was so terribly squeezed by the people crowding in upon her that she soon after expired.' Mrs Lee again kept her booth on the Bowling Green open until mid-October when she gave *Oroonoko* as a benefit for the Merry Trumpeter.[4]

Other booths, not depicted by Hogarth, were Miller, Mills and Oates's where *Jane Shore, with the Comical Humours of Sir Anthony Noodle and his man Weazle* was presented; Fielding and Hippisley's where, after *Love and Jealousy or the Downfall of Alexander the Great*, Mrs Pritchard repeated her performance of Loveit in *A Cure for Covetousness or the Cheats of Scapin* from Bartholomew Fair;[5] Yeates senior and junior's with a ballad

---

[1] Genest, *op. cit.* vol. III, p. 401.
[2] Above, p. 40; *Country Journal*, 8 September 1733; *Daily Post*, 10 September.
[3] *Country Journal*, 15 September; *Daily Post*, 10 September; below, p. 125.
[4] *Daily Post*, 16 October.
[5] Above, p. 39. Genest, *op. cit.* vol. X, p. 161.

opera, *The Harlot's Progress*.[1] On one of the Hogarth prints of Southwark Fair in the British Museum some verses are inscribed from which the following lines about the players may be quoted:[2]

> Stage players now of Smithfield take their leave,
> And hither come, more Shillings to receive.
> For this their Painted Cloths, full wide displayed,
> Tell ev'ry branch of the Dramatic Trade.
> Harper and Lee their Trojan horse display,
> Troy's burnt, and Paris kill'd nine times a day...
> The fall of Bajazet, alas! too true!
> Cibber and Bullock here present to view...
> On the Parades the Players march along
> Each proper habited, a shining throng.

1734

The Siege of Troy was revived by Lee and Harper in 1734 in a booth in Axe and Bottle Yard, which was a new site. They advertised that 'in its decorations, machinery, and paintings [it] far exceeds anything of the like kind that ever was seen in the fairs before, the scenes and clothing being entirely new'. The cast was Paris, Hulett; Menelaus, Roberts; Ulysses, Aston; Sinon, Hind; Captain of the Guard, Mackenzie; Bristle, Morgan; Butcher, Pearce; Tailor, Hicks; Cassandra, Mrs Spiller; Venus, Mrs Lacy; Helen, Mrs Purden; Cobler's Wife, Mrs Morgan. Terwin had a puppet show of the same name in Mermaid Court, but Lee and Harper were at pains to explain that theirs was 'the only celebrated droll of that kind... first brought to perfection by the late famous Mrs Mynns and can only be performed by her daughter Mrs Lee'.[3] At the Bowling Green booth was performed the droll of *The True and Ancient History of Maudlin, the Merchants Daughter of Bristol and her Constant Lover Antonio... With the Comical Humours of Roger, Antonio's Man.* This was followed by *The Intriguing Harlequin, or Any Wife Better than None.* Singing and dancing were by Miss Sandham, Woodward and Taylor, and a new dialogue was sung by Excell and Mrs Fitzgerald.[4]

[1] *Daily Post*, 10 September 1733.   [2] *Political and Personal Satires*, vol. II, p. 840.
[3] B.M., a collection of advertisements... relating to Southwark Fair.
[4] *Ibid*.

The Playhouse Bill was before the House of Commons in 1735, and among those who protested against it was Hannah Lee of the parish of St George's, Southwark, whose petition was presented on 21 April.[1] Mrs Lee stated that she and her mother, Anne Mynns, had resided in the parish upwards of thirty years, during which time their servants had annually performed drolls at Southwark Fair for the entertainment of those who resorted there, according to ancient custom. She claimed to have erected at her own expense 'Two Booths, and hath expended, in such Buildings, Cloaths, Scenes, Decorations, and other Necessaries, the sum of 2000 *l.* and upwards; which is her whole Substance and on which she subsists; and that being now infirm in Body, and old, she must be ruined, if the Bill should pass into Law'. She feared that it would prevent her exhibiting her annual entertainments and pointed out 'that her and her late Mother's Companies have always been Nurseries for the greatest Performers that ever acted on the *British* Stage, particularly the celebrated Mr *Powell* and Mr *Booth*, as well as great Numbers of the present Actors at the Theatres of *Drury Lane* and *Covent Garden*'. Her entertainments, she argued, were 'innocent and amusing' and honoured by the greatest in the land. She requested that she might be heard, through her counsel, against the section of the Bill that might affect her and asked the House to grant her such relief as seemed fitting. Her petition was rejected, but the Bill was withdrawn on 30 April, to be succeeded in 1737 by the Licensing Act.

[1] *House of Commons Journals* (1735), p. 470.

CHAPTER V

SOUTHWARK FAIR
1736–1762

1736–1739

THERE are no advertisements for play booths in 1735 when the
fair was limited to three days, though Mrs Lee was performing;[1]
nor did they advertise in 1736, though they were there, for the
Prince and Princess of Wales saw *King John* at Jones and Lacy's
booth.[2] There are again no records for 1737, but in 1738 they
were back in force despite the Licensing Act. Harper was no
longer with Mrs Lee. He had a stroke in the autumn, though he
lived on until 1 January 1742. Mrs Lee gave, at her Bowling
Green booth, *Merlin, the British Enchanter or St George of
England*, presumably a puppet show, since appropriate names
are given to the cast: Merlin, Oldman; St George, Champion;
Spanish Giant, Sig. Furioso. It was followed by *The Country
Farmer, or Trick upon Trick* and by the Lord Mayor's Show from
Whittington. The band of trumpets, French horns, violins, hautboys, bassoons and kettledrums was one of the attractions.[3]
Thereafter booth managers frequently advertised similar instruments. At Hallam's booth at the bottom of Mermaid Court, an
entertainment was put on called *The Man's Bewitch'd, or the
Devil to do about Her. With the Comical Humours of Squire Graygoose and his Man Doodle, my Lady Graygoose and Captain Atall.*
The Squire was played by Bencraft; Doodle by Dove; Atall, in
the character of Harlequin, by Rosoman; Lady Graygoose, in
the character of Columbine, by Mrs Dove. The pantomime was
performed by the same French dancers as at Bartholomew Fair
and the 'humours' had been seen at Hallam and Fielding's booth
at Tottenham Court Fair that season.[4] A band of music was
advertised and the booth was 'commodiously illuminated with

---

[1] Above, p. 73.   [2] *Grub-Street Journal*, 16 September 1736.
[3] *London Daily Post*, 12 September 1738.   [4] Above, p. 44; below, p. 126.

several large Moons and Lanthorns'. Numbers flocked to see
the entertainments. The Prince and Princess of Wales patronised
both Mrs Lee's and Hallam's booths and expressed their satisfaction.[1]

On 19 April 1739 the *Daily Post* reported that, on 10 April,
Yeates, the conjuror and puppet showman, had married Mrs
Lee, 'well known for her agreeably entertaining the Town with
Drolls at Bartholomew and Southwark Fairs etc. on which occasion a considerable fortune in South Sea Stock was made over
to the Bridegroom'. Whether this is true, a rumour or a satirical
quip, Mrs Lee retained her old name at the fair where she took
into partnership the dancer and harlequin, Phillips. They gave
the same medley, including the pantomime *Colombine Courtezan*,
as at Bartholomew Fair.[2]

In 1740 Lee and Phillips produced *Cephalus with the Death of
Procris* as it had been performed at Drury Lane, with Parry as
Cephalus, Miss Atherton from Drury Lane as Procris, and Mrs
Booth as Aurora.[3] This was followed by a revival, after three
years,[4] of the pantomime *Harlequin Faustus* with Phillips as
Harlequin; Closson, Servant; Topham, Pluto; Mrs Jones, Miller;
Mrs Lacy, Helen; and Mrs Phillips, Miller's wife. Yeates had
probably taken over Mrs Lee's second booth, as he is found this
year on the Bowling Green. He also transferred from puppets
to live shows and brought on from Bartholomew and Welsh
Fairs *The History of Orpheus and the Death of Eurydice and The
Metamorphosis of Harlequin*,[5] with additions to the cast of Mrs
Hickson, Sturges, Macguire, Mrs Hill, Price, and Mrs Jeffries.[6]
The fair must have lasted a fortnight, as advertisements appear
from its opening on 8 September to 20 September. The fair of
1741 was a short one but Mrs Lee, then in partnership with
Woodward,[7] presented the tragi-comedy of *The Prophetess: or,
The History of Dioclesian. With the Comical Humours of Geta,
Servant to Dioclesian*. It was followed by a new pantomime,

[1] *London Daily Post*, 11, 12 September 1738.
[2] Above, p. 46; *London Daily Post*, 7 September 1739.
[3] J. H[aslewood], *op. cit.* vol. IX, f. 60v.
[4] I have not traced a previous performance at Southwark.
[5] Above, p. 47, below, p. 129.   [6] *London Daily Post*, 5, 20 September 1740.
[7] *London Daily Post*, 15 September 1741.

Harlequin, the Man in the Moon with his Adventures at Southwark Fair, in which Woodward danced Harlequin; Mrs Dove, Columbine; other parts being filled by Vaughan, Warner, Miss White, Wallis, Peterson, Bambridge, Mrs Freeman, Mrs Smith and Mrs Carr. The show was open from 12 to 9 p.m. Fawkes and Pinchbeck, who displayed a machine showing the Siege of Carthagena, also presented an interlude called the *Baronet Bit*.[1]

On 10 September between one and two in the morning rogues broke into the booth of young Yeates, stole his wardrobe to the value of nearly £40 and incapacitated him from acting for a while.[2]

1742–1743

In 1742 Phillips and Mrs Lee were again in partnership[3] and brought from Bartholomew Fair a two-act comedy, *The Indian Merchant: or, the Happy Pair. Interspers'd with the Comical Humours of The Intriguing Chambermaid*, and a pantomime, *The Miser Bit; or Harlequin Reveller*. Both were performed by players from the theatres, among whom were Mr and Mrs Phillips, Mr and Mrs Dove, and Smith. On 21 September, the last day of the fair, at 6 p.m., for Mrs Phillips's benefit, *The Unhappy Favourite* and *The Mock Doctor* were played.[4]

In spite of the fact that he had been arrested the previous year,[5] Seward had a booth on the Bowling Green where, on 21–2 September he presented *King Edward the Fourth, or the Life of Robin Hood* together with *The Adventures of Harlequin or the Miser Bit*.[6]

A great theatrical booth on the Bowling Green was used for a series of performances in February 1743.[7] This is probably the New Theatre on the Bowling Green, opposite the old tiled booth, where at fair time *The Plotting Lovers: or The Old One Trick'd at Last* was revived, followed by *Harlequin Triumphant*[8] with Mr and Mrs Rosoman as Harlequin and Columbine, Warner as Clown, and Yeates as Squire. Part of the stage was formed into

---

[1] *Ibid*. 10 September 1741.   [2] *Morning Advertiser*, 14 September.
[3] Folder in Southwark Library with MS. notes; above, p. 51.
[4] *Daily Advertiser*, 20 September 1742.   [5] Above, p. 73.
[6] *Daily Advertiser*, 21 September.
[7] *London Daily Post*, 25 February 1742/3.
[8] *Daily Advertiser*, 8 September 1743.

boxes for the better reception of the ladies and gentlemen. Hughes and Scouten record a performance there of *Trick upon Trick*[1] but this is presumably only a sub-title for *Harlequin Triumphant*, as it had been so used at May Fair that year. *Trick upon Trick* had been given at Bartholomew Fair just previously.[2]

We first hear of a 'Great Theatrical Til'd Booth', which may have been a new or enlarged structure to be distinguished from the old tiled booth mentioned above. This latter may have been the tiled booth which Powell and Yeates had opposite Mrs Lee as early as 1726.[3] At the Great Tiled Booth was given the *True and Ancient History of the Blind Beggar of Bethnal Green. With the Comical Humours of Tom Strowd, a Country Farmer's Son, and Gudgeon his Man*. Comparison of the dramatis personae with that of John Day's old comedy shows that the droll was based on it. The cast was: Lord Mumford, Cushing; King, Woodhouse; Sir Robert Westford, Bambridge; Capt. Westwood, Malone; Gamester, Clough; Lady Westford, Mrs Bambridge; Arabella, Mrs Cushing; Widow, Mrs Motteux; Tom Strowd, Hacket; Gudgeon, Clarke. Singing and dancing were by Price, and Master and Miss Morris. The play was followed by a representation of the Battle of Dettingen with the English and French forces newly clothed and with new machinery and scenes.[4]

1744–1748

Theatrical booths were forbidden both at Southwark and Bartholomew Fairs in 1744. As a result, the Tiled Booth housed instead a company of Italian, Dutch and English tumblers who gave an entertainment entitled *The Force of Magick: or The Adventures of Harlequin*,[5] and Yeates had a Grand Temple of the Arts.

We hear of no further performances until 1746, when Lee returned with *Love in a Labyrinth or a School for a Wife*, followed by *Harlequin Invader, or Columbine Cameron* as at Bartholomew Fair.[6] After the fair was over, on 21 October, *The Beaux Stratagem* and *The Devil to Pay* were given at the 'Old Theatre'

---

[1] *Op. cit.* p. 205.   [2] Above, p. 52.   [3] *Daily Post*, 13 September 1726.
[4] *London Daily Post*, 8 September 1743.
[5] *General Advertiser*, 10 September 1744.   [6] Above, p. 53.

on the Bowling Green for the benefit of Daniel, who played Scrub.[1] The term 'Old Theatre' may refer to Mrs Lee's former booth as distinct from the 'New Theatre' of 1743. There seem to have been two permanent structures on the Bowling Green at the time.

Lee and Yeates were in partnership at the Great Tiled Booth in 1747 where they revived *The Siege of Troy* as at Bartholomew Fair.[2] Hughes and Scouten record a performance of *Trick upon Trick* on 24 September;[3] this may have been Yarrow's farce *Trick upon Trick; or, the Vintner Out-witted* or a revival of the pantomime of 1743.

In 1748 advertisements are discontinued after 12 September, but there was a revival in theatrical activity. The two Yeates's, Lee and Warner brought on *The Unnatural Parents* from Bartholomew Fair.[4] It was performed at the Great Tiled Booth with entirely new scenes and clothes and with a somewhat different cast, including Cuthbert, Cunningham, Harrison, Thompson, Mason, Adams, Mrs Peters, Mrs Pile and Mrs Jones. Bridges, Cross, Burton and Vaughan likewise brought from Smithfield their droll, *The Northern Heroes* and their afterpiece *The Volunteers: Or, the Adventures of Roderick Random and his Friend Strap*. As the duration of the fair was so limited, performances began early.[5] From Smithfield too came Hussey, who had a booth on the Bowling Green with *The Constant Quaker* and the pantomime of *Harlequin's Frolics*.[6]

1749–1751

Lee, Yeates and Warner announced in 1749 that 'The Proprietors have been at a great Expence in having their Booth repaired and surveyed, in order to accommodate the Gentry and others in an agreeable Manner, and to prevent any Accident that might happen thro' the Carelessness of Workmen'. This definitely proves that their Great Tiled Booth was permanent,

[1] *General Advertiser*, 21 October 1746.
[2] *Ibid.* 8 September 1747; above, p. 54.   [3] *Op. cit.* p. 205.
[4] *General Advertiser*, 8, 12 September 1748; above, p. 55.
[5] *Ibid.* 7 September; *Penny London Post*, 5–7 September; above, p. 54.
[6] Frost, *op. cit.* p. 144; above, p. 55.

since it was repaired and not re-erected. Mrs Lee's old droll of *Whittington* was revived, as at Bartholomew Fair.[1]

At Phillips's booth on the Bowling Green a droll entitled *The Industrious Lovers; or, The Yorkshire-Man Bit* was performed with the pantomime of *The Harlot's Progress. With the Escape of Harlequin into a Quart Bottle and Signor Jumpedo.* The pantomime had been given by Phillips at Bartholomew Fair[2] and there was only one change in the cast, Mrs Peters dancing the Maid instead of Miss Berry. This was once again a short fair and advertisements cease after 12 September.

After this Lee is heard of no more. If it was still Mrs Lee, she had probably retired or died, as she referred to herself as old in 1735. Indeed the well-known names were gradually disappearing from the fair. The limitation to three days did not make it worth while for the comedians from the theatres to come any more, and they were replaced by strollers or companies from the provinces.

Yeates and Warner had the booth in 1750 when they revived *Jephtha's Rash Vow* with the original music, as performed by Mrs Lee. Carr played Jephtha; Warner, Capt. Bluster; Mrs Grimwood, Princess Miriam; Mrs Smith, Nurse; other roles being taken by Clark, Jones, Coleman, Malone, Allen and Grimwood. At Yeates's Great Tiled Booth *The Unhappy Favourite*, followed by *The Mock Doctor*,[3] was given on 14 September. The fair began on 7 September and there are no advertisements after 12 September.

A company of comedians acted the droll, *King Edward IV. Or the Lives of Robin Hood and Little John. With the Comical Humours of the Pindar of Wakefield*, in the Great Tiled Booth in 1751.[4] There were no advertisements after the three days were up, except for the benefit of Phillips on 18 September when *Hamlet* was performed, followed by *The Lying Valet*.[5]

---

[1] *General Advertiser*, 6 Sept. 1749; above, p. 55.   [2] *Ibid.*; above, p. 56.
[3] *Ibid.* 10, 14 September 1750.
[4] *Ibid.* 7 September 1751.   [5] *Ibid.* 18 September.

1752–1755

The change over to the Gregorian calendar in 1752 meant that the dates between 2 and 14 September were omitted. The fair was opened on 18 September and confined to three days, with a threat of prosecution against anyone keeping a booth open or exhibiting a droll after that limit.[1] At the Tiled Booth, a droll entitled *The Rake Reform'd, or, The Happy Lovers* was presented, followed by Steward's performance on the slack wire.

At Bence's booth on the Bowling Green, *The Intriguing Chambermaid or, The Wanton Wife*, which may or may not have had any connection with Fielding's farce, was performed with a pantomime, *Harlequin Triumphant: or Pantaloon Outwitted*, with Harlequin, Gayward; Pantaloon, M. Devisse; Servant, Smith; Clown, Hussey; and Columbine, Madame Grimaldi.[2] The last named may have been the first wife of Signor Grimaldi, the great clown's father.

At the three-day fair in 1753, *The Sham Physician: or Trick for Trick* and *The Distress'd Sailor: with the Comical Humours of the Wapping Landlady* were given at the Tiled Booth.[3] The latter was probably the same piece as given at Smithfield with the sub-title, *The Merry Humours of the Ladies of Pleasure.*[4]

Four theatrical booths were advertised at Southwark Fair in 1754.[5] Harlequin Phillips presented at his Great Theatrical Booth on the Bowling Green a droll, *The Distress'd Merchant, or, the Jew of Venice*,[6] presumably taken from Lansdowne's adaptation of *The Merchant of Venice*. Phillips danced Harlequin in a new pantomime *The Escape of Harlequin, or Fribble Trick'd*, which concluded with a comic dance, *The Humours of Cloth Fair*. He advertised that he had been at great expense for machinery, habits and decorations and hoped for the usual indulgence from the nobility and gentry.

Yeates junior showed at his Great Tiled Booth *The Tender Husband, or The Artful Wife* with a new pantomime, *Harlequin*

---

[1] *Ibid.* 18, 22 September 1752.   [2] *Ibid.* 18, 22 September.
[3] *Public Advertiser*, 18, 24 September 1753.   [4] Above, p. 58.
[5] All information for 1754 and 1755 kindly supplied by Professor A. H. Scouten from files in the Folger Shakespeare Library.
[6] *Daily Advertiser*, 16, 18, 21 September; *Public Advertiser*, 23, 24 September.

Barber, or, Mezzetin in the Suds.[1] While the booth was filling a citizen of London entertained with balances on a slack wire in full swing. The scenes and clothes were new.

At Bence's booth 'Mrs Midnight' presented her Grand Carnival Concert with *The Old Woman's Oratory* and a pantomime burletta by a company of Lilliputians, entitled *The Birth of Harlequin or The Old Woman's Whim*.[2] In order to distinguish the booth she hoisted the English colours. The fourth booth was occupied by a company of comedians from Bath in *The Miser Outwitted, or, Phelim in the Suds*.[3] At performances on 23 and 24 September they added a new pantomime, *Canning's Escape*.

The three days allowed for the fair from 18 to 20 September were exceeded, in spite of a notice from the Borough of Southwark in the *Daily Advertiser* on the opening day which threatened prosecution of any players who kept their booths open after the permitted span. The players were again threatened with prosecution in 1755 if they kept their booths open longer than from 18 to 20 September;[4] but again the warning went unheeded and Warner and widow Yeates continued to advertise their show up to 22 September.[5] At the Great Tiled Booth they presented *The Unnatural Parents*; the same droll that Mrs Lee had performed twenty years previously, but now misleadingly described as an 'Historical Play'.

At the New Theatre, Bowling Green, Phillips's company presented *The Injur'd Merchant, or, The Extravagant Son* and as afterpiece *The Jew in Distress, or Harlequin Turn'd Sharper*.[6] Phillips was Harlequin and others who appeared were Mrs Vaux and Mrs St John.

1756–1760

In 1756 we find at Warner's Tiled Booth on the Bowling Green a droll entitled *The Lover's Metamorphosis: Or, More Ways than One to win Her*, followed by *The Stratagems of Harlequin*. The scenes, clothes, music and paintings were given out as new, and

---

[1] *Public Advertiser*, 16, 17 September; *Daily Advertiser*, 18–24 September 1754.
[2] *Daily Advertiser*, 19–24 September.
[3] *Ibid*. 21, 23, 24 September.
[4] *Ibid*. 19 September 1755.   [5] *Ibid*. 18–22 September.
[6] *Public Advertiser*, 18 September.

the band consisted of violins, bassoons and hautboys.[1] In 1757
Warner announced that his booth had been made 'very theatrical
and commodious'. His entertainment consisted of a droll, *The
Lover: Or, A Tit-Bit for a Nice Palate*, and a new pantomime,
Harlequin's Vagaries.[2] Warner was back in 1758 with a comic
entertainment, *The Old Widow Bewitch'd or, The Devil to do
about Her*, 'In which will be shewn the extraordinary Courtship
of Loadham the Fat, Pinchgut the Lean, and his Man Meager:
And the Adventures of Capt. Puff Culverin, and Dermot Magrah
Ballingbrogue the Irish Captain'. There was a representation of
the recent siege and capture of Cape Breton with the procession
of colours and standards.[3] The comedy may have been Mottley's
of that name, brought out at Goodman's Fields in 1730; more
likely it was a variant of *The Man's Bewitch'd, or the Devil to do
about Her* which Hallam had given at the fair in 1738.[4] We first
come on the famous low comedian, Edward Shuter, at the fair in
1759, when he brought on from Bartholomew Fair *The French
Flogg'd*.[5]

In 1760 he returned at the Tiled Booth with an 'Entertainment of Wit and Humour' which included Fielding's *Don Quixote
in England. With the Tragic Adventure of the Knight of the Woeful
Countenance, and the Comical Humours of his Merry Squire Sancho
Panza*. The entertainment concluded with a view of the monu-
ment erected to General Wolfe and a monody on his death.
Shuter, whose advertisements were touched with originality,
announced that it was 'An Entertainment entirely adapted to the
taste of all Ladies, Gentlemen, Bucks, Bloods, and Choice Spirits;
but more especially those who are fond of Liberty and Roast-
Beef'.[6]

Foote's Haymarket company also took a large booth at the
bottom of the Bowling Green where they performed a comedy
entitled *The Female Minor*. Foote's *Minor* had been brought out
that year and this may have been an adapted version of it. The
company took a superior line in choosing ' to wave [*sic*] the usual

---

[1] *Ibid*. 17 September 1756.   [2] *Ibid*. 17 September 1757.
[3] *Ibid*. 16 September 1758.   [4] Above, p. 97.
[5] *Public Advertiser*, 18–21 September 1759. Reference supplied by Professor
A. H. Scouten from Folger Shakespeare Library. Above, p. 61.
[6] *Public Advertiser*, 13, 16 September 1760.

pompous and bombastic Stuff generally crowded into Advertisements on these Occasions. They only beg Leave to say, that they humbly presume, their having been at an uncommon Expence, Care and Trouble in getting up this Comedy will entitle them to some Degree of Preference and Encouragement above those Paltry Performances usually exhibited at Fairs.' They provided a coach-way within six yards of the booth, avoiding the fairground.[1] An accident occurred when some mischievous persons 'fastened up two lighted links, at the back part of the booth where the Minor was acted...and at the same time ripping one of the boards away and crying out fire surprised the audience to that degree, that some young woman jumped out of the gallery into the pit, and broke her legs'.[2] It was lucky that there was no worse panic.

1761–1762

Foote's troupe reappeared in 1761 when at their Large Theatrical Ordinary they presented, in Foote's style, *Dishes of Wit and Savoury Courses of Humour*. The audience was 'only entreated as a common Fee to give 2s. 6d. 1s. 6d. 1s. and 6d. according to their different Degrees'.[3] This time they imitated Shuter's gastronomic advertising: 'Here are no French Kickshaws and Frigasees, but good substantial Food for an English Stomach:—The Treat is ready, the Cooks waiting and will be served up the Instant the Guests are seated.'

On 21–22 September they presented a new comedy in Foote's style: *The Whimsical Battle of the Greybeards, Or the Humorous History of a Covent-Garden Adventure,* 'Containing the ridiculous Behaviour of Shela O'Flannegan the first Irish Woman introduced at any Fair, the odd Resentment of Col. Crackcrown, and his whimsical Duel with the purblind Major Blinco, the Adventures of two Lovers who have been the Cause of the Comical Altercation. The Marriage of Sawney Macgregor, a Scotch Footman and Shela O'Flannegan: With the fortunate Conclusion of Peace, by a Methodist Cobler.'[4] This farrago was followed by a comic dance by Signor Florentina, said to be from the Opera House in Turin,

---

[1] *Public Advertiser,* 20 September 1760.   [2] *Ibid.* 25 September.
[3] *Ibid.* 17 September 1761.   [4] *Ibid.* 21 September.

and an epithalamium on the royal nuptials of George III and Princess Charlotte.

Warner also celebrated this event at his Tiled Booth with *George for England; Or, The Triumphs of Roast Beef:* ' In which will be exhibited the Reception of George for England at the Court of Solyman, the Ægyptian Emperor, the Love of the Fair Sabrina; and the Rivalship of Mamamouchi, the Persian General Interspers'd with the Humours of Don Duello Flanconado; and the extraordinary Incidents that befel Esquire Gundy alias Glumglug de Gull, and his Culinarian Armour.' This St George droll was followed by *The Triumphs of Hymen: And the Landing of the Queen,* for which new music and dresses were provided.[1] The wire dancer, Mathews, performed, and diversions were brought on from Sadler's Wells, where the season had finished.[2]

On 22 June 1762, the Court of Common Council ordered that Lady Fair should not be kept any longer.[3] We hear of no theatrical entertainments at Southwark that year but in 1763 the players again attempted to erect their booths.[4] The high constable with over a hundred petty constables descended on Suffolk Place, adjoining St George's Fields, and forced the men who were putting them up to demolish them. There was no lawful authority any longer for keeping Lady Fair.

[1] Above, p. 62.   [2] *Public Advertiser*, 22 September.
[3] *Annual Register* (1762), vol. v, p. [90].
[4] *St James's Chronicle*, 17–20 September 1763.

CHAPTER VI

MAY FAIR

1696–1698

MAY FAIR dates from 1688 when James II granted a charter to Sir John Coell and his heirs to hold a fair for fifteen days from 1 May in Great Brookfield Street in the parish of St Martin in the Fields. There had, however, been a previous fair, called St James's Fair, on this site since the time of Charles I.[1] The actual location is referred to in 1699 as being east of Hyde Park near Bartlet [Berkeley] House.[2]

The players were there in 1696,[3] when *King William's Happy Deliverance and Glorious Triumph over his Enemies or the Consultation of the Pope, Devil, French King and the Grand Turk, with the Whole Form of the Siege of Namur, and the Humours of a Renegade French-Man and Brandy Jean, with the Conceits of Scaramouch and Harlequin* was given at Miller's Loyal Association Booth at the upper end of the market near Hyde Park Corner. James II's enemy and successor had just escaped assassination in Barclay's Plot, and Namur had been recaptured by him the previous year.

Ned Ward visited May Fair in 1699 and has left us his customary vivid description.[4] He expected to find several strolling companies but there was only one 'amongst whom Merry *Andrew* was very busie in coaxing the attentive Crow'd into a good Opinion of his Fraternitie's and his own Performances; and when with Abundance of Labour, Sweat and Nonsense, he had drawn a great Cluster of the Mob on his Parade, and was Just beginning to encourage them to *Walk in and take their*

---

[1] John Timbs, *Walks and Talks about London* (1865), p. 39; R. W. L. Muncey, *Our Old English Fairs*, p. 59, which gives the date incorrectly as 1689.

[2] *Post Man*, 4–6 April 1699; H. B. Wheatley, *London Past and Present*. Berkeley House stood on the site of Devonshire House.

[3] *London Society* (December 1863), p. 539, an earlier version of an article in J. Timbs, *op. cit.*

[4] *The London Spy*, Part VII, 10 May 1699.

Places, his unlucky opposite whose boarded Theatre entertain'd
the Publick with the wonderful activity of Indian Rope-dancers,
brings out a Couple of chattering *Homunculusses* drest up in
Scaramouch Habit; and everything that Merry *Andrew* and his
Second did on the one side, was mimick'd by the little Flat-
nos'd Comedians on the other, till the two Diminutive Buffoons,
by their Comical Gestures, had so prevail'd upon the gaping
Throng, that tho' *Andrew* had taken pains with all the wit he had
to collect the Stragling Rabble into their proper order, yet like
an unmannerly Audience, they turn'd their Arses upon the
Players, and devoted themselves wholly to the Monkeys, to the
great vexation of *Tom-Fool*, and all the Strutting Train of
imaginary Lords and Ladies'. Ward also mentions puppet shows
'where a Senseless Dialogue between *Punchenello* and the *Devil*
was convey'd to the Ears of a Listening Rabble thro' a Tin
Squeaker'.

1700–1707

The following year, 1700, the entertainments are described as
similar to those at Bartholomew Fair.[1] In 1701 'All the nobility
of the town' flocked there to see the famous Lady Mary (Mrs
Finley) dance on the rope.[2] Penkethman spoke an epilogue to
Durfey's *The Bath* at Drury Lane, complaining that his nose had
been put out of joint by her popularity:

> For I must own, whilst the Rope-dancing sway'd,
> I did take Snuff, you should my Face degrade;
> 'Gad; I began to think my Charm decay'd;
> And that the Beaus resolv'd a new Vagary
> To go and live and die with Lady Mary.

'To empty Benches here, I made grimace', he continued. When
she fell and hurt her foot:

> Such dire concern was then, such desolation
> As if 't had been the downfal of the Nation.

The rope dancers of the fair had drawn away the patrons of the
playhouse.

---

[1] *Flying Post*, 25–7 April 1700.
[2] MS. letter of Brian Fairfax, quoted by J. Nichols in his edition of *The Tatler*,
vol. I, p. 418.

Miller had a booth in 1702[1] where he presented the droll *Crispin and Crispianus, or a Shoemaker a Prince. With the Comical Humours of Barnaby, and the Shoemaker's Wife*, with the best machines, singing and dancing yet seen in the fair. A famous ladder dancer performed feats never seen before 'to the admiration of all men'. Opposite Miller's booth was Barnes and Finley's rope-dancing company, who advertised that they were as large as that at the previous Bartholomew Fair. A rumour that Lady Mary had died was contradicted,[2] and she continued to perform. Mills and Bullock had a booth next door, and opposite were Penkethman and Simpson, though we do not know what entertainments they provided. There was trouble this May because the fair was so thronged with rogues and pickpockets that the magistrates sent the constables to interfere; but the soldiers took the part of the mob, and one John Cooper, a peace officer, was killed. This produced an agitation for the suppression of the fair. However, it came to nothing at that time, and Barnes and Finley's booth was functioning at the same spot with Lady Mary in 1703.[3] Though no comedians are recorded they were probably there, for the theatres shut during the time of the fair.[4]

Penkethman had a rope-dancing booth in Brookfield Market Place for sixteen days in 1704. Among the entertainments he spoke an epilogue, not on the customary ass, but 'on an Elephant between Nine and Ten Foot High, arrived from Guinea, led upon the Stage by six blacks'. Penkethman evidently owned ground at the fair as he advertised shops or booths for rent.[5]

Timbs cites an undated bill advertising a droll at Husband's booth called *The Fairy Queen, or Love for Love, and the Humours of the Hungry Clown*, which was 'intermingled with a most delightful merry Comedy after the manner of an Opera, with extraordinary varieties of Singing, and Dancing, by his Grace the Duke of Southampton's Servants'.[6] This company, about

---

[1] *Post Man*, 2–5 May 1702.   [2] *Post-Boy*, 7–9 May 1702.
[3] *Daily Courant*, 14 April 1703.
[4] Emmett Avery and A. H. Scouten, 'Tentative Calendar of Daily Theatrical Performances in London, 1700–1704/5', *PMLA* (1948), vol. LXIII, pp. 127, 171.
[5] *Daily Courant*, 27 April 1704, quoted by Alfred Jackson, 'London Playhouses, 1700–1705', *R.E.S.* (1932), vol. VIII, p. 301.
[6] *Op. cit.*

which little is known, was playing in Richmond in 1714.[1] The advertisement probably belongs to a decade earlier, for among the performers were Sorine (mispelt Sorias) as Scaramouch and Baxter as Harlequin who played these roles at Southwark in 1704.[2] The French comedian, Sorine, was also in England in 1702 and 1703. The pair became well known at the Paris fairs, and 'the English harlequin', Baxter, eventually obtained the privilege of the Opéra Comique, but proved a failure. When the privilege was withdrawn he retired to a hermitage and died in an odour of sanctity in 1747.[3] Other entertainers in the troupe were the equestrian, Evans, and the vaulter, Thomas Simpson.

In 1705 Penkethman and Finley advertised that for some time past they had given satisfaction to the quality in their separate booths and planned to keep up the grandeur of the fair with new and surprising entertainments which would be further specified on bills in and about the town.[4]

The next fair in 1706 saw a combination of the widow Barnes, Evans and Finley, who claimed to show 'the most famous rope dancer of Europe'.[5] Penkethman's booth had no rope dancing.

Penkethman came out with a novelty in 1707[6] in the form of 'Eight Dancing Dogs, brought from Holland'. His last show was between 8 and 9 p.m. as the Park broke up.

1708–1709

By 1708 Edward Shepherd, the architect who gave his name to Shepherd Market, was the owner of the fairground, the market, and a house for which he paid a guinea rates.[7] It may possibly have been Shepherd who was responsible for 'the New Play-House in May-Fair', mentioned in an undated handbill,[8] where was presented 'The True and Ancient Story of Maudlin the *Merchants Daughter* of Bristol, and *her Lover* Antonio, How they

[1] S. Rosenfeld, *Strolling Players*, p. 274.   [2] Above, p. 76.
[3] Information from I. Kyrle Fletcher; Avery and Scouten, *op. cit.*; J. A. Jullien des Boulmiers, *Histoire du Théâtre de l'Opéra Comique* (1769); E. Campardon, *Les Spectacles de la Foire* (1877).
[4] *Daily Courant*, 28 April, 1, 2, 3 May 1705.
[5] *Ibid.* 1 May 1706.   [6] *Ibid.* 10, 13 May 1707. Cf. above, p. 20.
[7] Peter Cunningham, *A Handbook for London* (1849), vol. II, p. 543.
[8] Harleian 5931.

were cast away in a Tempest upon the Coast of *Barbary*; where the Mermaids were seen floating on the Seas, and singing on the Rocks, foretelling this Danger'. The droll was performed by the Duke of Southampton's Servants and was again intermingled with a delightful merry comedy after the manner of an opera. This bill may be earlier than 1708, since the other visit of the Duke of Southampton's Servants to the fair dates from about 1704, but its 'Vivat Regina' places it some time before the death of Queen Anne in 1714. The playhouse was to be 'known by the Balcone adorn'd with Blue Pillars twisted with Flowers' and it may well have been the playhouse in the fair for which Christopher Reeves paid a poor rate in 1709.[1]

In 1708 was published *The Devil upon Two Sticks; or, the Town Until'd; With the Comical Humours of Don Stulto and Siegnior Jingo* ' As it is Acted in Pinkeman's Booth in *May-Fair*'. This is merely a prose narrative taken from Le Sage's *Diable Boiteux*, which was evidently dramatised as part of Penkethman's entertainments.

In November 1708 the Grand Jury of Westminster, encouraged by the proceedings against Bartholomew Fair which had been taken by the City Council, made a presentment of May Fair on the usual grounds of its tending to corrupt Her Majesty's subjects, violate her peace and even endanger her person.[2] At a session on 6 December, the Grand Jury of Middlesex followed suit.[3] In a rare tract issued in 1709 one of the reasons given for suppressing the fair was that multitudes of booths were not used for trading but 'for Musick, Showes . . . Stage-Plays and Drolls'.[4] On 28 April Queen Anne, as a result of the presentments, issued a proclamation forbidding the erection of booths for 'Plays, Shows, Gaming, Musick-Meetings, or other disorderly Assemblies'.[5] In the preamble the charge was made that 'several Booths have been constantly built and made use of, during all the time of holding the said Fair, for entertaining Loose, Idle, Disorderly People with Plays, Interludes and Puppet-Shows'

---

[1] Cunningham, *op. cit.*   [2] Timbs, *op. cit.* p. 42; Muncey, *op. cit.* p. 67.
[3] Strype, *A Survey of the Cities of London and Westminster* (1720), vol. v, pp. 1, 4.
[4] Cunningham, *op. cit.* The Guildhall copy was destroyed by enemy action.
[5] *London Gazette*, 28 April–2 May 1709.

instead of for the sale of goods. May Fair was not abolished, as was rumoured in the *Tatler*,[1] but the players were banished, and Penkethman took his strollers instead to Greenwich Fair.

1716–1743

There is no further record of drolls at May Fair until 1743 but it seems that some entertainments were given. An engraving of the fair from a water-colour of 1716[2] (Pl. IV) shows a rope dancer, some kind of dramatic entertainment on an open platform, fencing on another, and a show cloth suspended from an inn depicting Adam and Eve for the puppet show of *The Creation of the World*. In 1721 part of the fairground was built over[3] though the fair continued, and, in 1735, Edward Shepherd erected Shepherd Market.[4]

By 1742 entertainments of rope dancing, tumbling, vaulting and a pantomime were being given at the New Wells, May Fair in March.[5] Though not strictly a fair theatre, it usually functioned during the fair.

The players were definitely back at May Fair in 1743 when Yeates, Warner and Rosoman had a booth at the upper end of Little Brookfield.[6] They presented a dramatic piece, *The Lover his Own Rival*, which had been altered by desire perhaps from the ballad opera of that name by Langford, followed by the pantomime *Trick upon Trick* which the proprietors were to take on to the next Bartholomew Fair.[7] Rosoman played Harlequin, and Warner, the Clown John Trot; Mrs Cushing preceded Mrs Rosoman as Columbine, and Cushing was a Country Squire. A pantomimic dance was topically entitled *The Humours of May Fair*. The booth was 'form'd after the manner of an amphitheatre, with Boxes on the Stage for the better reception of Gentlemen and Ladies'. The performances lasted from 12 noon until 10 at night.

Seward brought on from Southwark Fair the droll of *King Edward the IVth*[8] which was followed by *Harlequin Triumphant*;

[1] 18 April 1709, no. 4.   [2] *London Society* (December 1863), p. 539.
[3] Muncey, *op. cit.* p. 67.   [4] Archivist, Westminster Public Library.
[5] *Daily Advertiser*, 12 March 1742.   [6] *London Daily Post*, 9 May 1743.
[7] Above, p. 52.   [8] Above, p. 99.

or, Trick upon Trick.[1] Great numbers of gentry resorted to his
theatrical booth, and he advertised that he was prepared to give
a private performance at an hour's notice. The Prince of Wales
visited the fair on 7 May[2] but, though he saw the wild beasts,
there is no mention of his having patronised the play booths.

1744

There were more booths than ever before in 1744. On 1 May
we first hear of Hallam's New Theatre adjoining the Market
House.[3] According to the advertisement this was 'a regular
theatre' in which 'Ladies and Gentlemen will be entertained in
a more decent and commodious manner than they can possibly
be at any Booth'. The charges were: stage 2s. 6d., boxes 1s. 6d.,
pit 1s., gallery 6d. This may have been the theatre in the second
storey of Shepherd Market House where John Carter saw a
performance of *The Revenge*.[4] The word 'adjoining' does not,
however, suggest a second storey and it is possible that it was
not until later that it was moved to that position. Rocque's map of
1746 does not show any building other than the Market House,
but neither does it show the New Wells, which certainly existed
at that time. The main offering was a droll, *The Royal Heroe; or
the Lover of his Country*, 'Intermix'd with several Comical and
Diverting Scenes call'd The Blundering Brothers. With the
merry adventures of Timothy Addlepot and Davy Dunce.' The
cast was: Royal Hero, Johnson; Justinian, Boman; Fernando,
Jones; Eumenes, Mrs Charke; Timothy Addlepot, Godwin; Col.
Britain, Gold; Antonio, Adams; Lieutenant, Symonds; Davy
Dunce, Smith; Goldsmith, Blogg; Leonora, Mrs Godwin; Lucia,
Miss Charke; Angelina, Mrs Smith. The pantomime which fol-
lowed was *Harlequin Sclavonian; Or Monsieurs in the Suds*, with
Adams as Harlequin; Robinson, Pierrot; and 'the celebrated
Mrs Careless', Columbine. The band was of kettledrums,
trumpets and French horns. On 3 May the droll was changed to
*The Captive Prince; Or, Love and Loyalty. With the Comical
Humours of Sir John Falstaff and Ancient Pistol*[5] with the follow-

---

[1] *London Daily Post*, 9 May 1743.   [2] *Ibid.*
[3] *General Advertiser*, 1 May 1744.
[4] *Gentleman's Magazine* (1816), p. 228.   [5] *General Advertiser*, 3 May 1744.

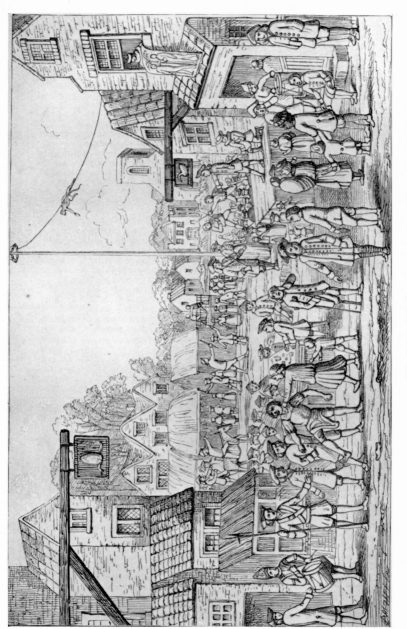

IV. May Fair in 1716

ing cast: Captive Prince, Miss Charke; Gloriana, Mrs Smith; Periander, Boman; Gonsalez, Dukes; Philotas, Edwards; Adlanca, Mrs Godwin; Doll Tearsheet, Mrs Freeman; Ancient Pistol, Mrs Charke; Falstaff, Smith; Shallow, Adams; Hostess Quickly, Godwin.

The theatre ceased to advertise after the close of the fair but reopened with a company of comedians on 7 June when *The Beaux Stratagem* was given. This was followed by *The Recruiting Officer* on 8 June and *The Careless Husband* for Mrs Charke's benefit on 27 June.[1] Tickets for the last were obtainable at taverns and at Mrs Charke's Soup-House facing the Silk-Dyers in Drury Lane. The notorious Charlotte Charke was such an attraction in this series of breeches' roles that she lived on the profits made at the fair and after until the ensuing Bartholomew Fair.[2] The theatre was again in use out of fair time for a series of plays in February 1745.[3]

At the fair of 1744 Yeates had a booth at the lower end of Brookfield where he revived the *True and Ancient History of the Blind Beggar of Bethnal-Green. With the Comical Humours of Tom Strowd and his Man Gudgeon*.[4] It concluded with a representation of the recent battle in the Mediterranean. Part of the stage was formed into boxes for the quality.

At Daniel and Smith's booth, the third from the Market House, was presented a droll, *Don Quixote de la Mancha*, 'With the comical Humours of his illustrious Squire Sancho Pancha, Governor of Baratravia, and Sir Polydorous Hunter, Knight of the Black Cap; containing the heroick Flights, notable Atchievments, and wonderful Actions of the Spanish Don; particularly the memorable Battle betwixt his Donship and the Windmill'.[5] The pantomime was *Harlequin Captive; or the Frenchman Bit*. Singing was provided by Conyers and Miss Clarke, and a Russian boy diverted the assembling company with tumbling.

The Wandering Prince of Troy at Middleton and Cushing's booth was 'Interspersed with the Comic Humours of the

[1] *Ibid.* 7, 8 June 1744 (B.M., Fillinham collection of cuttings, IV).
[2] C. Charke, *A Narrative of the Life of Mrs Charlotte Charke* (1929), p. 149.
[3] S. Rosenfeld, 'Shepherd's Market Theatre and May Fair Wells', *Theatre Notebook*, vol. V, p. 90.
[4] *General Advertiser*, 4 May 1744.   [5] *Daily Advertiser*, 30 April.

Carthagenian Landlady, Capt. Kielhaul and Nibble Bisket his Boatswain', to which was added the pantomime, *Le Mariage de Peasant*. Clothes and scenes were new, and the booth was fitted up in amphitheatre form with boxes on the stage. This popular entertainment drew crowds from afar who expressed their satisfaction at the representations 'and the Order, Regularity and Good-Humour with which they are performed'.[1]

At Punch's Theatre, Seward gave 'general Satisfaction to the Gentry, &c. with his comic Medley of Entertainments'.[2] He performed conjuring tricks followed by a puppet show: 'when Punch and his merry Family make their Appearance on the Stage, the Drolleries they exhibit are not to be heard with composed Countenances, but a universal Laughter spreads itself through the whole Audience, and the Booth rings with Shouts of Applause'.

The booths were drawing crowds, and it may have been this popularity that roused the authorities once again to endeavour to suppress them. The Grand Jury for Middlesex presented Hallam's New Theatre, 'where there are usually great Meetings of evil and disorderly idle Persons', in May 1744.[3] Many believed it would be closed down but it continued to advertise and play. It even reopened in February 1745[4] quite independently of the fair and in flagrant defiance of the law.

1745

Just before the fair was due to open, in April 1745, the city justices issued an order for suppressing disorders by the arrest of players. The following January, hearing that the players were again contracting for ground to erect their booths whilst others had taken rooms, parts of houses or yards for acting, the Middlesex County Sessions Court ordered the constables to apprehend them and announced that they would be subject to a fine of £50.[5] All this, as we shall see, had not the slightest effect, and in April

[1] *Daily Advertiser*, 1 May; *General Advertiser*, 7 May 1744.
[2] *General Advertiser*, 9 May.
[3] *Gentleman's Magazine* (1744), p. 278.
[4] For details of this season see *Theatre Notebook*, *loc. cit.*
[5] *Middlesex County Records. Calendar of Sessions Books* (1744–7), pp. 8, 36.

1746 the justices addressed a despairing letter to Lord Hardwicke, the Lord Chancellor, in which they admitted that the encouragement of the fairs was too powerful and the resort to them too popular for any attempts to crush them to be successful without backing and assistance from superior authority.[1] May Fair was the head and front of the offenders since it was the first of the long summer series and flourished with the connivance of many officials within the city of Westminster. If other fairs were suppressed, the justices would be accused of partiality. They asserted that 10,000 people assembled at May, Tottenham Court and Welsh Fairs, some of whom stayed into the early hours of morning. Vice and profanity, they alleged, gained ground; habits of drinking, gaming and swearing were inculcated, and gangs of thieves organised, whilst the poor grew poorer from squandering their money on the amusements. Even the constable who had been killed forty-four years previously was mentioned as evidence alongside unspecified 'great and heinous enormities' of the current fairs. The court then proceeded to throw the onus on the justices of the divisions in which the fairs were held.[2] It ordered them to issue warrants for the apprehension of players by the high constable with the assistance of petty constables and head boroughs. This order was to be printed and posted up so as to prevent players from contracting for ground on which to build their booths or sheds.

In April 1747 a further court order flung the opprobrious term rogues and vagabonds at the players and affirmed that their acting was illegal and occasioned quarrels, riots and tumults.[3] Once again the players had contracted for ground, and the responsibility for arresting them was cast on the divisional courts.

Shepherd did not ignore the justices' challenge and was at pains to publicise the fact that May Fair was conducted with decency and decorum 'as it remarkably has been every Year since the present Proprietor has had the Management thereof'.[4] He contended that he employed a large number of peace officers and assistants to prevent tumults and disorders. He was also careful

[1] *Ibid.* p. 51.   [2] *Ibid.* pp. 56, 57.
[3] *Ibid.* p. 94.   [4] *Daily Advertiser*, 2 May 1745.

to call attention to the legal standing of the fair by the following notice in the newspapers:[1] 'Whereas a Patent was granted by King Charles the First and confirm'd by King James the Second to the Proprietor of Great and Little Brook-Field, then in the Parish of St Martin in the Fields, now in the Parish of St George Hanover-Square, to hold a Fair during the Space of fifteen Days, to begin on the 1st Day of May next and of every May-Day for ever; The present Proprietor thinks it proper to apprize the Publick thereof, that it may not be thought that he attempts to do anything but by Virtue of the said Patent and no Ways to disturb the Publick Peace or act in Contradiction to the Laws of the Realm.'

Indeed it does not seem that the justices could abolish the fair in face of the patent, and all they might hope to achieve was to stop the players acting at it. That they completely failed to do so is evident from the number of booths of which we hear in 1745.

Middleton resurrected *Argalus and Parthenia*, one of Penkethman's drolls which had 'not been acted for thirty years'.[2] The pantomime, *Harlequin's Whim, or a True Touch of the Times*, was new. The advertisement he inserted amusingly concludes with the words 'this is no Puff'.

Jane Shore interspersed with *The Merry Cobler of Preston*, presumably a version of either Charles Johnson's or Christopher Bullock's farce, was shown at Hussey's booth, followed by a new pantomime, *Adventures of Harlequin* and later by *The Contrivances of Harlequin*.[3]

Yeates had the New Wells which he advertised as being a regular theatre. A new droll, *The Maiden Queen, or the Rival Generals*, interspersed with a comedy, *The Fair Hypocrite, or the Fond Husband*, was to be seen there, followed by *The Escapes of Harlequin*.[4] Performances by one Pinnington drew such crowds that he announced that those who did not wish to be incommoded by them might have a private performance any morning. The waxworks from Germany also proved very popular.[5]

---

[1] *Daily Advertiser*, 20 April 1745.
[2] *Ibid*. 7 May. There is no other record of this droll.
[3] *Ibid*. 6, 10, 13 May.   [4] *Ibid*. 10, 13 May.
[5] *Ibid*. 4, 6 May.

1746–1750

In 1746 Phillips and Hussey had a company at the New Wells.[1] Harlequin Phillips from Drury Lane had not appeared on the English stage for three years and his return in his favourite role of Harlequin in *The Harlot's Progress* must have been a great attraction. The pantomime was preceded by a comedy, *The Prodigal Son*, and followed by a grand chorus in honour of the Duke of Cumberland's recent victory at Culloden.

Charges at the Wells were: boxes 2s. 6d., pit 1s. 6d., gallery 6d., and the entertainments lasted from 12 noon until 10 p.m. If these times were kept the justices could hardly blame the players for the late hours of the fair. The Wells, as usual, continued to function long after the fair was over, with Phillips and Hussey's pantomimes and rope dancing by Miss Rayner.[2]

There are no advertisements for 1747 and, as this was the year that Edward Shepherd died, it is possible that no fair was held. After his death Elizabeth Shepherd paid the rates for the Market House.[3]

The New Wells reopened on 2 May 1748 with diversions and a pantomime, followed by Italian fireworks, as at the Haymarket.[4] A pint of wine for 1s. admitted to pit or boxes and half a pint to the gallery. On 3 May when *Miss in her Teens* was given the charges were: boxes 1s., pit 6d., and gallery 3d.—a considerable reduction on those of 1746.

Yeates again had the New Wells in 1749, where performances were given daily during the fair at 2, 5, 7 and 9 p.m. The shows were evidently longer, or less frequent, than the usual hourly ones. On 1 May was performed Mrs Lee's old droll, *The Unnatural Parents; or, The Fair Maid of the West, Also the Comical Humours and Adventures of Trusty, her Father's Man, and the Three Witches*.[5] The original dance by three wildcats of the wood was included. The scenes and clothes were new, and a good band was advertised. On 10 May the droll was changed to *Dorastus*

---

[1] *General Advertiser*, 1 May 1746.   [2] S. Rosenfeld, *Theatre Notebook*, vol. v.
[3] Information from the Archivist, Westminster Public Library.
[4] *General Advertiser*, 30 April, 3 May 1748.
[5] *Ibid*. 29 April 1749.

and Fawnia; Or, The Royal Shepherd and Sheperdess.[1] This was
a revival of the old Bartholomew Fair droll of 1703 based on
Greene's *Pandosto.* The conservatism of the fair offerings is well
demonstrated by these two pieces.

In 1750 at Shepherd Market, *Love and Empire; or Virtue
Triumphant* and *School for a Wife* were presented, and on 10 May
the programme was changed to *Tamerlane the Great* and a revival
of *Harlequin Fortune Teller.*[2] There are no further advertisements for shows. The date of the fair changed from 1 May to
12 May in 1753,[3] as a result of the change of calendar. In April
1763 the inhabitants of Curzon Street and the neighbourhood
signed a remonstrance against the disorders of the fair and, the
following year, Pearce, guardian to Shepherd's nephew Howell,
invoked the vestry's assistance in putting a stop to riotous proceedings.[4] The magistrates were recommended to prevent such
assemblies. The end came when the Earl of Coventry purchased
a house in Piccadilly in 1764 and, annoyed by the 'unceasing
uproar during the month of the Fair', used his influence to have
it finally abolished.

[1] *General Advertiser*, 10 May 1749.
[2] I owe this information, from the *Daily Advertiser*, 1, 10 May 1750, to Professor A. H. Scouten.
[3] *Public Advertiser*, 1 May 1753.
[4] Information from the Archivist, Westminster Public Library.

CHAPTER VII

SOME LESSER FAIRS

TOTTENHAM COURT FAIR

THE fair at Tottenham Court which, in the early eighteenth century, was on the outskirts of London, was held annually from 4 August for fourteen days, thus preceding Bartholomew and Southwark Fairs. It covered the fields on the right hand side of the road that led from St Martin's in the Fields to the old Adam and Eve tavern, which is shown in Hogarth's 'March to Finchley'.[1] It was one of the so-called Gooseberry Fairs.[2] We do not know when it was first held, but the players were there in 1717[3] when Leigh and Jubilee Dicky Norris from the Theatre Royal had 'the great Theatrical Booth at Tottenham Court during the Time of the Fair' from Monday 5 August to 13 August. They presented *The History of Jane Shore. With the Pleasant and Comical Adventures of Sir Anthony Noodle and his Little Man Weazle*. Mrs Spiller was the heroine and Norris was Weazle. This is the first time this droll is found at the fairs, though it became very popular thereafter. Singing and dancing, both serious and comic, were provided between the acts. But a warrant was issued by the justices for the apprehension of the players, as a result of which they were arrested and their booths pulled down and taken away.[4]

An order was made against the players at the Middlesex County Sessions in July 1718, and again in 1724.[5] In June 1725 the high constable of Holborn was ordered to give notice of the illegality of performing drolls there. Nevertheless, in July 1727 it was reported to the court that 'several common players of interludes' had erected booths and acted drolls for several years

---

[1] Geo. Clinch, *Marylebone and St Pancras* (1890), p. 161; G. W. Thornbury and E. Walford, *Old and New London*, vol. IV, p. 477; W. Wroth, *London Pleasure Gardens* (1896), pp. 127–8; R. Wilkinson, *Londina Illustrata*, vol. I.
[2] John T. Smith, *A Book for a Rainy Day* (1845), p. 26.
[3] *Daily Courant*, 5 August 1717,   [4] *Flying Post*, 22 August 1717.
[5] *Middlesex Sessions Books* (1722–7), pp. 160, 246.

at 'Tottenhoe alias Tottenhall alias Tottenham Court', and that some were contracting for ground on which to build booths. Constables were ordered to affix the prohibition in prominent places and, if the actors defied it, they were to be apprehended and punished.[1] On 14 November 1727 the Court of Aldermen of the City of London opposed John Thurmond's application to hold a fair annually in Murrells Fields in the village of Tottenhall for buying and selling all kinds of goods.[2] In all likelihood this was the dancer and pantomimist Thurmond,[3] who was a member of the Drury Lane company. But the authorities could not or would not enforce order. A writer in *The Craftsman* describes how 'there were *two Jack-puddings* entertaining the Popellace from a gallery on the Outside of one of the *Booths*; one of whom represented an *Englishman* and the other a *Spaniard*, and the Spaniard knocked down the Englishman'.[4] This referred to the Spanish war, and the writer was shocked at the ridicule of his countrymen in the unpatriotic knockabout. He protested that no example had been made of the perpetrators: 'It seems very extraordinary that a Parcel of *infamous Strollers* should be indulg'd contrary to *Law*, in debauching the Morals of the People, with their lewd and ridiculous Mummery.'

In 1728 Lee and Petit had a booth at the fair where actors from the theatres performed the *History of Maudlin, the Merchants Daughter of Bristol; and Her Constant Lover Antonio with the Comical Humours of Roger, Antonio's Man*.[5] Singing and dancing between the acts were provided by Sandham, Miss Sandham, Mrs Woodward and Taylor. In 1730 there were two theatrical booths.[6] The company from Goodman's Fields Theatre was at a booth next to the Turnpike, where they performed a droll written by Doggett entitled *Mad Tom of Bedlam: or, The Distress'd Lovers. With the Comical Humours of Squire Numscul.* Mad Tom was acted by William Giffard, Numscul by Penkethman the younger, other roles by Huddy, R. and W. Williams, Pearce, Machen, Eaton, Collet, Mrs Haughton, Mrs Thomas,

---

[1] *Middlesex Sessions Books* (1727–9), p. 24.
[2] Repertory 132, p. 6.   [3] See *D.N.B.*
[4] 25 August 1727, quoted, in Frederick Miller, *Saint Pancras Past and Present* (1874).
[5] *Country Journal*, 10 August 1728.   [6] *Daily Post*, 9, 10 August 1730.

Mrs Mountfort and Mrs Palmer. This was given for the Indian
King Ouka and his chiefs on 19 August. The company took the
droll on to Bartholomew Fair. Dancing was provided by La
Sieur Labisle, recently arrived from France, and Sandham; singing by a boy of twelve named Corse.

At Reynolds's Great Theatrical Booth 'A Comical Tragical
Farcical Droll', *The Rum Duke and the Queer Duke; Or, a Medley
of Mirth and Sorrow*, was presented with Mullart and Rosco as
the Dukes, supported by Jones, Stoppelaer, Dove, Mrs Mullart,
Miss Palms, Mrs Britton and others from the Little Haymarket.[1]
To this was added *Punch's Oratory: Or, The Pleasures of the
Town*, from Fielding's *Author's Farce*, with Reynolds as Punch;
Mrs Egleton, Joan; Jones, Dr Orator; Stoppelaer, Signor Opera;
Mrs Mullart, Goddess of Nonsense; Mrs Nokes, Mrs Novel.
Dancing was provided by M. St Luce and others. Scenes,
machines and other decorations were advertised as new. Performances were given between 1 and 10 p.m. On 11 August,
the afterpiece was changed to a pantomime, *The Miller's Holiday:
or Love in a Furz-Bush*, with Knott as Harlequin, and Reynolds
and Mrs Egleton as the Miller and his wife.

Yeates had a booth adjoining the Sun for his puppet version
of Theobald's pantomime, *Perseus and Andromeda*, in which
living singers participated.[2] He also showed two machines: the
Temple of Apollo and the Coronation.

The next year, 1731, comedians from Goodman's Fields and
the theatres royal performed at the New Theatre the droll
Amurath,[3] which young Penkethman had given the previous
year at Southwark.[4] This showed how the London Prentice 'slew
two furious Lyons, tearing out their Hearts in the Presence of
the Grand Signor and all his Court, when thrown into their Den
in order to be devoured: Also the Honours done him by the
Turkish Count in Recompence of his Valour'. Penkethman again
took the role of the London Prentice; and Huddy, Amurath; but
other roles were differently cast: Collet, Wantbrains; Hulett,
Achmet; Mrs Spiller, Selima; and Mrs Thomas, Zara. It was
followed by Coffey's ballad opera *Phebe, or the Beggar's Wedding*,

[1] *Ibid.* 4, 11 August 1730.   [2] *Ibid.* 10 August.
[3] *Ibid.* 3 August 1731.   [4] Above, p. 90.

with Mrs Spiller as Phebe; Jenkins, Hunter; Hulett, Chaunter; Huddy, Quoram; Penkethman, Cant; Collet, Snip; Mrs Thomas, Tippet; and Mrs Hulett as the Queen of the Beggars.

At Yeates's rival booth facing the King's Head could be seen the opera, *Damon and Phillida. With the Comical Humours of Simon and Mopsus*, with Taylor, Dove, Cross, Yeates junior, Jones, and Miss Yeates as the heroine.[1] Young Yeates performed conjuring tricks, and a curious piece of Italian machinery, nine feet high and eight feet wide with upwards of two hundred figures moved by clockwork, was shown. The performances were from 12 noon to 9 p.m.

Lee and Harper did not attend Bartholomew Fair in 1732 and instead showed the *True and Antient History of Whittington* 'with all the Pageantry Shew as has been in former times' at Tottenham Court.[2] Madge the Cook Maid was played by Harper, other parts by actors from the theatres. There was singing and dancing between the acts including a song, 'Mad Tom of Bedlam', by Platt. The booth was visited by Ach. Mahomet, Envoy Extraordinary from the Dey of Algiers, 'who seem'd mightily delighted with the Diversion'. *Whittington* was also reported as 'perform'd in the most splendid and magnificent Manner to a crouded Audience'.[3] Ach. Mahomet, accompanied by Prince William and the young princesses, also saw a new ballad opera, *A Wife Well Manag'd; or Cuckoldom Prevented; with Harlequin Doctor Faustus* at 'the great Booth in the Cherry-Tree Garden, the first Entrance of the Fair from Bloomsbury Fields'.[4]

Pinchbeck and Fawkes had a booth over against the Ship Ale-House with conjuring, a posture master aged eight, and various machines,[5] whilst Yeates showed entertainments of a similar nature.[6]

The Lee and Harper combination returned with Petit as a third partner in a booth behind the King's Head in 1733.[7] This is probably the tall wooden building which is shown behind this

[1] *Daily Post*, 9 August 1731.   [2] *Ibid.* 2 August 1732.
[3] Cutting, St Pancras Public Library, A xi, f. 16.
[4] *Daily Post*, 17 August 1732.   [5] *Ibid.* 10 August.
[6] *Ibid.* 14 August.   [7] *Daily Journal*, 4 August 1733.

tavern in Hogarth's 'March to Finchley'. It was probably permanent, as it is described two years later as 'Petty's Old Playhouse'. From 4 to 19 August they presented *Bateman or, The Unhappy Marriage, With the Comical Humours of Sparrow, Pumpkin and Slicer, going to the Wars. And a Diverting Scene of the Midwifes and Gossips at the Labour,* and *The Harlot's Progress* which they later took on to Southwark.[1]

The city authorities made determined efforts to suppress playing in Bartholomew and Southwark Fairs in 1735, and the Middlesex Sessions followed suit at Tottenham Court.[2] In spite of an order issued in July, several players succeeded in performing drolls and other shows, and even had the effrontery to advertise them in the newspapers. The Holborn justices were ordered to proceed against them and four announcements of the order were printed in the *Daily Advertiser*. One of the offenders was 'J. Petty' or Petit, who advertised at his Old Theatre a performance of *The Unnatural Parents* on Saturday 2 August and for all the following week.[3] Petit inserted a paragraph claiming a legal right to perform: 'This, the Proprietor attempts, pursuant to his Right, with due Deference to the Laws, and the strictest Decorum by which his Servants will continue to act Tragedies, Comedies &c. the whole Year, on all such Days as the Publick shall by their Encouragement make beneficial to the Undertaker'. Petit may have had a licence for a strolling company.

The order against players was renewed in July 1736, with as little effect.[4] Petit's 'old playhouse' at the end of Tottenham Court was in use again that year for the three-act dramatic entertainment, *The Birth of Merlin, the British Enchanter*,[5] which had been seen at Southwark Fair in 1724. Merlin's Cave and the Hermitage had been erected in 1735 at Richmond and representations of them were added. Playing continued until 20 August.

Fielding and Hallam had a booth near the Turnpike in 1738,

[1] Above, p. 94.
[2] *Middlesex Sessions Books* (1732–5), pp. 139, 164.
[3] *Country Journal*, 2 August 1735.
[4] *Middlesex Sessions Books* (1735–8), p. 35.
[5] *London Daily Post*, 5 August 1736; above, p. 85.

where they brought out a new entertainment, *The Mad Lovers; or Sport upon Sport, with the Comical Humours of Squire Graygoose and his Man Doodle, my Lady Graygoose and Capt. Atall.*[1] The same 'comical humours' were attached to another droll at Hallam's booth at Southwark later on in the autumn.[2] Bencraft played the Squire and Mrs Dove, Columbine in both but, at Tottenham Court, Doodle was taken by Penkethman, and Atall in the character of Harlequin by the French dancer De la Hays. Others who took part were Dove, Mrs Penkethman, and MM. and Mlles De La Grange and Le Brune. While the booth was filling, the audience was entertained by comic dancing and the posture master, M. Rapinière. There was a band, and illuminations of moons and lanthorns enabled the coaches of the quality to drive close to the door. Performances took place from 1 to 10 p.m.

Another order for suppressing the players was issued in July 1739.[3] It did not deter the famous Harlequin Phillips from setting up his booth and presenting his five-part medley,[4] consisting of a grand ball dance; a dialogue between Punch and Columbine; the 'Drunken Peasant' by himself; a song entitled 'The Beau'; and a Scaramouch dance which he and others had performed at the Paris Opera House for forty nights. A new grotesque pantomime followed, entitled *Harlequin's Distress, The Happiness of Columbine*, with Phillips as Harlequin. A new and complete band, new scenes, clothes and decorations were advertised. A coach-way which avoided the crowds led out of the main road.

At another booth a new entertainment was given called *Trick for Trick; Or an Odd Affair between Harlequin, his Associates, and the Vintner of York. Poor Harle in the Sudds at Last.* It was evidently a pantomime version of the well-worn farce of the vintner in the suds. It was followed by *A Ball, or the Humours of a Masquerade.*[5]

Phillips was in partnership with Mrs Lee in 1740,[6] when a miscellaneous entertainment was provided from 4 to 18 August,

---

[1] *London Daily Post*, 8 August 1738.   [2] Above, p. 97.
[3] *Middlesex Sessions Books* (1738–41), p. 36.
[4] *London Daily Post*, 8, 10 August 1739; for Phillips, see above, p. 46.
[5] *Ibid.* 6 August 1739.   [6] *Ibid.* 2, 18 August 1740.

after which the company was due to move on to Bartholomew Fair.[1] The Scaramouch dance was repeated from the previous year and other items were a grand scene of Jupiter and Juno in which Parry played Jupiter; a Scotch dialogue sung by Parry and Mrs Phillips; a new song in praise of Admiral Vernon by Parry, and a new sailor dance by Phillips and others. The pantomime was *Harlequin Happy; Or, Jack Spaniard Bit* in which Phillips was Harlequin; Parry, Spaniard; M. Closson, Pierrot; and Mrs Phillips, Columbine. All this was a topical reflection of the current Spanish war familiarly known as the War of Jenkins's Ear. The concluding grand dance was entitled *Vertumnus*, in which Phillips danced the title-role.

Yeates was back this year with a booth near the Swan; probably Yeates the younger, as he demonstrated dexterity of hand. After this a pantomime entertainment was given called *All Alive and Merry; Or the Happy Miller just Arriv'd. Being the Humorous Magical Mill that Grinds Old Men and Women Young again.* It is doubtful whether this piece had any connection with Samuel Johnson of Cheshire's *All Alive and Merry, or Men in Pursuit of Money.* The grinding mill was a popular legend. *Harlequin Grand Vol-gi Being the Comic of Cephalus and Procris,* which had been brought out at Drury Lane in 1730, followed. Rosoman was Harlequin; Yeates, a Noble Venetian; Warner, Pierrot, and Mrs Warner, Columbine. James, Price, Parker and Hill also took part in it or in the concluding Scaramouch dance.

We again hear of two booths in 1741.[2] At the Great Tiled Booth, near the Turnpike, Lee and Woodward revived *The Generous Freemason,* with Woodward as Noodle, Vaughan as Doodle, Cross as Clerimont, and other actors from both the theatres.[3] The pantomime was *Harlequin Sorcerer* in which Woodward danced Harlequin; Miss Robinson, who had never appeared before, Columbine; and Warner sustained his customary role of Clown. The other show was *The Rival Queens; Or the Death of Alexander the Great Intermix'd with a Comic, call'd A Wife well Managed or a Cure for Cuckoldom* at Middleton's booth, with Marshall as Alexander; Miss Carter, Roxana; Mrs Davis,

[1] No advertisements occur for them there in 1740.
[2] *London Daily Post,* 31 July 1741.   [3] Above, p. 33.

Statira; Middleton, Teague; Mrs Middleton, Diligence; and Peterson, Pattenden, Naylor, Beauford, Malone, Harrel and Young. Nat Lee's old ranting drama had already been utilised at Bartholomew Fair in 1732 and must have made an excellent droll. In the new pantomime, *The Adventures of Harlequin in Spain*, Signor Thomassin, lately arrived from Italy, danced Harlequin. He may have been one of the sons of the great Tommaso-Antonio Thomassin: Vincent-Jean who excelled in Punchinello roles or his young brother Joachim.[1] Charges were: boxes 2s. 6d., pit 1s. 6d., gallery 1s., upper gallery 6d.

Yeates, Warner and Rosoman had a booth near the Pound in 1743 where they performed *The Tragical History of King Richard III*, into which was introduced a representation of the Battle of Dettingen.[2] It was intermixed with *The Wanton Trick'd; or All Alive and Merry*, which probably had some connection with the piece performed in 1740.[3] *The Harlot's Progress* with Rosoman as Harlequin was the pantomime. A band consisted of hautboys, violins, bass viols, kettledrums and trumpets.

John T. Smith says that the fair was infested by the lowest rabble and was famous for its booths of 'theatrical performers who deserted the empty benches of Drury Lane Theatre, under the mismanagement of Mr Fleetwood, and condescended to admit the audience at sixpence each. Mr Yates and several other eminent performers, had their names printed on their booths.'[4]

This was, however, the last year in which we hear of the players' visits. A further order from the justices was made against the fair in January 1744 and was followed up by a report on this and other fairs, to the Chancellor, Lord Hardwicke.[5] This seems to have done the trick and the drolls were suppressed.[6] In 1748 Daniel French opened an amphitheatre in the Tottenham Court Road with an entertainment called *The Country Wake* which consisted of cudgel playing, boxing and wrestling,[7] but,

[1] *Nouvelle Biographie Générale*, vol. XLV, under Thomassin.
[2] *London Daily Post*, 3 August 1743. Advertisements until 16 August.
[3] Above, p. 127.   [4] *A Book for a Rainy Day*, p. 26.
[5] *Middlesex Sessions Books* (1744–7), pp. 17, 24, 51.
[6] D. Lysons, *Environs of London* (1795), vol. III, p. 342, n. 1.   [7] *Ibid.*

if there were players at the fair, they had not the temerity to
advertise.

An order for the suppression of the fair was issued in April
1748,[1] but in fact it continued until 1827.[2]

WELSH FAIR, CLERKENWELL

Welsh Fair, which was held in Spa Fields, Clerkenwell, was also
a Gooseberry Fair. It was originally held at Whitsuntide but,
by 1740 when we first hear of it in connection with dramatic
performances,[3] it had been transferred to the end of August.

Thomas Yeates advertised at his booth the entertainment of
Orpheus and Eurydice with *The Metamorphosis of Harlequin*,
which he brought on from Bartholomew Fair and was to take to
Southwark.[4] Yeates was also proprietor of the New Wells,
which had been functioning near the London Spa since 1737, and
he announced that, during Welsh Fair, he would revive there
*A Hint to the Theatres; or Merlin in Labour, With the Birth,
Adventures, and Restoration of Harlequin. Also an Addition of
Merlin's Cave, as in the Royal Gardens at Richmond, by Mr Devoto.*[5]
This was followed by a pantomime, *The Happy Miller Arriv'd;
Or, Let None Despair,* and a new entertainment, *The Siege of
Portobello. With the Demolition of their Forts and Castles.* But
the New Wells was not a special fair theatre, and the pieces were
given long before and after the fair, which seems to have ceased
on 30 August; it bore much the same relation to the fair as
Yeates's May Fair Wells did to May Fair.

Yeates had his booth again in 1741, where he gave *The
Persian Hero, or the Noble Englishman. With the Comical Humours
of Toby and Dorcas Guzzle.*[6] This droll may have been on the
same theme as *Darius King of Persia or the Noble Englishman,*
revived that year by Lee and Woodward at Bartholomew Fair,[7]
but the dramatis personae are quite different. In Yeates's piece

---

[1] *Middlesex Sessions Books* (1747–51), p. 53.
[2] G. Clinch, *op. cit.* p. 161.
[3] W. Pinks, *History of Clerkenwell* (1865), p. 152.
[4] *London Daily Post,* 29 August 1740.
[5] *Ibid.* 25 August. The piece had been given there in 1738.
[6] *Ibid.* 24 August 1741.   [7] Above, p. 49.

Collins played the Persian Hero; Mrs Hickson, Alcmena; Hollins from the Edinburgh Theatre, Toby Guzzle; Warner, Dame Hacket; Yeates, Ambrose Merryman; other parts by Cushing, Sturgess, Oakley and Smith. To this was added the comic part of *Orpheus and Eurydice or the Metamorphosis of Harlequin*, with Rosoman as Harlequin. The band consisted of violins, German flutes, trumpets and kettledrums. The booth had boxes at 2s., pit at 1s., first gallery at 6d., and upper gallery at 3d.

In 1742 entertainments were given at Queen Elizabeth's Wells in Spa Field during the fair.[1] Singing and dancing were followed by a new pantomime, *The Adventures and Marriage of Harlequin in Turkey*, with Woodbe as Harlequin, Ayres as Turk, Miss Cole as Columbine, and Towers as Clown. A note adds: 'The Company may depend on having the best of Liquours, by W. Williams.' Nothing else is known of Queen Elizabeth's Wells, but it was probably attached to a tavern and may only have existed to serve the crowds at the fair.

In 1744 the Middlesex justices issued warrants for the apprehension of players at the fair.[2] A notice was inserted in *The Daily Advertiser* of 2 August that, though the fair would be proclaimed for 23–5 August, in conformity with the Lord Mayor's wishes, all players would be prosecuted.

The New Wells seems to have passed to the management of Harlequin Phillips in 1743 and performances were still given there during the fair in 1744, when six hundred people witnessed the feat of Dominique who, for the first time in England, flew over the heads of twenty-four men with drawn swords.[3] This is reminiscent of the Bartholomew Fair playbill of 1701 and is another example of the conservatism of fair entertainments.

Though we do not hear of any further performances at the fair, they must have gone on, for further orders were issued against the players in April 1746 and 1747.[4] We learn from them that the fair had spread itself to three weeks and that the players had frequented it for many years past.

---

[1] Guildhall Library, a collection of cuttings in . . . connection with the metropolitan fairs.

[2] *Middlesex Sessions Books* (May 1744), p. 18.

[3] Pinks, *op. cit.* p. 168.

[4] *Middlesex Sessions Books* (1744–7), pp. 49, 51, 94.

The New Wells closed down after 1750, but the tavern advertised the usual entertainments of roast beef and spa ale during the fair in 1754. Welsh Fair eventually moved out to Barnet.

MILE END AND BOW FAIRS

In 1664 Charles II, at the request of Thomas Wentworth, Earl of Cleveland, instituted an annual Michaelmas Fair at Mile End Green or other convenient place within the Manor.[1] The fair was later amalgamated with Bow Fair, where it became known as the Bow Green Goose Fair. This later site is now covered by Fairfield Road and Bow Station.[2]

Two dramatic notices are extant for performances at the fair when it was still at Mile End.[3] The first is dated 1730 and advertises a company of comedians at a large, commodious room in the Artichoke-Yard during the time of the fair. The company was probably under the management of Yeates junior who performed in the play and gave his usual conjuring show. The piece was a ballad opera, *The Harlot's Progress*,[4] based on Hogarth's painting of the name and had no connection with Theophilus Cibber's pantomime, which was not brought out until 1733. The dramatis personae were Colonel, Julian; Spruce, Yeates junior; Waggoner, Thomas; Jew, Williams; Julio, Master Brown; Flogwell, Patterson; Constable, Bright; Bawd, Macguire; Moll Hackabout, Mrs Frost; Alice, Miss Yeates. Before the play a little Dutch girl, aged four, who had been instructed by Rimes of Sadler's Wells, danced on the stiff rope, and a little posture master and tumbler also performed. In the same yard were shown two ostriches from Arabia. Entertainments lasted from 12 to 8 p.m.

The second notice relates to the visit of Yeates senior and junior to the fair on 3 October 1738, this time with a puppet show of Carey's burlesque opera *The Dragon of Wantley*. The younger Yeates did his conjuring tricks, and the Grand Theatre of Arts, or Musical Machine Clock was displayed, 'which for its

---

[1] David Hughson, *London* (1809), vol. vi, p. 309.
[2] Poplar Public Library cuttings.
[3] B.M. Fillinham, collection of cuttings, vol. iv.
[4] See above, p. 95.

surprising Movements, and beautiful Musick on the Organ sur-passes all that was ever made of the kind'. These clocks with moving figures were popular at fairs then as now.[1]

Players must have continued attending Bow and Mile End Fairs, for edicts went out against them from the Middlesex Sessions.[2] Mile End Fair was presented by the Grand Jury of Middlesex in 1736 because it extended seven days beyond its sanctioned time. Both Mile End and Bow Fairs are mentioned in April 1746 and 1747 and are also included in a list of fairs against the holding of which orders were to be posted up in April 1752.

In the late eighteenth and early nineteenth centuries the fair was visited by Richardson, Saunders, Gyngell, Flockton and Scowton, all well known fairground troupes. In April 1822 at the Whitechapel Petty Sessions the justices invoked the Police Act by whose means they were enabled to suppress any fair within ten miles of London which had not the benefit of charter, prescription or other lawful authority.[3] Giles, who owned the ground, knew of none such and could therefore only plead im-memorial precedent. The case was postponed for a fortnight to investigate the authority by which the fair was held. Evidently none was discovered for it was suppressed in 1823. An elegy, after Gray, entitled *The Humours of Bow Fair*, bewailed its passing:[4]

> The Bow Bell tolls the knell of Bow Fair fun
> And Richardson winds slowly out of town;
> Poor old 'Young' Saunders sees his setting sun
> And Gyngell pulls his red, torn tawdry down...
> At Scowton's dire destruction will be seen!
> The trumpet will give up its tragic truths!
> The magistrate, desiring to be *Keen*
> Will put an end, as usual, to the Booths!...
> *One act* (the Vagrant Act) hath been its ruin.

It was once more revived on 23 August 1847, in a field adjoining the old spot, when its entertainments included an equestrian circus.[5]

[1] Cf. the success of the Guinness clock in Battersea Festival Gardens.
[2] *Middlesex Sessions Books* (1744/5–7), pp. 51, 94; vol. v, p. 254.
[3] B.M. Fillinham cuttings, vol. IV.
[4] *Ibid.*   [5] *Ibid.*

HOUNSLOW FAIR

The fair at Hounslow was of ancient origin. In 1296 Edward I granted a charter to the brethren of Holy Trinity to hold an annual fair on the eve and feast of Holy Trinity and the six succeeding days. When Lysons wrote in 1795 it was still held on Trinity Monday, but it seems gradually to have dwindled away.[1] Whether it was regularly frequented by the players is not known but there is one notice of their visit. On 13 June 1720 at Bullock and Pack's booth a new droll entitled *The False Friend. With the Comical Humours of Sir Timothy Timberhead and his Sister Jezibel* was performed by Bullock as Sir Timothy, and by actors from the playhouse.[2] This must be the same piece that was given by Bullock and the widow Leigh at Bartholomew Fair in 1719 as *The Constant Lovers or The False Friend*.[3] It was followed by an entertainment after the Italian manner called *The Tavern Bilkers* by Harlequin, Scaramouch and Punch, which may have been Weaver's pantomime of that name. Bullock announced that he had erected commodious boxes for the quality.

OTHER FAIRS

There were several other fairs at which the players appeared, though we know nothing of their performances. They are, however, mentioned in the Middlesex Sessions records. In May 1739 there was a presentment by the Grand Jury of booths and buildings which had been erected for acting plays at Moorfields, to which idle and disorderly people resorted and disturbed the peace.[4] John Yates, who on 4 May and other days had kept a booth for play acting, was one of the offenders. The constables of Finsbury and Tower divisions were bidden to issue orders to the petty constables to apprehend the offenders and take them before a justice or justices dwelling nearest to the place where the booths were erected. A similar order was made in April 1748, when players were included among those said to infest Moorfields daily.[5]

[1] *Environs of London*, vol. III, p. 37.   [2] B.M. Add. MS. 32249 (Latreille).
[3] Above, p. 23.   [4] *Middlesex Sessions Books* (1738–41), p. 36.
[5] *Ibid.* (1747–51), p. 12.

Other fairs frequented by players mentioned in the Sessions records are Paddington (1746 and 1747), Hampstead (1746 and 1747), Highgate (1746), and Acton and Sherking Fairs in the Kensington division (1754).[1] At the last people were alleged to stay until one and two in the morning. The players were accused, not only of encouraging vice, immorality and debauchery and ruining servants and apprentices, but of occasioning riots and tumults.

At the Surrey Quarter Sessions held at Southwark on 15 January 1771, an order was made to prohibit Wandsworth Fair and apprehend the players who had built booths and sheds and acted drolls for many years past. A similar order applied to Mitcham Fair on 15 January 1773. The players in these lesser fairs were probably impoverished strollers who have left behind them no records of their performances.

---

[1] *Middlesex Sessions Books* (1744–7), pp. 51, 56–7, 94; vol. vi, p. 45.

CHAPTER VIII

PLAYS AND DROLLS

THE drolls played at the fairs, though of no literary or intrinsic merit, are worth studying as an expression of popular taste and as folk drama on themes parallel to those of chapbook and ballad. Our knowledge of the plays is derived from the few that are extant, from the original plays from which drolls were abridged, from the long descriptive synopses in the advertisements, and from one or two eye-witness accounts. A good many are mere names, but in several cases even these are a guide to content.

Extant plays which I have examined are: *The Siege of Troy* (Bartholomew Fair; Southwark Fair, 1707);[1] *The Broken Stock Jobbers* (S.F. 1720); *The Unnatural Parents, or the Fair Maid of the West* (B.F., S.F. 1726); Walker's *The Quaker's Opera* (B.F., S.F. 1728); Chetwood's *The Generous Freemason, or The Constant Lady* (B.F., S.F. 1730); *Robin Hood* (B.F., S.F. 1730); *Wat Tyler and Jack Straw; or the Mob Reformers* (B.F. 1730); *Jephtha's Rash Vow* (B.F., S.F. 1733) and *The Devil upon Two Sticks: or, The Town Until'd* (May Fair, 1708) which is merely a resumé of the plot taken from Le Sage's *Le Diable Boîteux*. Others advertised as printed for sale in the booths but not traced are: *The Siege of Bethulia containing the Ancient History of Judith and Holofernes*, printed by G. Lee, 1721; Coffey's *Southwark Fair; or the Sheep Shearing* (S.F. 1729);[2] *Guy, Earl of Warwick; Whittington, Lord Mayor of London; The Devil to Pay*, all three printed by G. Lee, 1731; *Female Innocence* (S.F. 1732) and *The Devil of a Duke or the Conjuror's Bastard*, printed 1741.[3]

Old tales, familiar to the people from Bible, ballad and chapbook, were dramatised for puppet shows at Bartholomew Fair in the seventeenth century. *Fair Rosamond* dates back at least to

---

[1] First printed by S. Lee [n.d. ?1707], [n.d. ?1715], 1716, 1735. There is no evidence that the drolls in *The Strolers Pacquet Open'd* (1742) were ever played.

[2] The Guildhall Library copy was destroyed in the war.

[3] Peter Murray Hill, Catalogue 55, no. 266 records a copy.

1655[1] and John Locke mentions a puppet show of *Judith and Holofernes* in 1664.[2] Pepys saw performances of *Patient Grizill* in 1667 and *Whittington* in 1666.[3] In 1686 we also hear of *St George and the Dragon*[4] and, twelve years later, of *Jephtha's Rash Vow*.[5] From 1682[6] until well into the eighteenth century *The Creation of the World*, with its appendages of *Noah's Flood* and *Dives and Lazarus*, was one of the principal puppet attractions. We have seen that, already by 1676, such spectacular puppet shows, lavish of scenes and machines, were called 'operas'.[7] Thus *The Creation of the World* was described as a little opera and boasted two or three machines descending as well as Dives rising out of hell. This piece was in the miracle play tradition but significantly added a comic intermezzo, 'the merry conceits of Squire Punch and Sir John Spendall'. Before 1695 drolls were being given at Southwark on the folk themes of Robin Hood and the Blind Beggar of Bethnal Green. In the last year of the century Brown adds to the list the old 'humble stories' of *Crispin and Crispianus*, and *Bateman*, and an 'opera' on the theme of the *Trojan Horse*; while Ned Ward gives his account of a live performance of *Friar Bacon*.

But Bartholomew Fair in the seventeenth century also housed another kind of play besides the dramatisation of old tales or biblical stories: this was the satirical-political-topical type performed both by puppets and by live actors. Thus *The Coronation of Queen Elizabeth*, acted both at Bartholomew and Southwark Fairs in 1680 during the Popish plot hysteria, is a virulent anti-Catholic satire; so too must have been *The Whore of Babylon*[8] with the Pope and the Devil among its characters, and *The Irish Evidence* of 1682.[9] The topical *Siege of Namur*,[10] mentioned by Sorbière, was part of an anti-Catholic show entitled *King William's Happy Deliverance and Glorious Triumph over His Enemies, or the Consultation of the Pope, Devil, French King and*

[1] T. D'Urfey, *Wit and Mirth: or Pills to Purge Melancholy.*
[2] P. King, *Life of John Locke* (1830), p. 25.
[3] *Diary*, ed. Wheatley and Braybrooke (1904), vii, 8; viii, 110.
[4] Playford, *Second Book of the Pleasant Musical Companion.*
[5] Sorbière, *op. cit.* (1798), p. 27.   [6] Above, p. 7.
[7] Above, p. 5.   [8] Above, p. 8.
[9] Above, p. 7.   [10] Above, p. 9.

the Grand Turk, with the Whole Form of the Siege of Namur.[1]
Evelyn expressed his disgust with a show of *The Earthquake of
Jamaica* at Southwark in 1693,[2] and we have seen how the players
turned to dramatic account the agitation against Admirals
Delaval and Killigrew and were arrested for their pains.[3] What
the players from the theatres, then, found entrenched at the
fairs, when first they started to visit them, were drolls on old
folk-tale and biblical themes, satirical pieces on contemporary
events, and comic interludes with native or *commedia dell'arte*
characters.[4] The comedians did not for some time attempt to add
anything more sophisticated but had the good sense to continue
the tradition established by drolls and puppet plays. It is true
that an anonymous writer in 1702 said that the drolls and interludes had grown into comedies 'highly advanc'd in Wit, and as
much in Wickedness, by Parties detach'd (in Vacation-time)
from the Play-Houses'[5] but he is merely being satirical at the
playhouses' expense. Brown makes a similar satirical comparison between the 'operas' of the fair and the spectacles of the
theatre.[6] Both writers are condemning the theatres for putting
on shows little better than those of the fairs. That the fair
offerings remained crude and unsophisticated is demonstrated
by those which have survived. The actors from the patent
theatres, however, were more talented than the strollers on
whom the fairs had hitherto relied, and the low comedy element
was developed as a vehicle for comedians such as Penkethman
and Doggett. The scenes and machines, too, which the puppeteers had introduced into their shows in the late seventeenth
century were imitated in the booths of the comedians. But the
plays themselves showed little advance; there is no great difference in style between *The Coronation of Queen Elizabeth* of
1680 and *Wat Tyler and Jack Straw* of fifty years later.

Only the ancient biblical themes tended to disappear, except
for Jephtha, whose source was in the ballad rather than in the
Bible, Judith, Saul, and the Prodigal Son. Otherwise the old
favourites reappeared in new guise. *The Siege of Troy*, taken as

[1] Above, p. 108 for full title. [2] Above, p. 75.
[3] Above, p. 7. [4] Below, pp. 145, 148.
[5] Above, p. 15. [6] Above, p. 13.

a subject by Settle for his elaborate droll of 1707, held the stage until 1747; St George was the hero of *The Royal Champion* in 1728; *Bateman* was frequently revived up to 1733; the puppet stories of *Whittington* and *Jephtha's Rash Vow* were converted into two of the most popular drolls which held the boards up to mid-century; *Friar Bacon* with the Miller and his son Ralph was still being performed in Southwark in 1720; and *Hero and Leander*, the theme of Ben Jonson's puppet play in *Bartholomew Fair*, was actually performed there in 1728.

Similar folk tales were dramatised for use by the actors, and the traditionalism of the fairs ensured for these drolls a long survival.[1] Thus *Maudlin, the Merchant's Daughter of Bristol* was brought out at May Fair during Queen Anne's reign and revived up to 1734; *Jane Shore* is found at Tottenham Court in 1717 and is last heard of at May Fair in 1745; *The Blind Beggar of Bethnal Green* was seen at Southwark Fair before 1695 and was constantly revived under varying titles until 1748; *Valentine and Orson* appeared at Southwark in 1722 as *The Royal Revenge, or the Princely Shepherd* and in 1724 under its own name; *The Distressed Beauty or the London Prentice* was given at Bartholomew Fair in 1722, at Southwark in 1730 and at Tottenham Court, as *Amurath the Great...or the London Prentice's Glory*, in 1731; *Merlin, the British Enchanter* was given at Southwark in 1724 and revived in various versions up to 1738, when it became connected with St George; *Robin Hood and Little John*, known at Southwark Fair before 1695, became the subject of one of Lee and Harper's drolls, and was still going strong in 1751 as *King Edward IV or the Loves of Robin Hood and Little John*; *Guy, Earl of Warwick*, another Lee and Harper droll, is found in 1730 and 1731, and *Fair Rosamond* was brought out at Bartholomew Fair in 1734 and was still being shown there by Hallam in 1741. These drolls thus contributed to keeping alive the old folk tales. All had counterparts in ballads or prose romances, or in both. Many preceded the first collection of ballads in 1723,[2] which included poems on Fair Rosamond, Robin Hood, Whittington,

[1] For list of puppet plays on folklore subjects see G. Speaight, *op. cit.* p. 327.

[2] *A Collection of Old Ballads*, attributed to Ambrose Philips.

Jane Shore, Bateman, Judith and Maudlin; and all had appeared in the booths long before Percy's *Reliques* in 1765. Eighteenth-century chapbook counterparts are extant for Friar Bacon, Bateman, Guy, Earl of Warwick, the Blind Beggar of Bethnal Green, Whittington, Fair Rosamond, Jane Shore, the Devil upon Two Sticks, as well as for two other droll subjects, Dorastus and Fawnia (B.F. 1729), originally from Greene's novel *Pandosto*, and Argalus and Parthenia (M.F. 1745 as not acted for ten years) from Sidney's *Arcadia*.[1]

Elizabethan and seventeenth-century dramatists had used the Blind Beggar (Day), Jephtha (Chettle in a lost play), Jane Shore (Chettle and Day), Robin Hood (Munday and Chettle), Valentine and Orson (Hathwaye and Munday), Friar Bacon (Greene), British Enchanter (? Rowley), Maudlin (Sampson's *Vow Breaker or Faire Maide of Clifton*), Richard Whittington (1605, lost), Jack Straw and Wat Tyler (1638, lost), but there is little evidence to connect the drolls with these plays. The fair *Robin Hood* was quite a different version of the story from Munday and Chettle's *Downfall of Robert, Earl of Huntington*, though both equated Robin Hood with that nobleman. The fair 'opera' is in three acts in blank verse and prose with nineteen songs. In it Mathilda and Marina search the forest for their banished lovers the Earl and Darnel, alias Robin Hood and Little John. Thus the Maid Marian of the *Downfall* is split into two characters in the droll. The latter introduces the Pindar of Wakefield, who was early associated with Robin Hood, and Prim a puritanical miser, both of whom are used as comic relief. The action includes a fight between Huntington and Pembroke, who had wrongfully accused him and so caused his banishment. Pembroke, in a dying confession, absolves Huntington, and the droll ends with his honourable reinstatement.

The fair *Jephtha's Rash Vow* is a pocket heroic tragedy in rhymed couplets and prose. It adds to the story the love of Elon for Jephtha's daughter Miriam and his final madness and suicide; the comic love of the foolish Zekiel who writes and sings ridiculous verses; and a comic sub-plot of Captain Bluster and his man Diddimo who have a scene with mock devils and witches

---

[1] John Ashton, *Chap-books of the 18th Century* (1882).

in a cave. As Chettle's play on the subject has not survived it is impossible to tell whether the droll owes anything to it.

Friar Bacon, as described by Ned Ward,[1] has no resemblance to Greene's play, nor does the synopsis of *Maudlin* reveal any connection with *The Vow Breaker.*

It is evident that the droll writers elaborated the simple stories by invented episodes, such as the fight between Huntington and Pembroke, or characters, such as Elon and Zekiel, and that they further supplied comic underplots, such as those of Prim and Captain Bluster, for the low comedians in the troupes of actors.

There is, however, a little closer resemblance between Rowley's *Birth of Merlin or the Child hath found his Father* and the droll of *Merlin, the British Enchanter or the Child hath found his Own Father.* The droll is not extant but it is linked with the play not only by the sub-title but by the comical humours of Sir Nicodemus Nothing who is likewise a comic character in the play. Perhaps a droll had early been abridged from the play and had survived until the eighteenth century. The fair *Blind Beggar of Bethnal Green* must also have been to some extent based on Day and Chettle's play, for the dramatis personae are similar, though some of the characters have different names. Another droll based on an earlier play (this time a late seventeenth-century one) was *The Happy Gallant; or The Modern Wife* (B.F. 1735) which derived from Betterton's *Amorous Widow.*

To continue with the description of the folk and pseudo-historical drolls: Elkanah Settle's *The Siege of Troy* was not taken from his dramatic opera on the Troy theme, *The Virgin Prophetess,* brought out at Drury Lane in 1701, and merely shares with it an emphasis on spectacle. The scenic effects of the droll are dealt with elsewhere[2] and their elaborateness may account for Benjamin Victor's verdict that it was the best droll he ever saw.[3] It is written in a combination of rhymed couplets and blank verse for the classical heroes and prose for the mob, and it contains a number of songs and some concluding dances.[4] The mob scenes supply the low comedy of Bristle the Cobbler

---

[1] Above, p. 12.   [2] Below, pp. 161 ff.
[3] *The History of the Theatres of London and Dublin* (1761), vol. II, p. 74.
[4] See Morley, *op. cit.* pp. 285 ff. for a detailed description of the plot.

and his wife and make no pretence to be anything but English. They recall how Ben Jonson mocked at a similar tendency to introduce a contemporary setting in his Bankside *Hero and Leander* two hundred years previously. The populace could not be trusted to stand too much of the classical legend even though it was accompanied by scenic marvels; the comedians had to be brought on to amuse them with the rough and tumble life they knew.

Mrs Mynns followed *The Siege of Troy*, given in 1707, with a spectacular *Whittington* which may also have been written by Settle. When Pack, Spiller and Hall gave a droll on this subject in 1718 the emphasis had been transferred to the humours of Madge the Cook Maid and John the Butler. The droll was revived on at least four more occasions, the last being in 1749.

The Royal Champion or St George for England (S.F. 1728) showed how the national saint fell in love with Sabrina, daughter of the King of Egypt, and slew the dragon as well as a giant demogorgon. The same pattern of adventure is seen in *Guy, Earl of Warwick* (S.F. 1731) and the 'Perils he underwent for Love of Fair Phyllis; his killing the monstrous Dun Cow of Dunsmore Heath, the dreadful dragon, and the Giant Colebrand; and then rescuing the Fair Phillis from a Tower which was set on Fire by the Treachery of Colebrand's Servant in order to burn her'.[1] His subsequent adventures as a pilgrim appear to have been omitted but the customary comic element was supplied by the 'distresses' of his servant Rogero.

Not only English legend but English history provided themes for drolls. Thus we find *King Egbert, King of Kent and Monarch of England or the Vision of Seven Kingdoms* (B.F. 1719); *The Envious Statesman, or the Fall of Essex* (B.F. 1732); *The History of Henry VIII and Anna Bullen* (B.F. 1732); and the extant *Wat Tyler and Jack Straw* (B.F. 1730). The prologue to this last stresses the patriotic point:

> Why shou'd the Muse for Foreign Actions roam
> When she can find Heroick ones at Home.

[1] *Daily Post*, 23 August 1731.

A romantic element is introduced with Aurelia, who follows
Walworth in disguise, and the comic element is supplied by
Jack Straw and his camp follower Suky, who spout mock heroics
in the following vein:

> Whiter than new-peel'd Turnips is her Skin,
> Her breath far sweeter than the Smell of Gin.

The mob again plays its part and the low comedy scenes are in
prose. The Genius of England adjures Tyler to repent; the
wounded Walworth meets the faithful Aurelia; at Smithfield
itself, Tyler demands the crown; Straw is led on with a halter
round his neck; Tyler is stabbed by Walworth and dies and
Straw is finally dragged off. King Richard ends the droll with
appropriate patriotic sentiments.

This patriotic note was also sounded in drolls of contemporary
adventure in which the hero was an Englishman. We have already
noted two versions of the London Apprentice story. *The Tempest:
or the Distressed Lovers* (B.F. date unknown) showed 'how a
Nobleman of *England* was cast away from the Indian Shore and
in his Travel found the Princess of the Country with whom he
fell in love, and after many Dangers and Perils, was married
to her: and his faithful Scotchman, who was saved with him,
travelling thorow Woods fell in among Witches where between
'em is abundance of Comical Diversion'.[1] The theme recurs in
The French Flogg'd; or the English Sailors in America (B.F.
1759) 'Together with the Reception of Captain Briton at the
Indian Court, the Manners, Customs, Ceremonies, and Dresses
of the Inhabitants of that Country. With their smoaking the
Calumett of Peace, and presenting the English Commander with
the Wampum Belt, for his bravery in rescuing the Princess
Sachema from the French Banditti. Interspersed with the Droll
Behaviour and Odd Adventures of MacDermott Geoghaghan
Ballinbrogue And the Witch of the Woods; or, a Woman without a Head.'[2] The Indian Princess is rescued from French
banditti (since we were then at war with France) and the
Scottish Jockey has turned into the Irish MacDermott. In this
case the usual procedure of extracting a droll from a play was

---

[1] Harl. 5931, handbill.   [2] *Public Advertiser*, 1 September 1759.

reversed, and the droll, possibly rewritten,[1] was brought out at Covent Garden in 1767. In the printed text of that year, the Irishman's name has been changed to Macfinan, which suggests that there were other alterations.

Another rescue story was *The Ship-Wreck'd Lovers; or French Perfidy Punished* (B.F. 1759), 'Containing the Distresses of a young Lady that was stolen by a French Pirate; the Gallantry of an English Captain who rescued her; their unfortunate Shipwreck, and their being thrown upon a desolate Island; their Sufferings there through Famine; the unexpected Relief they met with on a Part of the Island governed only by Women; their being afterwards seized as Pirates; the Punishment inflicted on them by the Female Government and their amazing Delivery by the Queen's finding her Husband and her only Son whom she had lost and thought dead upwards of twenty Years'.[2]

Yet another gallant Englishman appears at the court of King Darius in *The Noble Englishman or the History of Darius, King of Persia and the Destruction of Babylon* (S.F. 1721). Eastern potentates were associated with drolls which bore no relation to their lives. Thus the name of the contemporary Persian tyrant, Thamas Kouli Kan (Nadir Shah) was seized upon for a droll, *Thamas Kouli Kan the Persian Hero; or the Distressed Princess* (B.F. 1741). He had been celebrated in two short histories the year previously, but nothing more than his name was taken from these. The episodes of his banishment, love for Princess Karanza, imprisonment, and deliverance from the funeral pile[3] were not derived from the histories but from the stock-in-trade of the romantic droll, and were later transferred to *The Adventures of Timur Coran or the Favourite of the Sun* (B.F. 1760). The titles, with their suggestion of rich and fabulous oriental courts, were a bait for the multitude, catering for their taste for romance and opulence.

The rationalism and scepticism of the cultured classes in the eighteenth century had not percolated to the patrons of the fairs. The unlettered, as in all ages, had an inherent love of marvels

---

[1] The piece may have been by G. A. Stevens, *Biographia Dramatica* (1812), vol. II, p. 251.

[2] *Public Advertiser*, 3 September 1759.   [3] Above, p. 48.

and wanted it satisfied with dragons, ghosts and witches, with strange adventures and exciting situations. Thus in the fairground booths the seeds of the romantic revival were kept warm against their time of flowering. The old legends were retained in the remembrance of the people, and new tales invented in melodramatic style more than half a century before the taste for melodrama developed in the theatres royal.

The satirical droll on contemporary events was not as popular in the eighteenth century as in the preceding decades. There was no Popish plot to inflame the passions of the populace. The South Sea Bubble was in a general way the subject of *The Broken Stock Jobbers; or Work for the Bailiffs* (S.F. 1720). The preface to the printed text states that its object was to expose the vice of gaming, and its moral rather than satirical character is emphasised in the announcement that 'No Person is here meant by Character; Things and Vices, not Men are mentioned'. The droll shows how all types of people, including the clergy, indulge in the vice of gambling. Whilst the mother gambles, the daughter dopes herself. How the workers' audience must have applauded the sentiment of the hero who spoke of 'the Drones of Quality. . . who fed on others Labour and suck'd the Sweets of the industrious Trader'.

The fair booths also provided the equivalent of our news-reels by spectacles showing the events of the day. Thus the capture of Montjuich by the Earl of Peterborough in 1705 was celebrated at Bartholomew Fair the following year in *The Siege of Barcelona, or The Soldier's Fortune: With the Taking of Fort Mont-Jouy.* With superb disregard for time and place 'an exact representation of the Battle of Dettingen' was pitchforked into *Richard III* (Tottenham Court, 1743); and, in 1758, an entertainment concluded with a representation 'of the Taking of Louisbourg, and the whole Island of Cape-Breton By Admirals Boscawen and Amherst'. The French Revolution found place at Bartholomew Fair in 1790 when *The Spaniard well Drub'd, or the British Tar Victorious* ended with a procession of 'the King, French Heroes, Guards, Municipal Troops &c. to the Champ de Mars, To swear to the Revolutional Laws, as established by the *magnificent National Assembly* on the 14th of July 1790'. Here the people's theatre was on the side of the revolutionaries.

Music and singing had always played an important part in fair offerings so it is small wonder that, when the ballad opera craze swept the town after the production of *The Beggar's Opera* in 1728, the booth managers cashed in on it immediately. Not only was *The Beggar's Opera* itself performed at both Bartholomew and Southwark Fairs that year, but Lee, Harper and Spiller brought out an imitation of it by Thomas Walker, the original Macheath, entitled *The Quaker's Opera*. This is closely modelled on its original, substituting a Quaker's son for the beggar, and taking as its hero, not a highwayman, but the notorious contemporary house- and prison-breaker Jack Shephard. He too is provided with rival mistresses and is betrayed by a cast-off one; and the scenes in Newgate and with the ladies of the town parallel those in *The Beggar's Opera*. Many ballad operas followed, most of which had been presented at the theatres: *The Beggar's Wedding, Damon and Phillida, Flora, The Country Wedding* and Coffey's *Southwark Fair* were at the fairs in 1729; and *The Devil to Pay* in 1731. Chetwood wrote *The Generous Freemason* especially for the fairs (B.F., S.F. 1730; T.C. 1741). It is in three acts and consists of two entirely divorced plots, though both are of masonic interest: one a romantic love and adventure episode at the court of Amurath and Zelmana, the other a comic interlude of the simple squire and his man who are tricked and gulled in scenes of slapstick. This was one of the few pieces that reached the theatre (Haymarket 1730) by way of the fair booths.

Full-scale pantomime, curiously enough, was more slowly adopted by the fairs, perhaps because the hour's show did not at first allow of afterpieces, and pantomimes alone would have insufficient dramatic or low comedy content. *Commedia dell'arte* characters are found in the fairs as early as 1667 when Pepys saw Polichinelle performing alongside an English Merry Andrew.[1] After Punchinella came Scaramouch and Harlequin whose 'conceits' were tacked on to a political droll at May Fair in 1696.[2] Ward described the rivalry between two Scaramouches and a Merry Andrew at a rope-dancing booth at the same fair in 1699.

[1] G. Speaight, *op. cit.* for the further history of Punch in the fairs.
[2] Above, p. 108.

It was, in fact, chiefly at the rope-dancing booths that the masks of the Italian comedy were popularised at the fairs. Thus an Italian Scaramouch rope dancer was seen at Bartholomew Fair in 1701 and a Scaramouch and Harlequin performed there in 1703.[1] The famous couple, Sorine and Baxter, presented an interlude between these two characters at Penkethman's rope-dancing booth at Southwark in 1704.[2] A mimic scene between Harlequin and a peasant at Southwark in 1717 shows that Harlequin was by then silent. The first full pantomime I have traced in the fairs is *The Tavern Bilkers* in 1720 at Hounslow, three years after Rich's triumph with the form at Lincoln's Inn Fields. This may have been Weaver's pantomime which, he claims, was the first English one.[3] That same year *The Italian Shadows* from Lincoln's Inn Fields was given at Southwark though not until after the fair had closed. Pantomimes did not become established in the fairs until about 1729–30 but thenceforth they were a regular feature. Harlequin and Columbine had assumed their popular dance-mime partnership. Some pantomimes were from the theatres but many were the fairs' own products. A few were based on classical stories such as the spectacular *Fall of Phaeton* (B.F., S.F. 1733)[4] and *The History of Orpheus and Death of Eurydice* (B.F., S.F., Welsh, 1740).

After playing nearly twenty years at the fairs, the players introduced pieces from the theatre repertory, presumably in abridged form. The custom of extracting scenes out of plays dated from before the Commonwealth, and Kirkman printed several of them in *The Wits*, 1672. The entertainments of the fairs were much shorter than those of the theatres; they lasted about an hour and were repeated to a succession of audiences many times during the day. Ward states that a show lasted three quarters of an hour and that on the parade 'the clod skulled audience were lugged by the ears for an hour'.[5] The poem *Bartholomew Fair*, 1717, contains the line 'A comic Droll here

---

[1] *Post Man*, 21–3 August 1701; *Daily Courant*, 23 August 1703; above, p. 16.
[2] Above, p. 76.
[3] J. Weaver, *The History of Mimes and Pantomimes* (1728), p. 45. *The Cheats or the Tavern Bilkers* was given at L.I.F. in April 1717.
[4] Printed with *Jephtha's Rash Vow*.
[5] *Op. cit.* August 1699, September 1699.

every Hour is shewn', which, allowing for a change of audience, would mean that the piece lasted about 45 to 50 minutes. Thus a play would have to be cut down by more than half. A version of *The Recruiting Officer* was frequently revived (S.F. 1720, 1722, 1729, 1730), and other comedies given at the fairs were *The Beaux Stratagem* (S.F. 1730), *The Busy Body* (S.F. 1726), and *A Bold Stroke for a Wife* (S.F. 1731). Tragedies included *Oedipus, King of Thebes* (S.F. 1724), *George Barnwell* (S.F. 1731), *Tamerlane the Great* (B.F., S.F. 1733), and *The Rival Queens* (B.F. 1732, T.C. 1741). Some of these were presented at special benefit performances which probably lasted the whole evening. Shakespeare was represented by *The Jew of Venice* (S.F. 1719), *Henry IV* (S.F. 1720), *Richard III* (T.C. 1748), and *The Tempest or the Inchanted Island* (B.F. 1749). A droll entitled *The Ephesian Duke, or Blunder upon Blunder* (B.F. 1743) was carved out of *The Comedy of Errors*, and *The Life and Death of King John* (B.F. 1749) was apparently confined to the Arthur and final scenes. *The Comical Humours of Sir John Falstaff*[1] was performed as a separate piece (B.F. 1733), as well as being tacked on to the droll of *The Captive Prince* (M.F. 1744). Sir Andrew Aguecheek, presumably only in name, turns up at the siege of Babylon attached to the droll of *Darius* (B.F. 1741).

Among shorter pieces that were seen at the fairs may be mentioned Gay's *What D'ye Call It* (S.F. 1716), Fielding's *Tom Thumb* (B.F., S.F. 1730) and *Covent Garden Tragedy* (B.F. 1742), Garrick's *Lying Valet* (S.F. 1743), and the *Operatical Puppet Show Punch's Oratory; Or, the Pleasures of the Town* (T.C. 1730) taken from the puppet show in Fielding's *Author's Farce*.

There remain for consideration comic drolls or sub-plots. Several titles are indicative of the popularity of tricks and stratagems as, for example, *The French Doctor Outwitted* (B.F. 1743), and *The Intriguing Footman or the Spaniard Outwitted* (B.F. 1742). The venerable comic theme of the vintner in the suds, whose source was Marston's *Dutch Courtezan*,[2] turns up as *The Imposter; or the Biter Bit* (B.F. 1734) and as the pantomime

---

[1] F. Kirkman, *op. cit.*, had published a droll version.
[2] Leo Hughes and A. H. Scouten, 'Some Theatrical Adaptations of a Picaresque Tale', *Studies in English*, 1945–6, University of Texas, pp. 98–114.

Trick for Trick; or an Odd Affair between Harlequin, his Associates and the Vintner of York (T.C. 1739). Molière was the fount of such entertainments as *The Humours of the Forc'd Physician* (B.F. 1732) and *A Cure for Covetousness, or The Cheats of Scapin* (B.F. 1733). More significant were the 'comical humours' that accompanied most of the drolls, low comic interludes which have always been an ingredient of folk drama. They consisted of the clowning of two or more characters, frequently those of a master and his man, a tradition which had descended from Roman comedy. These farcical intermezzi, adopted in many Elizabethan plays, lingered on in the popular drama of the fairground. As an example of direct descent we may cite the humours of Tom Strowd and Swash his man, which were part of Day and Chettle's *Blind Beggar of Bednal Green* and were retained, with the man's name changed to Gudgeon, in one of the droll versions of that piece (S.F. 1743). As we have noted in *Jephtha's Rash Vow* and *The Generous Freemason*, these comic scenes often had little or no connection with the main plot. The fair audiences required variety rather than coherence; a constant shift of scene, mood and actors to hold their attention, rather than intelligible action.

The jumble of various elements, remarked on by Ned Ward, can be further illustrated by *The Unnatural Parents; or the Fair Maid of the West. With the Comical Humours of Trusty her Father's Man and Dame Strikefire, the Wicked Witch of Cornwall* (B.F. 1727). The main plot is concerned with the distresses of the Fair Maid who has been turned out of doors by her parents; the sub-plot turns on Trusty's meeting with witches in a wood (a favourite droll episode),[1] and his being mistaken for the Fair Maid and dressed in her clothes by her mad sister. Other features are the descent of Venus in a chariot drawn by swans (a piece of machinery from *The Siege of Troy*), songs, and a final dance by Harlequins and Scaramouches.

The comic scenes later developed into separate playlets, and we also find plays interspersed with one another. Thus *The Rival Queens* was intermixed with *A Wife well Managed* (T.C. 1741); *Jane Shore* with *The Merry Cobler* (M.F. 1745); *The Maiden*

[1] Cf. *The Tempest*, above, p. 142.

Queen with *The Fair Hypocrite* (M.F. 1745), and *Richard III* with *The Wanton Trick'd or All Alive and Merry* (T.C. 1741).

Of the authors of the drolls we know little. Presumably the players employed hack writers, as Mrs Mynns employed Settle. Whether the actors themselves ever pieced together their playlets we do not know. Thomas Walker wrote a piece for Lee and Harper, and one of Doggett's drolls was performed years after his death. The Drury Lane prompter, Chetwood, was responsible for two fair plays, but with these exceptions nearly all the entertainments are anonymous. How far the actors extemporised it is not now possible to tell. Doubtless there was plenty of gagging. The comic scenes in the drolls were printed with the rest so that there was a script, but we do not know how strictly it was adhered to. Probably the comedians from the theatres and the more reputable companies learnt their roles, whilst the lesser strollers in the smaller fairs employed more extemporary methods. This was certainly the case in the nineteenth century. Richardson made his actors study their parts and so did later fair managers such as Thorne, Bennett and Douglas, but a fair stroller told Mayhew that he was 'more often told what character he's to take, and what he's to do, and he's supposed to be able to find words capable of illustrating the character';[1] he reckoned that for one actor who learnt his part ten did not. It seems likely that both methods descended from earliest times and that both were used in the eighteenth century.

What can we learn about the popular taste from this survey? First, it was conservative, clinging to the old tales. Secondly, it demanded the ancient relief of comic interlude, revelling in swiftly alternating contrasts of marvellous feats and knockabout farce, fustian and slapstick. Thirdly, it required an admixture of singing and dancing, so that all the elements of the Elizabethan jig survived in the booths to entertain the descendants of the Elizabethan groundlings. Crude as they are, the drolls are of interest because in form they preserved elements of an earlier age, whilst in content they helped to retain in the memory of the people the legends which were to fertilise the literature of the romantic movement.

[1] *Mayhew's Characters*, ed. Peter Quennell (1951), p. 213.

CHAPTER IX

THEATRES AND STAGING

THE usual playing place of actors at the fairs was the booth erected for the duration of the particular fair. The players contracted for ground on which to build their booths, just as the traders contracted for ground for their stalls. We have seen[1] that in the 1670's the showmen took 40 to 50 feet of ground for this purpose for which they paid about £5.

When the magistrates tried to suppress the drama at the fairs, they forbade the letting of ground for booths or sheds for plays and threatened those who contravened the prohibition with presentment at the sessions. The lessors were presumably the owners of the fairground but, on one occasion at least, Penkethman himself advertised ground for shops or booths at May Fair.[2] Had he hired more ground than he needed as a speculation? The ground acquired, the actors started to erect their booths about two weeks before the fair opened. Bullock, Miller and Mills, and Oates and Fielding began to put up their Smithfield booths on 10 August 1732 for the opening on 23 August;[3] and by 16 August Fielding's booth was sufficiently advanced for him to rehearse his droll there.[4]

The inn yard was a favourite site for the play booths, as it had been for stages before regular playhouses were built. The performance was, of course, no longer in the open yard but in a building erected in it. One of the advantages of a site in an inn yard or adjacent to an inn was that coaches could drive up to the door or to a private passage through the tavern and deposit people who did not want to run the hazards of the thronging crowds. Yates, for instance, at Bartholomew Fair, advertised in 1749 that gentlemen's coaches would be admitted to the yard of the George Inn,[5] and in 1759 he announced that there was

---

[1] Above, p. 5.
[2] *Daily Courant*, 27 April 1704.
[3] *Daily Post*, 11 August 1732.
[4] *Ibid*. 17 August 1732.
[5] *General Advertiser*, 21 August.

a commodious way opposite the sheep pens at the corner of Cow Lane where coaches could draw up to the door of his booth in the Greyhound Inn without being intercepted.[1] Passages to booths, whether in tavern yards or elsewhere, were of help in attracting the quality. These passages were illuminated and decorated. Illuminations consisted of globular lamps or of 'moons', as they are sometimes called, and lanthorns.[2] Walker at Southwark Fair in 1722 advertised a 'new and commodious passage for the reception of Ladies etc. paved and beautified with large open rooms on each side, adorned with Lamps. Also a proper number of Servants to guard the Company to their Coaches and prevent disturbances'.[3] A similar guard for keeping the passage clear was advertised by Yates and Shuter in 1758 at Bartholomew Fair.[4] Mud and dirt were other inconveniences that the quality wished to avoid, and this same year Dunstall, Vaughan and Warner announced that care would be taken to keep the passages to their booth in the George Inn yard clean, clear and well lit.[5]

Having considered the approaches let us turn to the actual booths themselves. They were not, as one might expect, tents but barn-like buildings constructed of wooden boards, tall and narrow in shape. They are well illustrated as to exterior in Hogarth's 'Southwark Fair' (Pl. III) and in Setchel's fan of Bartholomew Fair (Pl. I). Sometimes existing rooms in inns were converted, and the brick building on the left-hand side of the Hogarth print has the air of a more permanent structure and is probably one of these. In the May Fair print (Pl. IV) a show cloth of Adam and Eve is being hung out of the first floor window of a tavern with the sign of the Swan. Yates and Shuter took the newly erected concert hall in the Greyhound Inn in 1757, and this theatre was still in use in 1780 when Mrs Baker's company acted there. Richardson, who came to Bartholomew Fair in 1798, says that 'in those days the exhibitions were generally up inn yards, or in the upstairs of public-houses'.[6] He mentions that Mrs

[1] *Public Advertiser*, 3 September.
[2] *General Advertiser*, 21 August 1749; *London Daily Post*, 21 August 1738.
[3] *Daily Post*, 13 September.   [4] *Public Advertiser*, 5 September.
[5] *Ibid*. 30 August 1758.   [6] Pierce Egan, *op. cit.* p. 195.

Baker at the Greyhound was in a room up one flight of stairs
and the giant O'Brian at the King's Head was also shown in
a room upstairs. His own company had a similarly situated
theatre and his 'platform was built out of the one-pair-of-stairs
window, forming an arch over the gingerbread stalls, with a long
pair of stairs leading down into the fair'. The Hogarth illustration shows a platform over a china stall, but no outside stairs are
in evidence and the ascent must have been from within the
building. An upper room over the Market House was also used
at May Fair.

In January 1745/6 the *Middlesex Sessions Books* refer to the
players contracting for ground to erect sheds and booths and to
others taking rooms, parts of houses or inn yards for acting at
May Fair.[1] By far the most common procedure was to erect
a wooden booth. The size of the booths and their resemblance to
theatres were matters of pride. The King's players announced
in 1715 that they had erected the largest booth ever built at Bartholomew Fair,[2] and Mrs Lee advertised at Southwark Fair that
her booth was as near the perfection of a theatre as possible and
was decorated by ingenious workmen.[3] That the booths were
often of considerable size is confirmed by orders against them
which, from 1708 onwards, refer to their 'extraordinary Largeness'. We have seen that a hundred and fifty people were
accommodated on Penkethman's stage in 1717 at Southwark.[4]

Evidently, an attempt was made to keep a booth standing in
Bartholomew Fair in 1717, for, on 28 October, the Court of
Aldermen heard a petition from the inhabitants of Smithfield
praying for the show booth within the Rounds to be taken down
and no other erected, and this was duly ordered.[5] The first we
hear of a booth being still in use well after fair time is in 1720,
when plays were given in Hall's booth, Southwark Fair, at the
end of November.[6] Two years later what was probably the same
booth in Bird Cage Alley, since it was still owned by Hall, was
functioning in February 1723.[7] There is every reason, then, to

---

[1] January 1744/5–December 1747, p. 36
[2] Above, p. 22.   [3] Above, p. 84.
[4] Above, p. 72.   [5] Repertory 121, p. 429.
[6] Above, p. 80.   [7] Above, p. 83.

V. A fair balcony

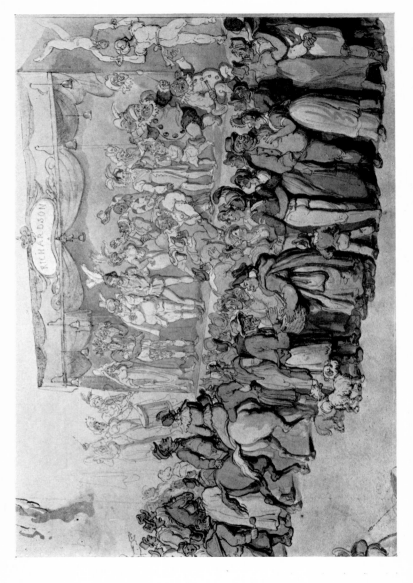

VI. Richardson's booth at Greenwich Fair

believe that this was a permanent building. In 1732 we find
plays being given in the Bowling Green in December, and in
1743 in February and March.[1] In the former year the house was
made warm and commodious for the winter and the passages
were relaid and ranged with lamps. We have seen that Powell
and Yeates had a tiled booth as early as 1726, and the tiles
which replaced boards for roofing probably indicated a permanent
structure. A tiled booth on the Bowling Green was still in use
in 1761.[2]

We have now to examine the most characteristic feature of
the fair booth, the parade or balcony on which the actors exhibited themselves in order to attract custom. This balcony was
common to fairs in Europe and was particularly highly developed
in the French fairs. A French example may be seen in Gabriel-
Jacques de Saint-Aubin's picture, 'The Parade', in the National
Gallery. The parade was, in fact, an integral part of the entertainments. As we have seen, these railed platforms were placed
at first-floor level when performances took place in a room on
the first storey of a house. In the booths, they were also well
above head level, as is evident from the pictures of them in
Hogarth's 'Southwark Fair', in Setchel's fan, and in the 'turn-
up' entitled 'Punch's Puppet Show'.[3] A reproduction by Philip
Norman of an undated drawing in Rendle and Norman's *The
Inns of Old Southwark* (Pl. V) shows a coach below the parade,
in which the quality are driving to the booth entrance. Before
the booth stands a girl drummer reminiscent of the famous
figure in the Hogarth picture. Jeering crowds are held back by
a guard with a long stick. The parade itself is furnished with a
bench at the back but most of the actors are lolling over the
balcony or conversing.

It was from the parade that the trumpeter blew to advise
patrons of the start of the show. On it actors strutted to show
off their costumes and attract onlookers; harlequins, perched on
the rails, pointed to the show cloths; Merry Andrews collogued
with clowns or pattered in soliloquy to the crowds below. Spy
describes how, when the actors had walked the length of the

---

[1] Above, pp. 93, 99.   [2] Above, p. 107.
[3] Reproduced in *Theatre Notebook*, vol. VII, p. 84.

gallery, 'each ascended to a seat agreeable to the dignity of their dress' whilst the Merry Andrews chattered, grimaced and mimed until it was time to call 'Walk in, gentlemen'.[1] 'Walk in' not 'walk up' for at that early time the entry was through a door on ground-floor level, as clearly shown in the Bartholomew Fair fan; sometimes it was directly under the parade, sometimes at the side of it. Women money-takers stood there behind a bar. 'Punch's Puppet Show', which, though dated 1792, may have been printed in 1772,[2] shows a member of the audience entering up a flight of steps leading to the parade and Mr Speaight opines that 'this is possibly the earliest illustration of the steps which the public were to be invited to "walk up"'. By the time that Richardson started to visit the fairs in 1797 the steps were usual. They are shown leading up to a small platform and then to a higher parade in the numerous prints of his theatre.[3] In Pugin's print the audience is walking up the steps both in front and at the side of the platform. In Rowlandson's water-colour of Greenwich Fair[4] in the British Museum (Pl. VI) the audience is mounting the parade by a step-ladder, which was probably an earlier form of ascent. The music on the parade is accommodated in a little built-up box such as is also visible in the menagerie parade at the side of Lane's print. The parade itself developed in the early nineteenth century from a balcony to a platform over which hung an elaborately draped and illuminated frontispiece. Richardson's cost £600.

The earlier balconies had also sometimes been decorated: one in May Fair, for instance, was adorned with blue pillars twisted with flowers. Flags often served as distinguishing signs in the booths and one is to be seen flying from the roof in the Hogarth print. At Southwark Fair in 1741 Fawkes and Pinchbeck advertised that their booth would have a large blue flag at the top. Barnes and Finley's rope-dancing booth at Bartholomew Fair in 1700 flew English and Dutch flags and, in the following

---

[1] E. Ward, *London Spy* (August 1699).

[2] George Speaight, 'Punch's Opera at Bartholomew Fair,' *Theatre Notebook*, vol. VII, p. 84.

[3] For example by T. Lane in Pierce Egan's *Life of an Actor* (1892), p. 193, and by Rowlandson and Pugin in *The Microcosm of London* [1808], vol. I, p. 52.

[4] The engraving in *Rowlandson's World in Miniature* (1816) is based on this.

years, an English flag. But what really distinguished one show
from another were the show cloths, generally painted with
pictures of the performances for the unlettered as well as with
the name of the booth proprietors and the show. This method of
advertisement, albeit on a smaller scale, is perpetuated today in
the photographs outside theatres. Hogarth and the Setchel fan
depict the cloths hanging above the balcony, but in 'Punch's
Puppet Show' they hang from its railings. When Penkethman
spoke an epilogue on an elephant at May Fair in 1704 he advertised this wonder 'by the Picture of the Elephant and Mr
Pinkeman sitting in state on his back on the outside of his booth'.[1]

Unfortunately, we know little of the interior arrangements of
the booths and the pictorial evidence is slight. The engraving
by Fourdrinier, after William Kent, at the head of Gay's fable
of the two monkeys who visited Southwark Fair,[2] appears not
to be an English theatre at all. There is no fore-stage and there
are no stage boxes. The stage is flanked by Corinthian columns
behind which is a draped curtain. The setting is of a formal
architectural kind and the performance is that of a tight-rope
walker. In the auditorium the audience is seated in a pit which
slopes down to the stage, and there are three tiers of boxes. The
engraving is in fact an enigma. Not only does it appear to
illustrate an auditorium and stage too elaborate for a temporary
booth, but the absence of fore-stage and proscenium doors has
no known parallel in this country at that time. We cannot, therefore, accept it as representing a booth interior.

The earliest representations are those of 'Punch's Puppet
Show' (Pl. VII)[3] which illustrate a puppet booth stage. In the
first interior scene Punch trundles his wife across the stage in a
wheelbarrow, much as he does in the show cloth of Punch's opera
in Hogarth's 'Southwark Fair'. At the back of the stage is the
court of France represented by the king and queen. They are
seated on thrones placed on a small platform two steps high
within a draped pavilion. Below the stage a conjuror shows his
tricks at a table watched by part of the audience, whilst another
part is looking at the performance on the stage. Since it seems

[1] *Daily Courant*, 27 April 1704.   [2] *Fables* (1727), p. 135.
[3] Sayer's Turn Ups, no. 14.

unlikely that three separate shows, Punch, the French court, and the conjuror, would be in progress simultaneously, the illustration is probably a composite one. In this case, the conjuror may represent the entertainment given while the booth was filling: if so, it took up space in the pit and the table must have been whisked away as the booth filled up. The other scenes depict the audience standing about or seated on a backless bench on which children are standing to get a better view. In one of them a band of four, consisting of a trumpet, violin and bombass and a Harlequin playing on the salt box, is placed directly below the stage. A draped curtain is raised well behind the front of the stage, leaving a fore-stage on which a dance of puppets is taking place; there is a backcloth of ships in battle. The stage itself is rather more than head high. Lighting is either from a chandelier or from one or two tiered hoops of candles and is centrally hung, except for the first scene of the French court where the hoops are on each side of the enthroned puppets.

No other views of the interior of a booth have come to my notice until 1810 when a print of an equestrian performance forms the frontispiece to *An Historical Account of Bartholomew Fair* published by John Arliss. A small circus ring is shown with two performers on horseback. A large central chandelier in two tiers is hung over the ring round which the audience is seated. It is not clear whether there is a ground floor tier of boxes, but there is definitely a balcony tier. These, however, only run down the two sides of the ring. At the rear is a large arch and a frame within it which may have been the proscenium of a stage or may merely be a back wall. The building has the air of a permanent structure and is well decorated. There is no evidence beyond the ascription at the foot of the print to prove that it represents an actual circus booth.

Rowlandson engraved a scene of the inside of a theatrical booth in the series 'Sports of a Country Fair' printed by Thomas Tegg in October 1810 (Pl. VIII). This shows an escaped tiger bursting through a canvas tent whilst a show was going on. Though a satirical print, it presumably bears a resemblance to a country fair booth, since it would need to be recognisable as such to make its point. It was probably a tent fit-up, though the ceiling does not appear to be canvas. The only bench is along

VII. Two scenes in a puppet booth

VIII. Interior of a country fair booth

the side wall and Dr Southern has conjectured that this may represent what was grandiloquently known as boxes. The rest of the audience must have stood. The stage is low and the proscenium arch contains the customary door and window, though whether practicable or not is uncertain. Behind the proscenium is a draped curtain and the scene is set with three castle booked wings and a backcloth of a castle with a bridge over a river. A hoop of candles illuminates the auditorium. It must be remembered that this represents a country fair booth of the early nineteenth century, which would be cruder than those of the principal London fairs. Another print in the series, showing the audience escaping from a fire down the steps leading from the booth balcony, depicts the usual timber building with entrance at first-floor level.

Failing pictorial evidence, we must depend on indications from advertisements as to parts of the house. Boxes seem to have been introduced at an early stage and are mentioned at Penkethman's booth at Southwark in 1716. At Penkethman and Pack's booth at Southwark in 1717 the boxes and pit were laid together,[1] and in 1721 at Bartholomew Fair Penkethman 'enlarged the Boxes and made them entirely commodious for the Quality'.[2] When Fielding built his booth at the George Inn Yard at Bartholomew Fair in 1733, he made a point that in boxes and pit 'the Audience receives every Sentence distinctly, as they are free from all the Noise and Confusion which perpetually incommode the Booths in the Field'.[3] How to keep out the noise of the tumultuous crowds outside must have presented a problem to those who had not the advantage of the comparative privacy of an inn yard.

Stage boxes are mentioned at Harper and Bullock's booth in Southwark in 1720, the only boxes in a booth which contained a pit and two galleries.[4] Much later, in 1743, at Yeates, Warner and Rosoman's booth at May Fair we again hear of stage boxes: 'The Booth is form'd after the manner of an amphitheatre, with Boxes on the Stage for the better reception of Gentlemen and Ladies', and in 1744 Yeates advertised that 'The Stage is form'd

---

[1] *Daily Courant*, 17 September 1717.   [2] *Ibid.* 23 August 1721.
[3] *Daily Post*, 8 August 1733.   [4] B.M. Add. MS. 32249.

into Boxes'.[1] It would seem, then, as though the amphitheatre referred not to the form of the auditorium in general but to a semi-circle of seats round the back and sides of the stage, such as was formed also on special occasions at the patent theatres. Booths usually had one gallery and sometimes two. There is no evidence as to their seating capacity. The prices varied, the usual being 2s. 6d. for the boxes, 1s. 6d. for the pit, 1s. for the gallery and 6d. for the upper gallery. Boxes were advertised for as much as 4s. for a benefit performance. The highest common price for the pit was 2s. 6d. and for the gallery 1s. 6d., but these charges were further augmented for benefits. Such prices were not cheap and must have precluded the poor, except from the upper gallery; they could see the puppets and monsters for a matter of a few pence. Towards the end of the century, when the regular London players no longer visited the fairs and the booths were occupied by strollers, the prices fell. In 1784 a Bartholomew Fair booth advertised seats at pit 1s., gallery 6d., upper gallery 3d.; and in 1790 Flockton charged 1s. for the pit and 6d. for the gallery.[2]

Of the lighting and decoration of the booths we know but little. At Hippisley, Bullock and Hallam's booth at Bartholomew Fair in 1734 the booth was illuminated with glass lustres after the manner of the *Ridotto al' Fresco*, Theophilus Cibber's panto-mime brought out at Drury Lane the previous year.[3] That decorations were not neglected is demonstrated by Warner and Fawkes's claim at the same fair in 1746 that their booth would be 'well illuminated and ornamented with variety of decorations'. What the decorations consisted of we do not know, but it was evidently thought worth while to ornament the booths, even for a three days' stay.

The establishment of Richardson's and other travelling theatres at the end of the century wrought changes in the form of the booths. These fit-ups had to be packed up and conveyed from place to place in caravans. This did not, however, prevent their being better decorated than of old. A writer about Bartholomew Fair in 1810 says: 'Very great improvements have lately been

---

[1] *London Daily Post*, 9 May 1743; *General Advertiser*, 4 May 1744.
[2] Guildhall Library, Granger 2. 1. 7.
[3] Guildhall Library, advertisement in J. P. Kemble, A collection of gleanings.

made in the arrangement and construction of the show booths, some of which appear highly decorated and of an evening are illuminated with coloured lamps.'[1] The structure may be envisaged as that used in portable theatres within living memory. When the audience entered the door at the back of the built-up parade, they found themselves at the back of the auditorium of the theatre which then sloped down in tiers corresponding to the steps which led up to the platform outside.[2] Accidents do not seem to have been frequent considering the hasty construction of the booths, and the mob that visited them. In 1725 the gallery fell at Lee's booth in Southwark Fair, causing the death of one spectator.[3] When the gallery of Phillips's booth collapsed in Bartholomew Fair in 1749, killing two people and injuring several others, the newspaper commented that it could only have happened through the carelessness of the workmen.[4] This caused Lee, Yeates and Warner to assure the public at Southwark Fair that their booth had been repaired and surveyed.[5] We have seen, too, how practical jokers gave a false alarm of fire at this fair in 1760, which resulted in a woman breaking her legs after jumping from the gallery into the pit.[6]

Scenery played an important part in many of the fair offerings. Spectacle had a natural appeal to the rough, unsophisticated, untutored crowds which visited the fairs; they needed something visual to marvel at as well as the patter of Merry Andrews and the crude jests of the comedians.

Some simple scenery was in use for the drolls of the Restoration period. *The Coronation of Queen Elizabeth*, which was played at both Bartholomew and Southwark Fairs in 1680, had three acts and several scenes.[7] The play opens with the 'noise of kettledrums and trumpets' and the curtain rises to discover 'the Queen sitting under a Cloth of State, in her Royal Robes' with attendant lords and ladies, 'two Bishops supporting her Crown, and two Popish Cardinals standing at a distance: the scene

---

[1] *An Historical Account of Bartholomew Fair* [1810], p. 18.
[2] See letter from Mr George Speaight and plan, *OSU Theatre Collection Bulletin* (Spring, 1957), vol. IV, no. 1, pp. 33–4.
[3] Above, p. 86.   [4] Above, p. 57.
[5] Above, p. 110.   [6] Above, p. 106.
[7] Morley, *op. cit.* pp. 200–1 reprints a large part of it.

imagined to be Whitehall'. The last phrase makes it clear that
no specific scenery was employed. All the characters exeunt at
the end of the scene. Scene ii is low comedy and presumably
is supposed to take place in the street. A flat was evidently
drawn in front of the Queen's throne, since for scene iii 'The
Scene draws off, and discovers the Romish conclave, the Popes,
Cardinals and Bishops, as in close consult'. This tableau would
have been prepared in place of the tableau of the Queen whilst
the low comedy scene was being played at the front of the stage.
Act ii opens in an unspecified place with two Cardinals to whom
a devil in the shape of a Jesuit enters. All exeunt and scene ii
takes place in the Queen's garden, where the crowd seizes her
would-be assassins. They all go off at the end, and for scene iii 'The
scene draws off, and discovers the Pope sitting by a Nun'. The
pattern was probably the same as in Act i with flats or a curtain
drawn over for scene ii and opened to reveal the tableau in
scene iii. This must have closed again at the end of the act as for
Act iii 'The Scene opens and discovers the Pope and Nun sitting
upon a Couch'. At the end of this scene the flats must have closed
again and scene ii opens with the crowd. In the middle of this
scene the Pope enters led by a Devil and after a few lines 'The
Scene suddenly draws off and discovers Hell full of Devils, Popes
and Cardinals, with the Ghosts of Moricena and Dulcementa
wounded: To them the Devil enters'. Probably the view of hell
closed as the Pope turned to go out and was prevented by the
entrance of the mob. It is obvious from this analysis that the
whole show was given with one pair of flats behind which scenes
could be prepared. The system was the same as that on the public
stage of the time though reduced to its most elementary form.

At the beginning of the eighteenth century the puppet stage at
the fairs was using much more elaborate effects involving
machinery. When *Noah's Flood* was added to Crawley's show of
The Creation of the World, we are told in the playbill 'The last
Scene does present Noah and his Family coming out of the Ark,
with all the Beasts, two by two, and all the Fowls of the Air seen
in a Prospect sitting upon the Trees. Likewise over the Ark is
seen the Sun rising in a most glorious manner, moreover a
multitude of Angels will be seen in double rank, which presents

a double prospect, one for the Sun, the other for a Palace, where will be seen six Angels ringing six Bells. Likewise Machines descend from above, double and treble with Dives rising out of Hell, and Lazarus seen in Abraham's Bosom besides several Figures dancing Jiggs, Sarabands and Country Dances.'[1] A version at Heatley's booth describes 'the Breaking of the Clouds, discovering the Palace of the Sun, in double and treble Prospects'.[2] Perspective scenery was used in this production, and the cloud shutters parted to reveal a two part perspective of the sun and a palace, while three cloud machines descended in the centre, one showing Dives, the second Lazarus in Abraham's bosom, and the third carrying the dancing puppets.

The puppeteers having contrived to show such elaborate effects, the live actors had to compete. The conjurations of Friar Bacon with a flying shoulder of mutton and other contraptions were, as we have seen,[3] immensely popular, and Brown mentions gods descending in machines, the raising of ghosts and apparitions, presumably through traps, and effects of thunder and lightning.[4]

Scenes and machines were advertised at Parker and Doggett's booth in 1703 and, about this time, Miller staged a *Tempest*[5] with a chariot drawn by sea horses in which sat Neptune and his Tritons, with singing mermaids, a scene which must have recalled the masque in Act v of the operatic *Tempest*. Elkanah Settle got up for Mrs Mynns in 1707 the most elaborate of all fair spectacles, *The Siege of Troy*. She claimed that the droll took ten months to prepare,[6] that it cost many hundred pounds,[7] and that 'In the whole several Scenes, Movements and Machines, it is no ways Inferiour even to any one Opera yet seen in either of the Royal Theatres'.

The pattern of scenes at the beginning was the same as that for *The Coronation of Queen Elizabeth*. 'Act i. The Curtain is drawn up, and discovers King Menelaus, Ulysses, Attendants, and Guards.' As in the *Coronation*, the formal opening is succeeded by a low comedy mob scene which in turn is followed by the opening of the scene to reveal a spectacle. The second or

---

[1] Harl. 5931, no. 274. [2] Harl. 5931, no. 272.
[3] Above, p. 13. [4] Above, p. 14. [5] Above, p. 16.
[6] Preface to first edition [? 1707]. [7] Epilogue.

both the first and second scenes were played on the fore-stage in front of the flats, which then were drawn to discover 'Paris and Helen, fronting the Audience, riding in a Triumphant Chariot, drawn by two White Elephants, mounted by two Pages in embroider'd Liveries. The side Wings are ten Elephants more, bearing on their Backs open Castles, umbraged with Canopies of Gold; the ten Castles fill'd with ten Persons richly drest, the Retinue of Paris; and on the Elephants Necks ride ten more Pages in the like rich Dress. Beyond over the Chariot, is seen a Vistoe of the City of Troy, on the Walls of which, stand several Trumpeters seen behind and over the Head of Paris, who sound at the opening of the Scene.'

It is clear from this description that there were five pairs of side wings and that these were not just painted cut outs of elephants, but were sufficiently built up for each castle to accommodate a human being and each animal's neck to be bestridden by a page. The centre of the stage was filled by the chariot drawn by the two elephants, probably profiled but in which Paris and Helen turned full face to the audience. On the backcloth was painted a prospect of Troy, in front of which there must have been practicable walls on which the trumpeters could stand and be seen over the head of Paris. But this was not all, for later in the scene 'Venus descends in a Chariot drawn by two Swans', and after a few lines 'The Ten Rich Figures in the Castles of the Elephants address themselves to the Goddess' in a musical chorus which ends the act. The scene was then shut to prepare for the spectacle which opens Act II: 'The Scene opens, and in a Wood without the Walls of Troy, appears the Trojan Horse, being a Figure of that Magnitude, that 'tis 17 Foot high to the top of his Back. The whole Figure magnificently adorn'd with all the Trappings, Furniture of a War Horse, set off with rich Gildings, Plumes of Feathers, and all other suitable Decorations. Under his Feet lies Sinon with a mangled Face all bloody, his Nose cut off, his Eyes out, &c. bound in Irons.' It may be surmised that the backcloth and walls remained for this scene but that the elephant wings were replaced by wood wings. The large decorated horse succeeded the chariot as centrepiece; its great height presupposes a high proscenium. Later the scene shuts leaving Ulysses outside. Thirteen lines spoken by him and Cassandra on the fore-stage were enough to enable an elaborate change to be made:

'The Scene opens and discovers the Temple of Diana, being a magnificent Structure richly adorn'd, the Capitals, Urns, Crescents, Festoons, and other carv'd Work, all gilt, consisting of ten pieces of Painting, in each of which, in a large Nych in each Front of these Paintings, are seen ten Statues of Heathen Gods, viz. Jupiter, Juno, Pallas, Apollo, Neptune, Thetis, Mars, Venus, Ceres and Mercury, each Figure near five Foot high, and all gilt. In the back of the Stage, in the Centre of the Temple, is a rich Altar-piece, bearing 3 Nyches in the Walls, in the middle of which on a Pedestal 18 Inches high, stands a young Woman drest in Cloth of Gold, representing the Statue of Diana, holding a Hunting Spear in her Hand; and on two other Pedestals of the same height on each Hand of her, stand two more young Women, in the like Golden Habit, representing two of her Nymphs, each with a Bow and a Quiver.

Over this Altar piece, and beyond the View of the Temple, are seen three beautiful Circles of Clouds, and on the Back Scene beyond them in a serene Heaven, is seen Diana driving in a Chariot drawn by two Hinds.'

The third set of wings formed the temple. The niches and statues appear to have been built as pieces in front of the wings.[1] The altar was probably a set piece (possibly using the same framework as the walls) with practicable niches in which three actresses could stand on pedestals. The backcloth was a heaven with a painting of Diana in her chariot and there was a sky border of clouds. It is not, however, clear whether the three circles were painted on one border or, as seems more likely, on three perspective borders.

Into this scene entered 'a Procession of Priests and Priestesses in Vestments, adorn'd with Silver Crescents' and Paris and Helen, with twelve pages bearing up their trains. Cassandra works a transformation by moving her wand 'and in the twinkling of an Eye, the Ten Golden Statues, in the Painting, are

---

[1] Cf. similar effect in Lediard's setting for *Great Britain Rejoicing* (1727), *Theatre Notebook*, vol. II, after p. 50, Pl. 6.

all turn'd to black, and the three Figures on the Pedestals are likewise stript of their Cloth of Gold and all drest in Black: and the whole Vistoe of the Heavens is changed to a flaming Hell'. Quite how this was effected we cannot tell. Perhaps the niches with the golden statues were swivelled round to show their obverse of black statues by the same type of machinery that worked the Greek periaktoi. The three pedestals at the back may have worked on the same principle with actresses dressed in black on the obverse. The back shutter of the heavens was drawn off to reveal a second shutter of hell and the sky borders must likewise have been changed. The success of the transformation depended on quick and precise timing. Cassandra's transformation is not seen by Paris and other Trojans. At the end of the act the shutters must once again have been drawn.

For Act III: 'The Scene opens and discovers the Town of Troy consisting of ten Pieces of Uniform Painting, representing a Street of Magnificent Buildings, terminating with a double Wall of the City, and over the wall is seen an upper Town. In the Center of this City stands the Horse, out of whose sides, in the sight of the Audience, two ladders slip, and immediately near forty Soldiers with their Officers, issue out of the Body of the Horse, all with their drawn Swords.' Doubtless the same walls and backcloth were used as in Act I with another set of wings. After only seven lines the scene shut again and a mob scene was played in front of it; then the scene, reopening, discovered the town without the horse. The Greeks enter with drawn swords in one hand and lighted flambeaux in the other and, whilst the king issues commands: 'the Soldiers run up and down the Streets seemingly setting the Town on Fire, whilst near forty Windows or Portholes in the Paintings all appear on Fire, the Flames catching from House to House, and all perform'd by illuminations and Transparent Painting seen scattered thro' the Scenes, both in the Upper and Lower Town'. This early use of the technique of the transparency is of great interest.[1] It would seem that some kind

[1] For discussion of the meaning of the term see Richard Southern, 'Lediard and Early 18th Century Scene Design', *Theatre Notebook*, vol. II, p. 49. Transparent scenes were in use by puppet shows at Smithfield at the turn of the seventeenth century.

of red transparent material was used for the windows of the houses both on the wings, which represented the lower town, and the backcloth which represented the upper. Candles or lamps must have been placed behind these and lit in succession so that the impression was given that more and more houses were catching fire. The effect was heightened by the stage business: 'Here enter several Trojans in various and distracted postures thro' the Flaming Streets, pursued by the Grecians, other Grecians running away with young Women in their Arms, all with several Shrieks and Cries.' Later, 'Helen Enters above' and 'Leaps down into the Fire'. How was this done? Did she enter on the walls and jump from them into the burning upper town between the set piece of the walls and the backcloth? The scene shuts and a mob scene distracts the audience whilst the last scenic effect is prepared behind. 'The Scene opens and discovers a Grove, terminating with a Triumphal Arch, with two Figures of Fame hanging beneath the Arch; and beyond the Arch, over a Tarras Walk, is seen a Beautiful Garden of six side Wings adorn'd with Statues, and ending in a Visto of Garden-work.' One may conjecture that the front wings were those of a grove, the second the uprights of an arch which spanned the stage and was completed by a border piece with the two hanging figures of fame. Beyond the arch was a raised platform representing the walk; the last three wings on each side represented the garden and statues, and the backcloth supplied the vista. The walk may have used the same platform as the walls with a replacement of the painting in front of it.

The whole show necessitated five wing changes and four back scenes (Troy, sky, hell, garden). The built-up pieces were the chariot, the walls, the horse, the altar, and the tarras walk. Trick scenery involving changing statues, transformation, and transparencies were within the scope of this fair company. The theatres royal could provide little more except trapwork. This is the most detailed description of the scenery and effects of an eighteenth-century fair performance that we have, and it leads us to revise a conception of all fair performances as very rough and ready. No doubt some were; yet the booth managers were capable of entertaining their patrons with a really elaborate show. It was probably in the following year, 1708, that Settle contrived *Whittington* for Mrs Mynns. Again it was an elaborate spectacle, though we have only the advertisement for it[1] and no text with scene directions. Settle, in his final scene of the Lord Mayor's Pageant, used parts of the scenery of the previous droll. In it were presented 'nine several Pageants, being Six Elephants and Castles, a magnificent Temple, and two Triumphant Chariots, one drawn by two Lyons, and the other by two Dolphins; in all which are seated above twenty Persons in various Dresses; with Flaggs, Scutcheons, Streamers, &c.' The elephants and castles, the temple and the two chariots had all been employed in *The Siege of Troy* but the white elephants and swans, which had drawn the chariots in that droll, were here replaced by lions and dolphins. Other 'stately and surprizing Scenes' were 'a Rowling Sea, bearing a large Ship under Sayl with *Neptune*, Mermaids, Dolphins, &c. Also a Prospect of a Moorish Country, so swarming with Rats and Mice, that they overrun the King and Queens Table at Dinner. Likewise a large diverting Scene of Tapestry fill'd with all living Figures.'

As we have seen,[2] Miller had already staged a Neptune in a chariot, and mermaids. Mrs Lee (who inherited from Mrs Mynns), Harper, and Spiller used Neptune, Tritons and floating mermaids in *Hero and Leander* in 1728; in Oates and Fielding's booth in 1730 in *The Generous Freemason*, Neptune rose to a symphony of soft music attended by Tritons; in W. Hallam's booth in 1739 there was a scene of Neptune's Palace with Tritons and sea nymphs, which was used again the following year as a concluding piece. It was evidently a popular effect. Mrs Lee also employed her mother's swan-drawn chariot in *The Unnatural Parents* at her booth with Harper in 1727.

Merlin, at Southwark in 1724, boasted 'scenes, machines, flyings, sinkings and risings proper to the Droll' as well as a shower of fire 'and the appearance of a Comet, with a fiery Dragon that prognosticated the birth of King Arthur'.[3] Only the principal characters, however, were 'new drest'. The sinkings presumably involved traps.

With the pantomimes came more elaborate and trick scenery.

[1] Harl. 5931, no. 278.   [2] Above, p. 161.   [3] *Daily Post*, 5 September 1724.

Lee and Harper's *Fall of Phaeton* in 1733 included the staging of another conflagration. Phaeton ascends in his chariot and his unruly horses set the world on fire. Jupiter descends on an eagle and Phaeton is struck out of the chariot into the river.[1]

Unfortunately we know nothing of who painted the scenes for fair shows; whether the actors brought scene painters with them from the theatres, or whether the lesser strollers employed more than a carpenter or actor who could daub something when necessary. We have seen that Settle was employed by Mrs Mynns for props and machinery, and Hogarth and Oram may have been employed by her daughter. Lee, Harper and Spiller's new scenes for *The Perjured Prince* (B.F. 1728) were painted by 'an excellent artist, approved of and commended by the best masters'. The scenes for the *Emperor of China Grand Vol-gi* (B.F., S.F. 1731) were similarly announced as 'new painted by a great master'.

Scenery was used for its own sake and frequently attached to more than one entertainment, as we have seen with Hallam's Neptune's Palace. Scenery and machinery combined to depict topical events abroad which were shown as separate items in the programme. Thus the battle of Dettingen (S.F. 1743) was illustrated 'With the taking of the White Household Standard, blowing up the Bridge, destroying and drowning most of the French Army'. This was probably a live show but scenic effects by clockwork were also shown.[2] At Godwin and Reynolds's booth at Bartholomew Fair in 1747, for example, a prospect of Bergen op Zoom with its fortifications, and a representation of the French besieging and the Dutch defending it from their batteries, was so displayed. This was followed by a prospect of Venice in a calm sea with a ship sailing, men rowing in barges, and pleasure boats, down to such details as swans feathering themselves, so the figures must have been on quite a large scale. In 1758 the capture of Louisburg and Cape Breton was exhibited by Yates and Shuter at Bartholomew Fair.[3] This type of model clockwork scene persisted into the twentieth century, and I can remember a very effective one of the earthquake at Messina in one of the exhibitions that were such a feature of Edwardian life.

---

[1] Above, p. 40.   [2] Above, p. 100.   [3] Above, p. 60.

Puppets, too, continued to exploit scenery and, at the Patagonian theatre at Bartholomew Fair, 1780, there was exhibited 'a Beautiful Scene of the Prospect of that part of the River Thames that Commands Ranelagh and Chelsea Hospital, with a Grand View of the Regatta'.[1]

Processions were as popular on the fair stages as they were in the patent theatres. The Lord Mayor's show, which was first represented in Mrs Mynns's *Whittington*, was introduced into *Wat Tyler* in 1730 and shown as a separate spectacle at Southwark in 1738. A procession of the Princess and Timur Koran to the funeral pile formed part of the droll of *Timur Koran* in 1760.

We know but little about the costumes worn by the fair players. During the Commonwealth, when the drolls were performed by stealth, Kirkman tells us that the costumes cost little and 'painted cloaths many times served the turn to represent Rich Habits'.[2] We have seen,[3] however, that Mrs Mynns dressed her characters in *The Siege of Troy* in gold and silver, and, though this may have been exceptional, it does show what a strolling company in a fair booth was capable of. The fairs followed the theatres in advertising habits proper to the characters as early as 1731 for the *Emperor of China Grand Vol-gi*, and, at a revival of *The Siege of Troy* in 1747, the clothes, scenes and decorations were 'finish'd according to the Taste of the Antient Greeks'. That the quality and number of costumes in a fair booth were not to be despised is confirmed by the value of nearly £40 put on Yates's wardrobe in 1741.[4]

Music played its part in the fair shows from early days. Kirkman mentions the fiddlers. Drummers and trumpeters, employed to beat the people in on the parades or among the crowds, most likely played also within at the representations. The first mention of a band I have found is in 1729 when the songs in the opera of *Hunter* and the music between the acts were supplied by a good band of instruments accompanied by a chamber organ. Indeed the advent of the ballad operas the previous year necessitated more elaborate music than had been used previously. From this time on, references to the bands are fairly frequent.

[1] Guildhall Library, Granger, 2. 1. 7.   [2] *The Wits*, Preface.
[3] Above, p. 84.   [4] Above, p. 99.

Kettledrums and trumpets were still the favoured instruments but we also hear of French horns, violins, hautboys and bassoons. A complete band was often announced as an attraction.

From all this it is evident that fair booths differed considerably in their resources. The poorest of them must have been crude, crowded and uncomfortable; the best were large and, later, permanent structures with equipment for elaborate staging.

The acting could not have been altogether despicable when comedians of the rank of Penkethman, Doggett, Norris, and Shuter were frequent visitors. Many famous players such as Macklin, Mrs Horton and Mrs Pritchard started their London careers at the fairs and many strollers who never attained fame graduated to the patent theatres from them. The fact, too, that the quality, and even royalty, patronised the booth entertainments shows that they had attractions for the upper and middle classes used to the amenities of the patent theatres. Most of the drolls themselves were, however, crude enough and conservatively traditional both in subject matter and style. They were undoubtedly written for the multitude yet succeeded in amusing their social superiors. The fair theatres never assumed the same importance in England that they did in France but they had a life of their own, distinct from that of the regular theatres whether metropolitan or provincial. By their traditionalism they preserved elements from older times and folk lore from immemorial ones. They should take their singular place in our theatrical history.

LIST OF REFERENCES

MS. material, collections of cuttings, etc., are listed under the names
of the institutions which own them.

Location of books, etc., is given only when not in the British Museum.

Place of publication is given only when abroad.

An asterisk indicates that I have not seen a copy.

MANUSCRIPTS

British Museum. F. Latreille MSS. Add. MSS. 32249–52; 47617.

Corporation of London Records Office. Bartholomew Fair Account
Book. MS. 155. 10.

—— Journals of the Court of Common Council.

—— Miscellaneous papers relating to Bartholomew and Southwark
Fairs. Miscellaneous MS. 11. 24.

—— Repertories of the Court of Aldermen.

Guildhall Library. A collection of cuttings, playbills, MSS. notes, and
other material relating to Bartholomew Fair and Pie Powder
Court. MS. 1514.

—— Smithfield Court Book containing the proceedings in the Court
of Piepowder from 1790 to 1854. MS. 95.

Latreille MSS. *See* British Museum.

Public Record Office. Assizes Book 31/1 f.

Southwark Library. Folder with MS. notes on the fair.

BOOKS, NEWSPAPERS, MISCELLANEOUS COLLECTIONS

*An Account of the Last Bartholomew-Fair, and the Late City Order for
Regulating the Same: with Two Letters to a Citizen of London on
that Occasion.* 1702. Guildhall Library, press-mark A. 1. 1.

The Annual Register.

ASHTON, J. *Chap-books of the 18th Century.* 1882.

ASTON, A. *A Brief Supplement to Colley Cibber.*

—— *The Fool's Opera; or, The Taste of the Age . . . To which is prefix'd
A Sketch of the Author's Life, Written by Himself* [?1731].

AVERY, E. and SCOUTEN, A. H. 'Tentative Calendar of Daily Theatrical
Performances in London, 1700–1704/5.' *PMLA*, vol. XLIII, no. 1.
1948.

BAGFORD. *See* British Museum.

Bartholomew Fair: An Heroi-Comical Poem. 1717.

Biographia Dramatica. Compiled D. E. Baker, I. Reed and Stephen Jones. 1812.

BLUNDELL, N. *Blundell's Diary and Letter Book, 1702–28.* Ed. M. Blundell. 1952.

BOLTING, B. 'Christopher Smart in London.' *Research Studies of the State College of Washington,* March 1939.

BOSWELL, E. *The Restoration Court Stage, 1660–1702.* Harvard University Press, 1932.

BOULMIERS, J. A. JULLIEN DES. *Histoire du Théâtre de l'Opéra Comique.* Paris, 1769.

British Museum. Bagford, J. A collection of titlepages and fragments of printed books formed by John Bagford. Harl. 5931. Press-mark N.L. 4.c.

—— A collection of advertisements, prints etc. principally relating to Southwark Fair. Press-mark 840 m. 26.

—— Fillinham, I. A collection of cuttings from newspapers, advertisements, playbills etc. Press-mark 1889. b. 10.

—— H[aslewood], J. Collections relating to the drama, vol. IX. Press-mark 11791. dd. 18.

The Broken Stock-Jobbers; or, Work for the Bailiffs. 1720.

BROWN, F. C. *Elkanah Settle, his Life and Works.* University of Chicago Press, 1910.

BROWN, T. *Letters from the Dead to the Living.* 1702.

CAMPARDON, E. *Les Spectacles de la Foire.* Paris, 1877.

CAMPBELL, T. *Life of Mrs Siddons.* 1834.

Catalogue of Prints and Drawings in the British Museum. Political and Personal Satires.

CHAMBERS, R. *The Book of Days.* 1888.

CHARKE, C. *A Narrative of the Life of Mrs Charlotte Charke.* 1929.

CHETWOOD, W. R. *A General History of the Stage.* 1749.

—— *The Generous Free-Mason: Or, The Constant Lady.* 1731.

CHURCHILL, C. *The Rosciad.* 1761.

CIBBER, T. *The Lives of the Poets of Great Britain and Ireland.* 1753.

CLINCH, G. *Marylebone and St Pancras.* 1890.

A Collection of Old Ballads. 1723.

The Coronation of Queen Elizabeth, with The Restauration of the Protestant Religion: or, The Downfal of the Pope. 1680.

The Country Journal.

The Craftsman.

CUNNINGHAM, P. *A Handbook for London, Past and Present.* 1849.

The Daily Advertiser.

The Daily Courant.

The Daily Journal.

The Daily Post.

DANIEL, G. *Merrie England in the Olden Time.* 1842.

DAVIES, T. *Dramatic Miscellanies.* 1784.

Dawks's Newsletter.

DENNIS, J. *Select Works.* 1718.

The Devil upon Two Sticks: or, The Town Until'd. With the Comical Humours of Don Stulto and Siegnior Jingo. 1708.

A Dialogue between Sly and Lovett. Sung at Fielding's Booth at Bartholomew Fair. [1733].

DOWNES, J. *Roscius Anglicanus.* 1708.

DUFFETT, T. *New Songs.* 1676.

D'URFEY, T. *Wit and Mirth: or Pills to purge Melancholy.* 1719–20.

EGAN, P. *The Life of an Actor.* 1892.

EVELYN, J. *The Diary of John Evelyn.* Ed. E. S. de Beer. 1955.

The Fall of Phaeton. See *Jephtha's Rash Vow.*

Farrago: or Miscellanies in Verse and Prose, 1739.

Fillinham. *See* British Museum.

The Flying Post.

FROST, T. *The Old Showmen.* 1874.

GAY, J. *Fables.* 1727.

The General Advertiser.

GENEST, J. *Some Account of the English Stage.* 1832.

The Gentleman's Magazine.

Granger 2. 1. 7. *See* Guildhall Library.

The Grub-Street Journal.

Guildhall Library. A collection of cuttings, woodcuts, advertisements, showmen's bills, booth bills, songs, and various memoranda in connection with the metropolitan fairs. Press-mark A. 5. 2.

—— A collection of hand-bills relating to Bartholomew Fair. 1779–1804. Press-mark Gr. 2. 1. 7.

—— Kemble, J. P. A collection of gleanings from periodicals and newspapers, 1711–61; consisting principally of advertisements respecting theatrical performances, Bartholomew, Southwark, and other fairs...in London and the provinces, collected and arranged in chronological order by J. P. Kemble. Press-mark A. 6. 6.

—— Osborne, A. B. Bartholomew, frost and suburban fairs, consisting of portraits, rare views, cuttings, music etc. 1718 to 1890. Collected by A. B. Osborne. Press-mark Gr. 3. 3. 1.

Harleian 5931. *See* British Museum.

H[aslewood], J. *See* British Museum.

An Historical Account of Bartholomew Fair. [1810.]

The History and Origin of Bartholomew Fair. 1808. Guildhall Library. Press-mark A. 1. 1.

HODGSON, N. 'Sarah Baker.' *Studies in English Theatre History.* Society for Theatre Research. 1952.

HOGAN, C. B. 'The New Wells, Goodman's Fields, 1739–1752.' *Theatre Notebook*, vol. III, no. 4. 1949.

HONE, W. *The Every-Day Book and Table Book*, vol. III. 1827.

—— *Year Book*. 1832.

House of Commons Journals. 1735.

HUGHES, L. *A Century of English Farce*. 1956.

—— and SCOUTEN, A. H. *Ten English Farces*. University of Texas Press, 1948.

—— 'Some Theatrical Adaptations of a Picaresque Tale.' *Studies in English*, 1945–6. University of Texas Press.

HUGHSON, D. *London*. 1809.

JACKSON, A. 'London Playhouses, 1700–1705.' *Review of English Studies*, vol. VIII, no. 31. 1932.

Jephtha's Rash Vow: or, the Virgin Sacrifice... To which will be added the Fall of Phaeton. 1733.

KEMBLE, J. P. *See* Guildhall Library.

KING, P. *The Life of John Locke*. 1830.

KIRKMAN, F. *The Wits or Sport upon Sport*. 1672.

KIRKMAN, J. T. *Memoirs of Charles Macklin*. 1799.

LATREILLE, F. 'Henry Fielding and Timothy Fielding.' *Notes and Queries*, 5th series, vol. III. 1875.

The London Chronicle.

The London Daily Post.

The London Gazette.

London Society. 1863.

The Loyal Protestant and True Domestick Intelligence.

LUTTRELL, N. *A Brief Historical Relation of State Affairs*. 1857.

LYSONS, D. *The Environs of London*. 1795.

MACAULAY, T. B. (Lord). *The History of England*. 1858.

MALCOLM, J. P. *Anecdotes of the Manners and Customs of London during the Eighteenth Century*. 1808.

Mayhew's Characters. Ed. P. Quennell. 1951.

MCKECHNIE, S. *Popular Entertainments through the Ages*. 1931.

The Microcosm of London. [1808.]

Middlesex County Records. Calendar of Sessions Books. [1911.]

MILLER, F. *Saint Pancras Past and Present*. 1874.

Mist's Weekly Journal or Saturday's Post.

MORLEY, H. *Memoirs of Bartholomew Fair*. 1892. Books and Papers by Henry Morley, vol. III.

The Morning Advertiser.

The Morning Chronicle.

MUNCEY, R. W. L. *Our Old English Fairs*. [1936.]

NICOLL, A. *A History of English Drama*. Vol. I, *Restoration Drama*, 1955. Vol. II, *Early Eighteenth Century Drama*, 1952.

Nouvelle Biographie Générale. Ed. J. C. F. Hoefer. Paris, 1855–62.

The Observator.

O[hio] S[tate] U[niversity] *Theatre Collection Bulletin,* vol. IV, no. 1. 1957.

Order of the Court of Common Council that booths and other erections of Bartholomew Fair shall be used only for purposes of merchandize. 1702.

Order of the Court of Common Council that Lady Fair in the borough of Southwark shall not be allowed to extend beyond the three days appointed by charter. 1735. Guildhall Library, Taylor Broadsides Sc. G. 2. 5, no. 123.

The Original London Post.

A Pacquet from Wills. 1701.

A Peep at Bartholomew Fair. [1837.]

PENNANT, T. *Some Account of London.* 1793.

The Penny London Post.

PEPYS, S. *The Diary of Samuel Pepys.* Ed. H. B. Wheatley and Lord Braybrooke. 1904.

PINKS, W. J. *The History of Clerkenwell.* 1865.

PLAYFORD, J. *The Musical Companion.* 1673.

—— *The Second Book of the Pleasant Musical Companion.* 1686.

POPE, A. *The Dunciad.* 1728.

Poplar Public Library. Cuttings book.

The Post-Boy.

The Post Man.

The Public Advertiser.

RENDLE, W. and NORMAN, P. *The Inns of Old Southwark.* 1888.

*RIDER, D. *Diary, 1715–1716.* Ed. W. Mathews. 1939.

RIMBAULT, E. R. 'Gleanings for the History of Bartholomew Fair.' *Notes and Queries,* 2nd series, vol. VIII. 1859.

Robin Hood. 1730.

ROSENFELD, S. *Strolling Players and Drama in the Provinces, 1660–1765.* 1939.

—— 'The Players in Cambridge, 1662–1800.' *Studies in English Theatre History.* Society for Theatre Research. 1952.

—— 'Shepherd's Market Theatre and May Fair Wells.' *Theatre Notebook,* vol. V, no. 4. 1951.

—— 'Was Hogarth a Scene Painter?' *Theatre Notebook,* vol. VIII, no. 1. 1953.

ROWLANDSON, T. *Rowlandson's World in Miniature.* 1816.

The St James's Chronicle.

St Pancras Public Library. Cuttings. Press-mark A XI, f. 16.

The Secret Mercury.

The Siege of Troy. [? 1707]; [? 1715]; 1716; 1735.

SMITH, J. T. *Antient Topography of London*. 1815.
—— *A Book for a Rainy Day*. 1845.
SORBIÈRE, S. DE. *A Journey to London in the Year 1698*. 1698.
SOUTHERN, R. 'Lediard and Early Eighteenth-Century Scene Design.'
Theatre Notebook, vol. II, no. 3. 1948.
SPEAIGHT, G. *The History of the English Puppet Theatre*. 1955.
—— 'Punch's Opera at Bartholomew Fair.' *Theatre Notebook*, vol. VII,
no. 4. 1953.
The Stroler's Pacquet Open'd. 1742.
STRYPE, J. *A Survey of the Cities of London and Westminster*. 1720.
SUMMERS, M. *A Bibliography of the Restoration Drama*. [1935.]
The Tatler. Ed. J. Nichols. 1786.
Théâtre des Boulevards ou Recueil des Parades. Ed. M. Gilles [Corbie].
1756.
THORNBURY, G. W. and WALFORD, E. *Old and New London*. [1873–8.]
TIMBS, J. *Walks and Talks about London*. 1865.
The Unnatural Parents, or the Fair Maid of the West. [?1727.]
VICTOR, B. *The History of the Theatres of London and Dublin*. 1761.
—— *Original Letters*. 1776.
VOITURE, V. DE. *The Works of Monsieur Voiture*. 1705.
WALFORD, C. *Fairs, Past and Present*. 1883.
A Walk to Smithfield. 1701.
WALKER, T. *The Quaker's Opera*. 1728
WARD, E. *The London Spy*.
Wat Tyler and Jack Straw: or the Mob Reformers. 1730.
WEAVER, J. *The History of Mimes and Pantomimes*. 1728.
WEBB, E. A. *The Records of St Bartholomew's Priory*. 1921.
The Weekly Journal or British Gazetteer.
WESTON, T. *Memoirs of that Celebrated Comedian...Thomas Weston*.
1776.
WHEATLEY, H. B. *London Past and Present*. 1891.
*WIGNELL, J. *Poems*. 1762.
WILKINSON, R. *Londina Illustrata*. 1819.
WINGENT, R. M. *Historical Notes on the Borough*. 1913.
Wit and Drollery. 1682.
WROTH, W. *London Pleasure Gardens*. 1896.
YOUNG, E. *Two Epistles to Mr Pope Concerning the Authors of the Age*.
Dublin, 1730.

INDEX

I. PERSONS AND SUBJECTS

It is not always possible to distinguish between actors of the same name. When no Christian name is known I have listed all actors of the same name under that name unless there is evidence that more than one person is involved.

Owing to variations in the spelling of proper names, the same person may be entered in two places. I have made a cross-reference when I have felt this to be likely.

With families of actors it is impossible to be certain which one is meant unless an initial is given or the date precludes others. Unless I could be reasonably sure that the reference is to a particular member of the family I have entered it under the surname only. Thus entries under Hallam may also refer to Adam or William Hallam. In the case of Lee, I cannot be sure that Mrs Lee is not meant in every case so all entries for Lee are under her name.

I am greatly indebted to Mr C. B. Hogan's invaluable indexes to his *Shakespeare in the Theatre*, vols. i and ii, for most of the more obscure actors' Christian names.

Abraham, showman, 67
Achurch, Thomas, actor, 90
Acton fair, 134
Actors, emoluments of, 10, 16, 60, 63, 89
Adams, actor, 48, 52, 101, 114, 115
Aldridge, showman, 67
Aldworth, vintner, 34
Allen, actor, 55, 59, 102
Amelia, Princess, 46
Amherst, John, admiral, 60, 144
Anne, Queen, 16, 112, 138
Appleby, puppet showman, 67
Appleby, rope dancing showman, 75, 76
Archer, actor, 51
Arliss, John, publisher, 156
Arthur, John, actor, 45-6, 47, 48, 90
Astley's, 69
Aston, Anthony, actor, 14, 19, 41
Aston, Walter, actor, 28, 36, 38, 40, 95
Atherton, Miss, actress, 37, 40, 98
Audiences, at drolls, 12-13, 23; at parades, 10-11; at a puppet show, 156; behaviour of, 12, 86-7, 116; middle class among, 38, 48-9, 65, 82, 169; mixed nature of, 46; on the stage, 72, 78, 169; quality among, 19, 25, 46; tastes of, 143-4, 148, 149
Ayres, James, actor, 89, 91, 130

Baker, Miss S., dancer, 65
Baker, Mrs Sarah, showwoman, 64, 65, 69, 70, 151-2
Balcony, *see* Parade
Balducci, Signor, showman, 45
Ballad operas, 35, 38, 41, 64, 123; popularity of, 30-3, 87-8, 145
Ballads, 135, 138-9
Bambridge, actor, 40, 42, 99, 100
Bambridge, Mrs, actress, 43, 51, 100
Banks, Thomas, scene painter, 69
Bannister, showman, 67
Barcock, actor, 34, 38, 92
Bardin, Peter, actor, 34, 36, 38, 42
Barnes, showman, 10, 15 n. 2, 75, 76, 110, 154
Barnes, Mrs, showwoman, 17, 111
Barnett, Mrs, actress, 32
Bartholomew Fair, 75, 109, 115, 124, 158, 159, 167; accidents at, 57; amateur actors at, 2, 22-3; arrest of players at, 7; attempt to abolish, 3-4, 63-4; Betterton's visit to, 14; boxes at, 25, 62, 157; date of, 9, 58, 70, 121; decline of theatrical entertainments at, 44, 57, 65, 70; depicted in Setchel fan, 26; description of acting at, 11, 12-13, 15, 18; entertainments from other fairs at, 113, 123; entertainments from, taken to other fairs, 76, 81, 85, 87, 91, 92, 94,

Bartholomew Fair (*cont.*)
  97, 99, 100, 102, 103, 105, 110, 120,
  128; Garrick's visit to, 57; Greyhound Inn Theatre at, 60, 61, 64,
  65, 66, 69, 151; Hogarth and Oram
  paint scenes for, 84; in the nineteenth century, xi, 70; licences to
  play at, 66–9; limitation to three or
  four days, 1, 2–3, 23, 44, 45, 46, 70,
  71; origin of, 1; passage to booths at,
  29, 42, 58, 66, 150–1; Patagonian
  Theatre at, 168; payments for
  ground at, 5–6; playbills of, 2, 8, 12,
  15, 16, 17, 21, 75, 130; plays and
  players at, 1–70, 95, 101, 123, 135–
  48 *passim*; riot at, 63–4; Settle
  employed at, 20, 21; size of companies at, 37, 49; suppression of
  plays at, 1–4, 14, 44, 52, 57, 63, 70,
  125, 152; times of performances at,
  30, 32, 35, 39, 47, 61, 64, 69;
  visited by royalty, 24, 29, 37, 46–7,
  65
Bath, 16; comedians from, 104; morris
  dancers, 52
Baxter, Mrs, actress, 18, 78
Baxter, Richard, harlequin, 76, 111,
  146
Bayley, George, showman, 14 n. 1
Beauford, actor, 128
Bellgard, dancer, 44
Bembridge, *see* Bambridge
Bence, showman, 59, 103, 104
Bencraft, James, actor, 36, 44, 47, 52,
  97, 126
Bencraft, jr., actor, 38
Bennet, actor, 53
Bennet, Miss, actress, 48
Bennett, showman, 149
Bernal, puppet showman, 68
Berry, Edward, actor, 34, 36, 40, 42,
  52
Berry, Miss, dancer, 102
Betterton, Thomas, 14, 59, 140
Bickerstaff, John, actor, 18
Billington, Mrs, singer, 66
Binks, actor, 42
Birmingham, players at, 44
Blackford, Alderman, 3
Blackmore, puppet showman, 67
Blake, showman, 9
Blakes, Charles, actor, 48, 52
Bland, Mrs, actress, 52

Blogg, actor, 114
Blower, puppet showman, 67
Blundell, Nicholas, 23
Board, actor, 45
Boheme, Anthony, actor, 24, 27, 80, 81,
  82
Bolton, Mrs, actress, 66
Boman, John, actor, 32, 42, 114, 115
Boneway, Mlle, dancer, 53
Booker, actor, 19
Booth, Barton, actor, 76, 77, 96
Booth, Mrs, actress, 49, 98
Booths, 2, 3, 40, *150–9*; accidents in,
  57, 86, 106, 159; permanent, 80, 83,
  93, 101, 152–3; tiled, 100, 101, 102,
  103, 104, 105, 107, 127, 153
Boscawen, Edward, admiral, 60, 144
Boucher, Thomas, actor, 31
Boulogne, English players at, 68
Bow Fair, 131–2
Bowman, actor, 68
Bowman, Mrs, singer, 27, 82
Brassey, actor, 55
Bray, Mrs, actress, 30
Brett, Miss Anne, dancer, 37
Bridges, actor, 54, 57, 101
Bridges, Mrs, actress, 54
Bridgewater, R., actor, 28, 29, 84
Bright, actor, 131
Bristol, players at, 44
Britton, Mrs, actress, 123
Brogden, actor, 34
Broke, Mons. de, dancer, 51
Brouard, machinist, 81
Brown, showman, 67, 69
Brown, Master, actor, 131
Brown, Tom, 13–14, 136, 161
Browne, actor, 85
Bruodin, actor, 56
Buchanan, actor, 85
Buchanan, Mrs Elizabeth, actress, 31
Buck, Timothy, actor, 85
Bullock, Christopher, dramatist, 118
Bullock, Hildebrand, actor, 23, 24
Bullock, Mrs Jane, actress, 36
Bullock, Miss, dancer, 24
Bullock, William, actor, 29; arrest of,
  72; booth holder, 31, 33, 36, 38, 45,
  81, 82, 83, 157; partnership with T.
  Cibber, 39, 93–4, 95, with Hall, 35,
  with Hallam and Hippisley, 42, 158,
  with Leigh or Mrs Leigh, 23, 24,
  79, 80, with Miller and Mills, 150,

Bullock, William (*cont.*)
with Mills, 110, with Pack, 133, with Penkethman, 17, 77, with Spiller, 28, 85; roles, 18, 23, 31, 33, 36, 40, 45, 76, 79, 85, 133
Burnett, actor, 33, 34
Burney, actor, 34
Burton, Edmund, actor, 54, 101
Butcher, actor, 28, 85
Butcher, Mrs, actress, 85

Canterbury, players at, 44
Cantrell, Mrs, actress, 31, 33, 40
Careless, Miss, actress, 40
Careless, Mrs, actress, 89, 114
Carey, Henry, composer and dramatist, 34, 45, 47, 131
Caroline, Princess, 47
Carr, actor, 102
Carr, Mrs, actress, 99
Carter, John, 114
Carter, Miss, actress, 127
Cartwright, actor, 47
Cash, *see* Coysh
Catchpole, puppet showman, 69
Chambers, Robert, 65
Chapbooks, 135, 139
Chapman, Miss, actress, 33, 36
Chapman, Thomas, actor, 33, 35, 36, 41, 42, 43, 45, 46, 47, 49, 50, 52, 53, 85, 89
Charke, Mrs Charlotte, actress, 38, 39, 42, 51, 59, 114, 115; her puppets, 51 n. 2
Charke, Miss, *see* Harman, Mrs
Charke, Richard, actor and dancer, 32, 34, 89
Charles I, King, 108, 118
Charles II, King, 1, 131
Charles, trumpeter, 89–90, 91, 92–3, 94
Chettle, actor, 54
Chetwood, William Rufus, dramatist, 4, 33, 35, 46, 85, 88, 91, 135, 145, 149
Churchill, Charles, 63
Cibber, Colley, actor and dramatist, 32, 33, 88, 92, 93–4, 95
Cibber, Theophilus, actor and dramatist, 20, 29, 39, 40, 91 n. 2, 94, 131, 158
Circus, 66, 132, 156
Clark, actor, 33, 92, 102; *see also* Clarke, Nathaniel
Clark, showman, 67

Clark, Mrs, actress, 32, 33, 35, 38, 90
Clarke, Miss, actress and singer, 52, 115
Clarke, Nathaniel, 31, 100; *see also* Clark
Clerkenwell New Wells, 129, 130, 131
Cleveland, Thomas Wentworth, Earl of, 131
Clockwork, 37, 124, 131–2, 167; *see also* Musical picture
Closson, Mons., actor and dancer, 98, 127
Clough, Thomas, actor, 49, 100
Coe, 83
Coell, Sir John, 108
Coffey, Charles, dramatist, 31, 87, 91, 123, 135, 145
Coker, actor, 24
Coker, Mrs, actress, 45, 91
Cole, E. D., actor, 37
Cole, Miss, dancer, 40, 45, 130
Coleman, actor, 102
Collet, actor, 34, 122, 123, 124
Collier, dancer, 92
Collins, actor, 130
Commedia dell'arte, 4, 11, 30, 137, *145–6*
Conjuring, 18, 58, 67, 116, 124, 127, 131, 155–6; bottle conjuror, 56
Connell, actor, 64
Conyers, singer, 115
Cook, Mrs Mary, actress, 29, 82
Cooper, John, 110
Corse, boy singer, 123
Cory, John, actor, 29, 85
Costello, Patrick, actor, 55
Costumes, cost of, 96, 99, 103, 168; description of, 22; Doggett's 15; dressmaker for, 69; Macklin's, 89; new, 31, 36, 54, 79, 82, 91, 95, 100, 101, 104, 166; of dancing dogs, 79; parade, 10, 60, 95; Roman, 26; Setchel fan, 26; *Siege of Troy*, 54, 77, 84, 95, 162, 164, 168; Spanish, 17, Turkish, 17
Court of Aldermen, 1, 3, 71, 73, 122, 152
Court of Common Council, 1, 2, 3, 15, 74, 107
Covent Garden Theatre, 45, 47, 49, 50, 56, 59, 96, 143
Coventry, George William, Earl of, 120
Coysh, John, actor, 6, 19
Crawley, William, puppet showman, 14, 75, 160

Croft-Murray, Edward, 26
Crofts, actor, 48
Cross, Mrs Frances, *née* Shireburn, 30, 31, 32, 49, 54
Cross, Richard, actor, 36, 38, 39, 40, 47, 49, 54, 57, 92, 101, 124, 127
Culloden, battle of, 53, 119
Cumberland, William, Duke of, 49, 53, 119
Cunningham, W., actor, 101
Cushing, John, actor, 56, 100, 113, 115, 130
Cushing, Mrs John, actress, 56, 100, 113
Cuthbert, actor, 101

Dancers and dancing, 13, 49, 52, 56–7, 75, 77, 97, 110; at Bartholomew Fair, 27, 28, 31, 34, 43, 47, 50; at Southwark Fair, 80, 89, 92, 95; at Tottenham Court Fair, 127; ballet, 43, 58; burlesque, 92; comic, 103, 106, 126; country, 9, 35, 38, 91; foreign, 8, 28, 30, 32, 43, 49, 56–7, 59, 97, 106, 123; in grotesque characters, 30, 33, 41; morris, 52; pantomime, 40, 44; puppet, 161; Scaramouch, 127; trick, 8
Dancing dogs, 20, 79, 111
Daniel, actor, 101, 115
Daniel, George, 8, 12
Daniel, Mrs William, actress, 55
Davenport, actor, 33, 38, 90
Davidge, puppet showman, 67
Davis, actor, 51, 53
Davis, dressmaker, 69
Davis, Mrs, actress, 127
Day, John, dramatist, 100
De Ferron Ville, Mons., dancer, 37
De la Grange, dancer, 44, 126
De la Grange, Mlle, dancer, 44, 126
Delaval, Sir Ralph, admiral, 7, 137
DeLorme, Mlle, dancer, 34, 38, 43
Dettingen, battle of, 51, 52, 100, 128, 144, 167
Devisse, Mons., dancer, 103
Devonshire, showman, 68
Devoto, Anthony, puppet showman, 5
Devoto, John, showman, 5
Dibdin, Charles, dramatist, 64
Diggs, Richard, actor, 24, 78
Dighton, actor, 50
Diswell, puppet showman, 68

Dodson, Miss, actress, 49
Dodson, Mrs, actress, 52
Dogget, actor, 55
Doggett, Thomas, 3, 12–13, 15, 16, 17, 18, 19, 30, 34, 83, 122, 137, 149, 161, 169
Dominique, acrobat, 130
Dorset, Lionel Sackville, Duke of, 38
Douglas, showman, 149
Dove, Michael, actor, 32, 35, 45, 47, 51, 90, 97, 99, 123, 124, 126
Dove, Mrs, dancer, 44, 45, 47, 51, 52, 97, 99, 126
Downes, actor, 33
Drolls, *135–49*; development of, 15, 70; duration of, 11, 13, 23, 33, 119, 146–7; suppression of, 1–4, 14, 48, 52, 63, 73, 75, 112, 121–2, 125, 128
Drury Lane Theatre, 69, 109, 122, 140, 149; compared with Bartholomew Fair, 14; entertainments from, 39, 46, 64, 91, 127, 158; Lilliputians from, 45; players engaged for, 42, 76, 77, 96; players from, 6, 24, 25, 32, 38, 39, 41, 48, 49, 50, 55, 56, 59, 83, 98, 119; players secede from, 93, 128; shut during Bartholomew Fair, 9 n. 2, 10
Drury, Robert, dramatist, 49
Dublin, 49
Duffett, Thomas, 5
Dukes, actor, 115
Dulton, actor, 35, 90
Dulton, Mrs, actress, 90
Dunstall, John, actor, 48, 50, 70, 151
Dunstall, Mrs John, actress, 48
D'Urfey, Thomas, dramatist, 4, 109
Dyer, singer, 24

Eaton, actor, 86, 89, 91, 122
Edinburgh Theatre, 130
Edward I, King, 133
Edward IV, King, 71
Edwards, 4
Edwards, actor, 115
Edwards, Miss, actress, 85
Edwards, Miss, child dancer, 45
Egerton, Mrs, actress, 50
Egleton, Mrs Jane, formerly Mrs Giffard, actress, 27, 32, 36, 79, 81, 83, 89, 123
Egleton, John, actor, 27, 81, 83, 86

Elmy, Mrs Mary, *née* Morse, actress, 37, 42
Elsam, Mrs, actress, 83, 86, 89
Epsom, players at, 19
Este, William, actor, 42
Evans, actor, 36, 92
Evans, equestrian, 111
Evelyn, John, 75, 137
Evenel, actor, 51
Excell, actor, 34, 36, 95

Fairs, limitation of, 1, 3, 9, 42, 44, 70, 71, 72–4, 81, 102, 103, 104
Faux, *see* Fawkes
Fawkes, Isaac, conjuror and showman, 26, 37, 70, 83
Fawkes jr., showman, 37, 46, 51, 52, 53, 99, 124, 154, 158
Fell, Mrs, actress, 59
Ferg, Master, dancer, 45
Ferguson, Miss, actress, 49, 51
Field, Mrs, actress, 55
Fielding, Henry, dramatist, 40, 51, 103, 105, 123, 147
Fielding, Timothy, actor, 30, 31–2, 34, 35, 37, 38, 39, 42, 87, 89, 91, 93, 94, 97, 125, 150, 157, 166
Finley, rope-dancing showman, 15 n. 2, 111, 154
Finley, Mrs (Lady Mary), rope dancer, 109, 110
Fireworks, 54, 55, 88, 119
Fisher, dancer, 32
Fitzgerald, Miss, actress, 32
Fitzgerald, Mrs, actress, 40, 95
Fleetwood, Charles, manager of Drury Lane, 129
Flint, Miss, actress, 66
Flint, Mrs, actress and showwoman, 66, 68, 69
Flockton, puppet showman, 65, 66, 67, 68, 132, 158
Florentina, Signor, dancer, 106
Fluyder, Sir Samuel, Lord Mayor, 63
Folkestone, players at, 68
Foote, Samuel, 63, 105–6
Forrester, Mrs, actress, 35, 42
Fourdrinier, Pierre, engraver, 155
Fowler, Miss, actress, 68
Francis, Miss, dancer, 24, 27, 32, 80
Freeman, actor, 52
Freeman, Mrs, actress, 99, 115
French, Daniel, showman, 128

French fairs, 11, 76, 153, 169
Frimble, Mrs, actress, 59
Frisby, actor, 59
Frost, Mrs, actress, 131
Furnival, actor, 91
Furnival, Mrs, actress, 91

Garrick, David, 42, 54, 57, 147
Gay, John, 86, 147, 155
Gayward, actor, 103
Geast, William, 90
George, actor, 55
George III, King, 62, 107
Gibbins, rope dancer, 86
Giffard, Henry, actor, 31, 33, 79, 87, 88
Giffard, Mrs Jane, *see* Egleton, Mrs
Giffard, William, actor, 34, 122
Gilbert, actor, 88
Giles, fairground owner, 132
Gloucester, William, Duke of, 65
Godwin, actor and showman, 51, 52, 114, 115, 167
Godwin, Mrs, actress, 114, 115
Gold, actor, 114
Goodbehere, 4
Goodman's Fields New Wells, 47, 49, 105
Goodman's Fields Theatre, 31, 34, 48, 50, 122, 123
Goodshaw, Mrs, actress, 32
Grace, Mrs Anne, actress, 34, 36, 37
Grafton, Charles Fitzroy, Duke of, 47
Graham, Mrs, actress, 55
Grand Jury, presentment by, 2; *see also* Middlesex *and* Westminster
Granier, actor, 45
Granier, Master and Miss, child dancers, 49
Gray, James, actor, 47, 49, 51
Green, actor, 50, 56
Greene, Robert, dramatist, 16, 120, 139, 140
Greenwich Fair, 21, 113, 154
Greenwood, Thomas, scene painter, 69
Grey, actor, 37
Griffen, actor, 66
Griffin, Benjamin, actor, 23, 39, 40, 76, 94
Grimaldi, Mme, dancer, 103
Grimwood, actor, 102
Grimwood, Mrs, actress, 102
Gulick, Mrs, actress, 24, 82
Gyngell, showman, xi, 68, 132

Habito, Mrs, actress, 51
Hacket, actor, 100
Haines, Joseph, actor, 8, 14, 78
Hale, Sacheverel, actor, 39, 42, 46
Hale, Mrs Sacheverel, actress, 42, 45
Hall, actor, 56
Hall, puppet showman, 69
Hall, Jacob, rope dancer, 5, 7
Hall, John, actor, 29, 30, 31, 33, 35, 36, 41, 44, 79, 80, 81, 82, 83, 91, 141, 152
Hallam, actor, 42, 43, 45, 56, 59, 94, 97–8, 105, 114, 116, 125, 126, 158
Hallam, Adam, 36, 37, 39, 40, 49, 92, 138
Hallam, Master, 42
Hallam, William, 39, 40, 45, 47, 49, 50, 166, 167
Hamilton, Masters J. and W., dancers, 45
Hampstead Fair, 134
Hampton Court, 79
Handel, G. F., 36
Hardwicke, Philip Yorke, Lord Chancellor, 117, 128
Harlequin, at rope dancers' booth, 16; in dance with countryman, 93; in interludes with Scaramouch, 76, 108, 111, 145–6, 148; in pantomimes, 35, 41, 44, 45, 47, 50–6 passim, 59, 64, 66, 68, 87, 90, 92, 97, 99, 103, 113, 119, 126–30 passim, 133; on parades, 26, 153; scene with peasant, 78
Harman, actor, 59
Harman, Mrs Catharine, née Charke, 59, 114, 115
Harper, actor, 59
Harper, John, actor, benefits for, 80, 81; death of, 97; partnership with Bullock, 81, 157, with Mrs Lee, 25–6, 29, 30, 33, 35, 36, 37, 40, 46, 83–95 passim, 124, 138, 145, 149, 166, 167; roles, 25, 27, 28, 30, 33, 36, 40, 81, 82, 88, 89, 90, 94; starts career at Southwark Fair, 80
Harper, Mrs, actress, 59
Harrel, actor, 128
Harrington, actor, 48
Harrison, actor, 85, 101
Hart, showman, 67
Harvard University Library, Theatre Collection, 8, 64

Haughton, dancer, 85
Haughton, Mrs, actress, 29, 34, 47, 85, 86, 122
Havard, William, actor, 34
Haydn, F. J., 79
Haymarket, Little Theatre, 27–8, 30, 31, 33, 35, 39, 45, 56, 58, 59, 64, 68, 82, 90, 145
Haymarket, Queen's or King's Theatre, 19, 54, 105, 119, 123
Hays, dancer, 44, 45, 47, 126
Heatley, Matthew, puppet showman, 14, 161
Hemskirk, dancer, 46
Henley-on-Thames, players at, 68
Henry I, King, 1
Henshaw, Robert, licenser of fair plays, 74
Hewet, John, actor, 40, 94
Heydon, Miss, actress, 64
Hicken, actor, 66
Hicks, actor, 35, 40, 92, 94, 95
Hicks, Mrs, actress, 69
Hickson, Mrs, actress, 55, 98, 130
Highgate Fair, 134
Highmore, John, patentee of Drury Lane, 3
Hill, actor, 127
Hill, Mrs, actress, 47, 51, 98
Hind, actor and dancer, 38, 95
Hind, Mrs, dancer, 38
Hippisley, John, actor and dramatist, 33, 35–6, 37, 38, 39, 42, 45, 46, 47, 49, 50, 52, 53, 91, 94, 158
Hippisley, Miss, actress, 55, 56
Hobbs, Mrs, actress, 24
Hogarth, William, 55, 84; his ' March to Finchley', 121, 125; his 'Southwark Fair', 93–5, 151, 152, 153, 154, 155, 167
Holinds, puppet showman, 69
Hollins, actor, 130
Holtham, actor, 50
Hone, William, 2, 12
Horton, Mrs Christiana, actress, 76, 169
Houghton, actor, 33
Hounslow Fair, 133, 146
Howell, 120
Howis, puppet showman, 68
Huddy, Philip, actor, 27, 28, 29, 34, 36, 37, 42, 83, 85, 90, 122, 123, 124

Hulett, Charles, actor, 27, 28, 30, 32, 36, 40, 42, 82, 88, 89, 90, 91, 94, 95, 123, 124
Hulett, Mrs, actress, 91, 124
Humphries or Humphreys, actor, 68
Husband, Benjamin, actor, 110
Hussey, showman, 53, 54, 55, 101, 103, 118, 119

Ingall, Mrs, actress, 55; see also Jinghall
Inns or taverns, 150–2; Angel, 83; Black Boy, 31; Buffalo, 39; Crown, 16, 32, 34; Cyder Cellar, 8; George, 29, 30, 32, 34, 36, 37, 38, 42, 45, 52, 53, 54, 55, 56, 58, 59, 60, 61, 62, 66, 68, 69, 150, 151, 157; Golden Lion, 75; Greyhound, 6, 23, 28, 48, 54, 60, 61, 62, 64, 65, 66, 68, 69, 151, 152; Half Moon, 81, 87, 88, 91; Harts Horn, 23, 26, 27; King's Arms, 48, 76; King's Head, 8, 48, 56, 58, 69, 152; King's Head, Tottenham Court, 124; Mitre, 8; Queen's Arms, 75, 76, 81, 82, 83, 84, 86, 87, 89; Red Lyon, 8; Ship, 124; Sun, 49; Sun, Tottenham Court, 123; Swan, 58, 59, 65, 68, 151; Swan, Tottenham Court, 127
Ipswich, players at, 44
Ives, actor, 68

Jack Pudding, 7, 9, 122
James II, King, 108, 118
James, Harris, actor, 49, 85, 127
Janno, dancer, 43, 47
Jeffries, Mrs, actress, 98
Jenkins, actor, 91, 92, 124
Jevon, Thomas, dramatist, 11
Jinghall, Mrs, actress, 47; see also Ingall
Jobson, showman, 65, 67, 68, 69
Johnson, actor, 51, 52, 56
Johnson, showman, 67, 68
Johnson, Benjamin, actor, 21, 114
Johnson, Charles, dramatist, 118
Johnson, Samuel, of Cheshire, dramatist, 43, 127
Jonas, showman, 67, 68, 69, 70
Jones, actor, 35, 36, 38, 40, 59, 66, 90, 97, 102, 114, 123, 124
Jones, Miss, actress, 55, 59, 90
Jones, Mrs, actress, 32, 90, 98, 101

Jones, puppet showman, 69
Jonson, Ben, 5, 138, 141
Julian, actor, 47, 48, 131

Kent, William, 155
Kilby, Mrs Elizabeth, actress, 32, 34
Killigrew, Henry, admiral, 7, 137
Kirkman, Francis, 146, 168
Knapp, actor, 81
Knapp, Mrs, actress, 25
Knott, actor and dancer, 35, 87, 123

Labisle, Sieur, dancer, 123
Lacy, actor, 42, 89, 97
Lacy, Mrs, actress, 36, 89, 95, 98
Lady Fair, see Southwark
Lady Isabella, rope dancer, 76
Laguerre, John, actor, 41, 45, 46
Laguerre, Louis, painter, 41, 93
Lamball, Mrs, actress, 50, 52
Lane, T., 154
Langford, Abraham, dramatist, 113
Laver, James, 26
Lawrence, showman, 67
Le Brune, dancer, 44, 126
Le Brune, Mlle, dancer, 44, 126
Le Coudrière, dancer, 30
Lee, see Mrs Hannah Lee
Lee, George, printer, 33, 36, 41, 88, 91, 135
Lee, Mrs Hannah, showwoman, and Lee, booth holder, 23, 25, 28, 73, 82, 86, 88, 97, 100, 104, 119; booth of, 86, 152, 159; employs Settle, 20; last visit to fairs, 102; partnership with Harper, 25–6, 29, 30, 33, 35, 36, 37, 40, 46, 83–95 passim, 124, 138, 145, 149, 166, 167; with Petit, 122, with Phillips, 46, 98, 99, 126, with Spiller, 24, 26, 29, 145, 166, with Woodward, 49, 127, 129, with Yeates, 53, 55, 101; petitions against Playhouse Bill, 96; reported marriage to Yeates, 98
Lee, Nathaniel, dramatist, 38, 128
Lee, S., printer, 76, 135 n. 1
Leigh, Mrs Elizabeth, actress, 23, 24, 40, 80, 133
Leigh, Francis, actor, 23, 73, 79, 80, 121
Leigh, Francis jr., 37, 40
Leigh, John, actor, 79, 80, 81, 82
Leigh, Mrs, see Lee

Le Sage, Alain, 112, 135
Licensing Act, 3, 44, 48, 53, 64, 96, 97
Lilliputian company, 45, 59, 104
Lillo, George, dramatist, 36, 91
Lincoln's Inn Fields Theatre, 9 n. 2, 14, 23, 24, 27, 30, 33, 43, 77, 80, 81, 87, 89, 146
Littleton, actor, 45
Livier, dancer, 43
Locke, John, 136
Logee, puppet showman, 67
Loggan, Thomas, fan painter, 26
London, city of, 71; fire of, 35
London Spy, see Ward, E.
Long Dens, Mons. de, dancer, 28
Lord Mayor of London, 2, 3, 14, 63–4, 74, 88
Lord Mayor's show, 21, 34, 97, 166, 168
Louisa, Princess, 47
Lowder, actor, 48, 55
Lussingham, publican, 8
Luttrell, Narcissus, 75

Macguire, actor, 98, 131
Machen, actor, 32, 56, 122
Machines, 20, 33, 47, 57, 75, 95, 110, 136, 148, 161, 166, 167; Coronation, 123; descent by, 14; Grand Theatre of Arts, 131–2; Italian, 124; new, 16, 17, 30, 35, 54, 81, 84, 88, 100, 103; puppet, 137; Siege of Carthagena, 99; Temple of Apollo, 58, 123; see also Clockwork
Mackarnea, actor, 55
Mackenzie, actor, 48, 95
Macklin, Charles, actor, 89, 169
Maddox, showman, 77
Mahomet Achmed Vizaro Mussulmo, Turkish rope dancer, 54, 56
Mahomet, Ach., 124
Malone, actor, 51, 100, 102, 128
Mann, Miss, actress, 32, 33, 41, 87, 88
Marr, Harry, actor, 47, 48
Marshall, actor, 85, 127
Marshalsea prison, 74
Marston, John, dramatist, 147
Marten, John, actor, 48
Martin, Mrs Elizabeth, actress, 42
Mary, Lady, see Finley, Mrs
Mary II, Queen, 12, 75
Masena, puppet showman, 67
Mason, actor, 101

Masons, 36, 145
Massey, actor, 56
Mathews, wire dancer, 107
May Fair, 20, 108–20, 135, 138, 139, 145, 151, 152, 154, 155, 157
May Fair New Wells, 113, 114, 118, 119, 129
Mears, Miss, actress, 37
Merrivale, actor, 85
Merry Andrew, 4–5, 9, 10–11, 16, 18, 26, 46, 58, 81, 87, 108–9, 145, 153–4, 159
Middlesex County Sessions, 116–17, 121–2, 125, 130, 132, 133–4, 152; Grand Jury, 116, 132, 133
Middleton, actor, 115, 118, 127, 128
Middleton, Mrs, actress and dancer, 27, 83, 128
'Midnight', Mrs, entertainer, 58, 59, 70, 104,
Mile End Fair, 131–2
Miller, showman, 10, 16, 23, 110, 161, 166
Miller, Josias, actor, 23–4, 25, 27, 29, 30, 31, 36, 37, 38, 41, 77, 81, 82, 83, 85, 92, 94, 150
Miller, Mrs, actress, 56, 89
Mills, John, actor, 18, 36, 37, 41, 92, 94, 110, 150
Mills, William, actor, 36, 38, 55
Milward, actor, 29, 30, 41
Mitcham Fair, 134
Moffett, Mrs, actress, 30
Molière, J.-B. P., 37, 39, 40, 147
Molloy, Charles, dramatist, 60 n. 4
Monk, Mrs, actress, 69
Monmouth, Duke of, his company, 6
Moore, actor, 59
Moorfields Fair, 133
Moreau, Miss, dancer, 54
Morello, puppet showman, 67, 68, 69
Morello, Charles, puppet showman, 67
Morgan, actor, 27, 30, 33, 36, 52, 77, 82, 86, 88, 89, 90, 94, 95
Morgan, Mrs, actress, 27, 28, 30, 31, 36, 82, 85, 86, 89, 91, 94, 95
Morley, Henry, 5, 7, 8, 20, 26, 41, 56
Morrell, showman, 69
Morris, Master and Miss, dancers, 100
Morse, Mrs, see Elmy
Motteux, Mrs, actress, 100
Mottley, John, dramatist, 105
Mountfort, actor, 32

Mountfort, Mrs, actress, 32, 34, 88, 123
Moyle, Walter, 9
Mullart, Mrs Elizabeth, actress, 35, 36, 37, 41, 43, 49, 51, 91, 123
Mullart, William, actor, 33, 35, 36, 37, 41, 43, 49, 50, 88, 90, 91, 123
Mun, Mrs, actress, 31
Music, 34, 46, 79, 82, 87, 145, 166, 168; ballad tunes, 31–2, 35, 38, 52, 91; concerts, 53, 58, 64; flourish, 11; Neapolitan, 42; new, 104, 107; on parades, 5, 154, 168
Music booths, 8, 13, 14–15
Musical band, 42, 53, 62, 88, 119, 126; instruments employed in, 23, 26, 37, 69, 92, 97, 105, 114, 128, 130, 156, 159, 168–9
Musical picture, 23, 28, 83, 85
Mynns, actor, 19
Mynns, Mrs Anne, showwoman, 19–20, 21, 23, 24, 70, 76, 95, 96, 141, 149, 161, 166, 167, 168

Nanfan, Master, actor, 48
Naylor, actor, 50, 128
Nevit, actor, 66
Newhouse, dancer, 27, 80
Newmarket company, 6
Newstead, Mrs, actress, 90
Nichols, actor, 40, 45
Nivelon, Mons., dancer, 50
Nokes, Mrs, actress, 32, 35, 88, 90, 123
Noland, puppet showman, 69
Norris, Henry (Jubilee Dicky), 18, 23, 24–5, 27, 28, 76, 77, 78, 79, 81, 85, 121, 169
Norris, Henry jr., 79, 85
Norwich, company of comedians, 65, 70; players at, 6

Oakley, actor, 130
Oates, Miss Anne, actress, 38
Oates, James, actor, 24, 27, 30, 31, 33, 34, 36, 37, 38, 41, 42, 45, 47, 56, 81, 82, 83, 85, 88, 92, 94, 150, 166
Oates, Miss, actress, 34, 36, 38, 41, 42
O'Brian, giant, 69, 152
Ogden, John, actor, 23, 24, 33, 36, 85
Ogden, Mrs, dancer, 31, 33
'Opera', 5, 13, 19, 20, 28, 35, 37, 43, 90, 110, 136, 137, 139
Oram, William, painter, 84, 167
Orfeur, actor, 27, 83, 85

Orfeur, Mrs, actress, 27, 85
Osbaldiston, actor, 45
Otway, Thomas, 39, 41
Ouka, Indian king, 123
Oulton, W. C., dramatist, 68
Owen, Lewy, actor, 64, 65

Pack, actor, 59, 78, 79, 133, 141, 157
Paddington Fair, 134
Page, actor, 51
Paget, William, actor, 34, 41, 47, 50
Palmer, money-taker, 57
Palmer, Mrs, actress, 32, 37, 123
Palms, Miss, actress, 35, 90, 123
Pantomimes, 145–6; at Bartholomew Fair, 28, 35, 40, 44–8 passim, 51, 55, 56, 59, 65, 66, 67, 70, 158; at Hounslow Fair, 133; at May Fair, 113–19 passim; at Southwark Fair, 73, 81, 88, 90, 92, 97–105 passim; at Tottenham Court Fair, 123, 126, 127, 128, 147; staging of, 166–7
Papillion, singer, 91
Parade, 10–11, 12, 17, 60, 93, 95, 146, 152–3, 168
Paris, dancers from, 28, 30, 32; equilibrist from, 52; fairs, 111; Opera House, 126
Parker, actor, 27, 127
Parker, showman, 12, 16, 75, 161
Parker, Mrs Anne, actress, 27
Parker, Robert, showman, 6
Parry, actor, 98, 127
Pattenden, actor, 128
Patterson, actor, 131
Pearce, 120
Pearce, actor, 32, 95, 122
Peckham, actor, 92
Peep-show, 26
Pelling, actor, 47, 80
Penderey, Thomas, actor, 77
Penkethman, William, actor, 3, 22, 26, 80, 137, 152, 169; arrest of, 72, 78; at Greenwich Fair, 21, 113; benefit for, 78; booth holder, 9, 12, 18, 21, 28, 76, 83, 84, 112, 146; death of, 29; epilogues spoken by, 34, 109, 155; his dancing dogs, 20, 111; his medley, 15; his musical picture, 23, 28, 85; his Richmond theatre, 23, 27, 28, 33, 79; partnership with Blake, 9, with Boheme, 27, 82, with Bullock, 17, 77, with Miller, 23–4,

Penkethman, William (*cont.*)
  25, 27, 81, with Norris, 24, 25, 29,
  79, 81, with Pack, 78, 157, with
  Simpson, 17, 110; rents ground at
  May Fair, 150; roles, 24, 25, 27, 78,
  87
Penkethman, William jr., actor, 33, 34,
  36, 37, 41, 44, 85, 87, 88, 90, 122,
  123, 124, 126
Penkethman, Mrs William jr., actress,
  44, 126
Penley, actor, 68, 69, 70
Penley, Mrs W., actress, 68
Pennant, Thomas, 67
Pepys, Samuel, 4–5, 74, 136, 145
Perin, John, showman, 6
Perknelly, showman, 67
Perrin, *see* Perin
Peterborough, Charles Mordaunt, Earl
  of, 18, 144
Peters, Mrs, actress, 101, 102
Peterson, Joseph, actor, 55, 91, 99, 128
Petit, showman, 122
Phillips, posture master, 37, 39, 92
Phillips, Constantia, 57, 124, 125
Phillips, 'Harlequin', 46, 51, 56, 57,
  98, 99, 102, 103, 104, 119, 126, 127,
  130, 159
Phillips, Mrs, actress, 47, 51, 56, 98,
  99, 127
Phillips, William, Merry Andrew, 46
Phillpot, Mrs, actress, 36
Phipps, actor, 24
Phoenix, actor, 55
Pickle-herring, 13, 15, 17
Pie Powder Court, 66, 68, 69
Pigeon, actor, 92
Pile, Mrs, actress, 101
Pinchbeck, Edward, showman, 51, 52,
  70, 73, 99, 124, 154
Pinner, George, actor, 56
Pinnington, performer, 118
Pitt, actor, 31, 89
Platt, actor and singer, 56, 59, 91, 124
Playbills, fair, 15, 17, 21, 64, 75
Plomer, Mrs, actress, 29, 36, 85
Polichinelle, 4, 5, 145; *see also* Punch
Pope, Alexander, 20
Portinary, puppet showman, 67
Potter, actor, 66
Powel, publican, 8
Powell, 4
Powell, actor, 31, 51

Powell, puppet showman, 67, 100, 153
Powell, George, actor, 96
Powell, Mrs, actress, 49
Price, actor, 47, 98, 100, 127
Price, Miss, actress, 38, 91, 92
Prices, for entertainments, 40, 51, 58,
  59, 64, 68, 78, 106, 114, 119, 128,
  130, 158
Prince of Wales, Frederick, 37, 97, 98,
  114
Prince of Wales, George, 24, 29, 83,
  92
Princess of Wales, Augusta, 97, 98
Pritchard, Mrs Hannah, actress, 39, 42,
  94, 169
Pritchard, William, actor, 42
Pugin, Augustus, 154
Pullen, Mrs, actress, 31
Punch, 14, 41, 45, 46, 51, 109, 116,
  126, 133, 136, 155–6; *see also*
  Polichinelle
Punch's Puppet Show, 153–4, 155
Puppets, 11, 43, 67, 68, 75, 98, 158;
  Punch's, 51, 116; scenery, 136, 160–1,
  168; shows, 14, 15, 22, 23, 37, 58,
  65, 70, 71, 74, 95, 97, 109, 112, 113,
  123, 131, 135, 137, 138, 147; stage,
  155–6
Purden, Mrs, actress, 50, 88, 94, 95

Queen Elizabeth's Wells, 130
Quin, James, actor, 78

Rahere, 1
Rainton, sen., actor, 36, 40
Rapinière, Mons., posture master, 45,
  126
Ratcliffe, Mrs, actress, 25, 81
Ray, John, actor and singer, 30, 32, 45,
  50, 82, 88, 89
Rayner and Pullen's company, 31
Rayner, dancer, 53
Rayner, Miss, rope dancer, 53, 119
Rayner, Mrs, actress, 31
Redman, actor, 49, 56
Reeves, Christopher, 112
Reynolds, Richard, actor, 30, 31–2, 33,
  34, 35, 56, 87, 90, 123, 167
Rice, Mrs, actress, 33, 36
Rich, John, 24, 146
Richards, actor, 49
Richardson, John, showman, xi, 69, 70,
  132, 149, 151, 154, 158

Richmond, 24, 29, 125; players in, 111; Theatre, 23, 27, 28, 33, 79
Rider, Dudley, 77
Ridout, Isaac, actor, 42
Rimes, rope dancer, 131
Roberts, actor, 66
Roberts, John, actor, 28, 36, 49, 84, 88, 94, 95
Roberts, Mrs John, actress, 28, 32, 34, 36, 40, 41
Robinson, actor, 66, 114
Robinson, Miss, dancer, 127
Rochester, players at, 65
Roebuck, actor, 59
Rogers, Mrs, actress, 38
Rogers, Thomas, actor, 77, 82
Root, Elnathan, publican, 8
Root, Michael, publican, 8
Rope dancing, at Bartholomew Fair, 5, 7, 8, 10, 14–18 passim, 23, 26, 28, 36, 40, 49, 53, 54, 56, 59, 67, 146, 154; at May Fair, 110, 111, 113; at Mile End Fair, 131; at Southwark Fair, 71, 75, 76, 77, 83, 85–7, 92, 103, 104, 107; Dutch, 7, 83, 131, 154; Italian, 28, 40, 59, 85, 92, 146; popularity of, 109; Turkish, 54
Rosco, James, actor, 32, 35, 36, 42, 89, 90, 91, 123
Rosoman, actor, 47, [52, 97, 99, 113, 127, 128, 130, 157
Rosoman, Mrs, dancer, 52, 99, 113
Rowe, Nicholas, dramatist, 24
Rowlandson, Thomas, 154, 156
Rowley, William, dramatist, 85, 140
Royal Circus, 66
Rugg, actor, 64
Russell, actor, 32
Ryan, Lacy, actor, 41, 78

Sadler's Wells, 47, 64, 89, 107, 131
Saffery, Cornelius, showman, 6
Saffery, Mrs, showwoman, 6
Saint-Aubin, G. J. de, painter, 153
St James's Fair, 108
St John, Mrs, actress, 104
St Luce, Mons., dancer, 32, 34, 123
Salway, Thomas, actor, 33, 36, 38, 42
Samuel, puppet showman, 67, 68, 69
Sandham, dancer, 122, 123
Sandham, Master and Miss, dancers, 82, 95, 122
Saunders, showman, xi, 132

Saxe, Marshal, 53
Scaramouch, 8, 16, 41, 45, 46, 76, 108, 109, 110, 126, 127, 133, 145, 146, 148
Scenery, 33, 45, 47, 58, 75, 81, 137, 159–68; scenic effects, 13, 16, 20; expenditure on, 96; gilded, 84; in machine, 58; new, 17, 30, 31, 35, 36, 54, 77, 79, 88, 91, 95, 100, 101, 104, 116, 119, 123, 126; scene painters, 36, 69, 84, 167; transparencies, 57, 58, 68, 69, 164–5
Schoolding, actor, 79, 81
Scotborough, actor, 46
Scowton, showman, 66, 67, 69, 132
Setchel, J. F., his Bartholomew Fair fan, 26, 151, 153–4, 155
Settle, Elkanah, dramatist and machinist, 19–20, 21, 138, 140, 141, 149, 161, 166, 167
Seward, James, showman, 68, 73, 99, 113–14, 116
Shadwell, Thomas, dramatist, 41
Shakespeare, William, 40, 42, 53, 56, 85, 147
Shepherd, Charles, actor, 24, 25, 78
Shepherd, Edward, fairground owner, 111, 117–18, 119
Shepherd, Elizabeth, 119
Sheridan, Thomas, dramatist, 53
Sherking Fair, 134
Shiels, John, composer, 34
Shireburn, Miss Frances, see Cross, Mrs
Shore, Richard, showman, 6
Shuter, Edward, actor, 57, 59, 60, 61, 62, 63, 66, 70, 105, 106, 151, 167, 169
Sidney, Sir Philip, 139
Simes, showman, 67
Simmons, Mrs, actress, 51
Simpson, actor, 56
Simpson, Thomas, vaulter, 16, 17, 110
Sims, Miss, actress, 69
Slater, Mrs, actress, 66
Sleep, John, publican, 8
Smart, Christopher, 58
Smith, actor, 27, 29–30, 31, 32, 33, 34, 40, 43, 49, 54, 56, 99, 103, 114, 115, 130
Smith, dancer, 31, 89
Smith, J. T., 57, 128
Smith, Miss, actress, 91
Smith, Mrs, actress, 99, 102, 114, 115

Smith, Richard, showman, 73
Smollett, Tobias, 54–5
Sorbière, S. de, visits to fairs, 9, 136
Sorine, French actor, 76, 111, 146
Southampton, Duke of, his company, 110–11, 112
Southby, puppet showman, 68
Southbys, clowns, 69
Southern, Dr Richard, 157
Southwark Fair, 20, 28, 154, 155, 157, 167; accidents at, 86, 94, 106, 159; arrest of players at, 72; benefits at, 78, 80, 81, 83, 86, 89–90, 91, 92, 94, 100; date of, 9, 73, 74, 103, 121; entertainments from other fairs at, 20, 27, 30, 72, 82, 85, 88, 92, 94, 98, 99, 100, 101, 102, 105, 126, 129; entertainments from, taken to other fairs, 26, 35 n. 2, 36, 113, 123, 125; Great Tiled Booth at, 99–105 passim; Hogarth's picture of, 93–5, 151, 153, 154; limitation to three days, 71–4, 80, 81, 97, 101–4 passim; New Theatre on Bowling Green at, 99, 101, 104; Old Theatre at, 92, 93, 101; origin of, 70; passages to booths at, 81, 87, 153; permanent booths at, 80, 83, 93, 101, 152–3; playbills of, 75; players' careers started at, 80; plays and players at, 7, 71–107, 135–48 passim; 159, 166, 168; proclaimed by Lord Mayor, 88; robbery of wardrobe at, 99; Settle employed at, 20; suppression of, 3–4, 63, 107; suppression of plays at, 73, 75, 100, 125; times of performances at, 78, 88, 91, 92, 93, 99, 101; visited by royalty, 83, 86, 89, 92, 97, 98
Southwark Quarter Sessions, 71, 72, 73, 134
Spackman, actor, 49, 50
Speaight, George, 154
Spelman, Mrs, actress, 40
Spiller, James, actor, 24, 26, 28–9, 30, 31, 77, 78, 79, 81, 83, 85, 86, 87, 141, 145, 166, 167
Spiller, Mrs James, actress, 27, 28, 30, 33, 40, 77, 78, 79, 88, 91, 95, 121, 123, 124
Steel, Mrs, actress, 49
Steele, Richard, 17
Stephens, Samuel, actor, 49
Sterling, Mrs James, actress, 85

Stevens, Mrs Priscilla, actress, 34
Steward, rope dancer, 103
Stoppelaer, actor, 35, 36, 37, 40, 42, 87, 123
Stoppelaer jr., actor, 42
Storer, Charles, actor, 54
Stourbridge Fair, xi, 6, 64
Strype, John, 71
Sturges, actor, 98
Sturgess, actor, 55, 130
Sturmer, showman, 68
Sturmer, Mrs, showwoman, 68
Subbeys, showman, 68
Summers, Montague, 7
Surrey Assizes, 73
Symonds, actor, 91, 114

Talbot, Mrs, actress, 37, 40, 42, 45, 47
Taswell, actor, 49, 50, 55
Taverns, see Inns
Taylor, actor, 48, 50, 91, 95, 122, 124
Taylor, Mrs, actress, 36, 49, 91
Tegg, Thomas, printer, 156
Templer, Mrs, actress, 33, 36, 37
Tench, dancer, 32
Tench, H., actor, 40
Tenoe, actor, 36, 38
Terwin, puppet showman, 95
Theobald, Lewis, dramatist, 123
Thomas, actor, 32, 131
Thomas, Mrs, actress, 32, 88, 122, 123, 124
Thomassin, Signor, dancer, 128
Thompson, actor, 101
Thorne, showman, 149
Thornhill, Dr, mountebank, 81
Thumoth, Burk, trumpeter, 37
Thurmond, John, 122
Thwaites, actor, 69
Thynne, Miss, actress, 51
Tillemans, Pieter, painter, 23
Tollet, Miss Henrietta, actress, 91
Topham, actor, 98
Tottenham Court Fair, 34, 45, 46, 94, 97, 117, 121–9, 138, 144, 145, 147, 148, 149
Towers, actor, 130
Transparencies, see Scenery
Tucker, Mrs, actress, 51
Tumbling, 38, 40, 43, 47, 49, 59, 66, 76, 77, 83, 85, 86, 91, 92, 100, 113, 115, 131
Turbutt, Robert, actor, 48, 50, 51
Turin Opera House, 106

Usher, N. L., actor, 54

Vallois, Mrs, actress, 51
Vaughan, actor, 48, 50, 54, 60, 70, 99, 101, 127, 151
Vaughan, actor, 69
Vaux, Mrs, actress, 104
Vernon, Edward, admiral, 127
Victor, Benjamin, 80, 140
Villeneuve, Mrs, actress, 47
Vincent, Mrs Elizabeth, actress, 85
Violante, Mme, rope dancer, 86

Wakelin, showman, 64
Wakelin, Miss, actress, 64, 65
Wakelin, Mrs, showwoman, 64
Walford, actor, 85
Walker, actor, 56, 59
Walker, Mrs, actress, 59
Walker, Thomas, actor, 25, 30, 77, 82, 84, 87, 90, 135, 145, 149, 151
Wallis, actor, 42, 51, 99
Walters, actor, 59
Walton, actor, 66
Wandring Spy, 17–18
Wandsworth Fair, 134
Ward, Edward (Ned), visits fairs, 10–13, 60, 108–9, 136, 140, 145, 146, 148, 153
Ward, John, actor, 85
Ward, Miss, actress, 88
Ware, actor, 49
Warner, Jemmy, actor, 47, 50, 52, 53, 54, 55, 60, 99, 101, 102, 104, 105, 107, 113, 127, 128, 130, 151, 157, 158, 159
Warner, Mrs, actress, 47, 127
Waters, actor, 45
Waters, Mrs, actress, 45
Wathen, actor, 35
Waxworks, 18, 118
Weaver, John, dancing master, 133, 146
Wells, puppet showman, 67
Welsh Fair, 98, 117, 129–31, 146
Westminster Grand Jury, 112
Weston, Thomas, actor, 60
Wetherilt, Mrs Elizabeth, actress, 25, 31, 36
Wetherilt, Robert, actor, 31, 36, 37, 42, 82, 92
Whitechapel Petty Sessions, 132
White, actor, 56

White, puppet showman, 67, 68
White, Miss, actress, 99
Wignell, J., dramatist, 62
Wilcocks or Willcox, actor, 32, 85, 89
Wild, showman, 69
Wilks, ?Robert, 25
Wilks, William jr., 24, 77, 85
William, Prince, 124
Williams, Charles, actor, 24, 25, 28, 29, 81, 82, 85, 131
Williams, Miss, dancer, 50, 89
Williams, Robert, actor, 32, 88, 122
Williams, William, actor, 32, 34, 88, 122
Williamson, Mrs, actress, 35, 40
Willis, Mrs Elizabeth, actress and dancer, 18, 23, 25, 27, 28, 29, 31, 33, 79, 80, 82, 85
Wilson, showman, 67, 68
Windsor, players at, 19, 68
Winstone, Richard, actor, 42, 49
Wolfe, James, general, 105
Wood, actor, 51
Woodbe, dancer, 130
Woodhouse, actor, 100
Woodward, actor and dancer, 49, 50, 51, 95, 98, 99, 127, 129
Woodward, Mrs, dancer, 43, 122
Wright, actor, 92
Wright, Mrs Christiana, 50

Yarrow, Joseph, dramatist, 57, 101
Yates, George, puppet showman, 65
Yates, John, showman, 133
Yates, Miss, actress, 56
Yates, Richard, actor, 45, 47, 50, 51, 55, 56, 57, 59, 60, 61–2, 63, 66, 70, 128, 150, 151, 167
Yates, Mrs Richard, actress, 48, 50
Yeates, junior, showman and conjuror, 70; booth holder, 55, 98, 103; conjuring by, 58, 124, 127, 131; death of, 59; partnership with Lee, Warner and Yeates sen., 101, with Yeates sen., 43, 94, 131; role, 131; wardrobe stolen, 99
Yeates, Miss, actress, 124, 131
Yeates, Mrs, showwoman, 59, 104
Yeates, Thomas sen., showman, 48, 70; booth holder, 47, 94, 101, 115, 124, 129; charged with illegal performance, 73; his machines, 37, 58, 100, 123, 124, 131–2; his puppets,

Yeates, Thomas (*cont.*)
36–7, 43, 58, 86, 123; partnership with Lee and Warner, 55, 101, 159, with Phillips, 51, with Powell, 100, 153, with Rosoman and Warner, 52, 113, 128, 157, with Warner, 102, 153; proprietor of Clerkenwell New Wells, 129, of May Fair New Wells, 118, 119; reported marriage to Mrs Lee, 98; role, 130
Young, actor, 128
Young, Edward, 20

II. ENTERTAINMENTS

Preliminary descriptive phrases to titles such as 'The true and ancient history of' are omitted.

When the same piece was played under different titles, cross-reference is made under each title to the others used.

The many variant sub-titles are omitted. Sub-titles are included only when they distinguish two different types of piece (i.e. droll and dance) with the same title or when they are used, in other instances, as full titles.

Adventures and Marriage of Harlequin in Turkey, 130
Adventures of Half an Hour, 59
Adventures of Harlequin, 99, 118
Adventures of Harlequin in Spain, 128
All Alive and Merry, 43, 53; as subtitle to *The Wanton Trick'd*, 128
All Alive and Merry; Or the Happy Miller just Arriv'd, pantomime, 127
All in Good Humour, 68
Gli Amanti Gelosi, 59
Amorous Contention, dance, 47
Amorous Parley, 65
Amorous Widow, 59, 140
Amours of Harlequin, 55
Amurath the Great, 90, 123, 138; see also *Distressed Beauty*
Argalus and Parthenia, 118, 139
Armenian Queen, 5
Author's Farce, 123, 147

Le Badinage Champêtre, ballet, 43
Ball, 126
Banish'd General, 36, 92
Baronet Bit, 99
Barren Island, 41
Bartholomew Fair, 5, 138
Bateman, 13, 16, 31, 77, 94, 125, 136, 138, 139
Bath, 109
Beaux Stratagem, 89, 100, 115, 147
Beggar's Opera, 30, 31, 87, 145
Beggar's Wedding, 31, 87, 88, 145, 168; as sub-title to *Hunter*, 32; to *Phebe*, 123

Birth of Harlequin, 104
Birth of Merlin, the British Enchanter, see *Merlin*
Blind Beggar of Bethnal Green, 27, 55, 85, 100, 115, 138, 139, 140, 148; as sub-title to *Injur'd General*, 25, 81; to *New Wonder*, 75
Bold Stroke for a Wife, 91, 147
Brave Irishman, 53
Broken Stock-Jobbers, 81, 135, 144
La Broomstickado, ballet, 58
Busy Body, 83, 86, 147

Calisto, 5
Camp, 64
Canning's Escape, 104
Captive Prince, 114, 147
Careless Husband, 115
Cephalus with the Death of Procris, 98, 127
Cheats of Scapin, 42, 50, 51 n. 2; as sub-title to *Cure for Covetousness*, 38, 94, 148; see also *Harlequin Scapin*, *Scaramouch Scapin*
Colombine Courtezan, 46, 98
Comedy of Errors, 52, 147
Comical Humours of Sir John Falstaff, Justice Shallow, Ancient Pistol and Others, 40, 147; as sub-title to *Captive Prince*, 114
Consequence of Industry and Idleness, 55
Constant Lovers, 23, 42, 76, 133
Constant Quaker, 55, 101
Contrivances of Harlequin, 118
Coronation of Queen Elizabeth, 7, 74–5, 136, 137, 159, 161

Country Farmer, 97
Country Wake, 128
Country Wedding, 33, 44, 145
Creation of the World, 8, 14, 18, 58, 75, 113, 136, 160
Crispin and Crispianus, 13, 110, 136
Cruel Uncle, 52
Cupid and Psyche, 46, 76, 98
Cure for Covetousness, 38, 94, 148; see also *Cheats of Scapin*
Cure for the Spleen, 15

Damon and Phillida, 32, 124, 145
Darius, King of Persia, 27, 49, 129; as sub-title to *Noble Englishman*, 82, 143; see also *Persian Hero*
Descent of the Heathen Gods, 56
Devil of a Duke, 49, 135
Devil of a Wife, 11
Devil to Pay, 91, 100, 135, 145
Devil upon Two Sticks, 112, 135, 139
Dishes of Wit and Savoury Courses of Humour, 106
Distressed Beauty, 27, 82, 138; see also *Amurath the Great*
Distress'd Merchant, 103; see also *Jew of Venice*
Distressed Sailor, 58, 103
Distress'd Virgin, 17; see also *Unnatural Parents*
Dives and Lazarus, 7–8, 14, 136
Don Carlos, 41, 42
Don John, 41
Don Quixote de la Mancha, 115
Don Quixote in England, 105
Dorastus and Fawnia, 16, 33, 119–20, 139
Downfall of Robert, Earl of Huntington, 139
Dragon of Wantley, 45, 131
Dutch Courtezan, 147

Earthquake in Jamaica, 75, 137
Emperor of China Grand Vol-gi, 35, 91, 167, 168
Enchanted Urn, 66
England Triumphant, 59
English Mirror, 62
Envious Statesman, 37, 141
Ephesian Duke, 52, 147
Escape of Harlequin, 103
Escapes of Harlequin, 118
Escapes of Harlequin by Sea and Land, 45

Everything in Season, 65
Exile of the Earl of Huntington, 75; see also *Robin Hood*

Fair Bride, 62
Fair Hypocrite, 118, 149
Fair Lunatick, 57
Fair Rosamond, 4, 42, 49, 135–6, 138, 139
Fairy, 59
Fairy Queen, 110
Faithful Couple, 83
Fall of Phaeton, 40–1, 94, 146, 167
False Friend, 133; as sub-title to *Constant Lovers*, 23
Farrier Nick'd, 41
Female Innocence, 92, 135
Female Mirror, 105–6
Flora, 33, 35, 36, 88, 145
Force of Magick, 100
French Doctor Outwitted, 52, 147
French Flogg'd, 61, 105, 142–3
Friar Bacon, 12–13, 18, 80–1, 136, 138, 139, 140, 161
Frolicksome Lasses, 54
Fryar Bacon, see *Friar Bacon*

Gardens of Venus, dance, 41
Generous Freemason, 33, 37, 88, 135, 145, 148, 166
George Barnwell, see *London Merchant*
George for England, 107
Glorious Queen of Hungary, 51
Guy, Earl of Warwick, 36, 89, 135, 138, 139, 141

Half-Pay Officers, 60 n. 4.
Hamlet, 102
Happy Gallant, 59, 140
Happy Hero, 53
Happy Miller Arriv'd, 129
Harlequin Barber, 103–4
Harlequin Captive, 115
Harlequin Disaffected, 51
Harlequin Faustus, 98; as sub-title *Harlequin Dr Faustus* to *A Wife Well Manag'd*, 124
Harlequin Fortune Teller, 120
Harlequin Grand Vol-gi, 127
Harlequin Happy, 127
Harlequin Incendiary, 53
Harlequin Invader, 53, 100
Harlequin, the Man in the Moon, 99

Harlequin Scapin, 47
Harlequin Sclavonian, 114
Harlequin Sorcerer, 127
Harlequin Triumphant, 99, 100, 103, 113
Harlequin Turn'd Philosopher, 45
Harlequin Wanderer, 65
Harlequin's Contrivance, 35, 90
Harlequin's Distress, 126
Harlequin's Frolic, 65
Harlequin's Frolics, 55, 101
Harlequin's Vagaries, 105
Harlequin's Whim, 118
Harlot's Progress, ballad opera, 95, 131
Harlot's Progress, pantomime, 39, 56, 94, 102, 119, 125, 128; see also *Ridotto al' Fresco*
Henry IV, 41, 81, 147
Hero and Leander, 30, 138, 141, 166
Herod and Mariamne, 35, 83
Hint to the Theatres, 129
Hob, 33, 83
Humours of Cloth Fair, dance, 103
Humours of the Forc'd Physician, 37, 148
Humours of Harlequin, 33, 87
Humours of May Fair, dance, 113
Hunter, 32; see also *Beggar's Wedding*

Imposter, 42, 147
Inchanted Island, 59
Indian Merchant, 51, 99
Industrious Lovers, 102
Infernals, ballet, 49
Injur'd General, 25, 81; see also *Blind Beggar of Bethnal Green*
Injur'd Merchant, 104
Injur'd Virtue, 76
Intriguing Chambermaid, 103; *Comical Humours of the*, 51, 99
Intriguing Footman, 51, 147
Intriguing Harlequin, 95
Irish Evidence, 6
Italian Shadows, 43, 80, 81, 146

Jane Shore, 24, 29, 41, 83, 94, 118, 121, 138, 139, 148; as sub-title to *Loves of King Edward IV*, 50
La Je Ne Sca Quoi, 58
Jealous Husband, 28
Jephtha's Rash Vow, 9, 15, 17, 40–1, 79, 94, 102, 135, 136, 138, 139–40, 148
Jew in Distress, 104

Jew of Venice, 80, 147; as sub-title to *Distress'd Merchant*, 103
Jovial Jack Tars, 57
Judith and Holofernes, 136, 139; see also *Siege of Bethulia*
Julius Caesar, 65

King Edward IV, 99, 102, 113, 138; see also *Robin Hood*
King Egbert, 24, 141
King Henry VIII and Anne Bullen, 37–8, 141
King John, 56, 97, 147
King Saul and the Witch of Endo, 82
King William's Happy Deliverance, 108, 136–7

Lady Pentweazle's Vagaries, dance, 58
Libertine, 41
Life and Death of Harlequin, 68
London Merchant, 36, 91, 147
Love and Empire, 120
Love and Jealousy, 38, 94
Love for Love, 81
Love in a Labyrinth, 53, 100
Love Makes a Man, 92
Lover, 105
Lover his Own Rival, 113
Lover's Metamorphosis, 104
Lover's Mistake, 65
Love's Mistress, 16
Loves of Harlequin and Columbine, 28
Loves of King Edward the Fourth, 50; see also *Jane Shore*
Love's Triumph, 24, 79
Lying Valet, 102, 147

Mad Lovers, 126
Mad Tom of Bedlam, 34, 122
Maiden Queen, 118, 148–9
Man's Bewitch'd, 44, 60 n. 4, 97, 105
Le Mariage de Peasant, 116
Matrimonial Squabble, 49
Maudlin, the Merchant's Daughter of Bristol, 24, 33, 95, 111–12, 122, 138, 139, 140
Le Médecin Malgré Lui, 37
Merchant of Venice, 103; see also *Jew of Venice*
Merlin, dance, 92
Merlin, the British Enchanter, 85, 97, 125, 138, 139, 166
Merry Andrew, 4–5

Merry Beggars, 59
Merry Cobler of Preston, 118; 148
Metamorphosis of Harlequin, 47, 129; as sub-title to *Orpheus and Eurydice*, 98, 130
Miller's Holiday, 123
Minor, 63, 105
Miser, 40, 94
Miser Bit, 51, 99
Miser Outwitted, 104
Miss in her Teens, 54, 66, 119
Mock Doctor, 99, 102
Modern Madness, 57
Modern Pimp, 43, 49

Neck or Nothing, 64
New Wonder, A Woman Never Vex'd, 75; see also *Blind Beggar of Bethnal Green*
Noah's Flood, 14, 75, 136, 160
Noble Englishman, 82, 143; as sub-title to *Darius, King of Persia*, 27, 49, 129; to *Persian Hero*, 129
Noble Soldier, 79, 80
Northern Heroes, 54, 101
Nuns Turn'd Libertines, 90

Oedipus, King of Thebes, 85, 147
Old Bachelor, 65, 80
Old Creation of the World, see *Creation of the World*
Old Widow Bewitch'd, 60, 105
Old Woman's Oratory, 104
Oroonoko, 83, 94
Orpheus and the Death of Eurydice, 47, 98, 129, 130, 146

Parting Lovers, 47
Patient Grizill, 4, 23, 136
Perjured Prince, 31, 38, 167
Perseus and Andromeda, 45, 123
Persian Hero, 129; see also *Darius, King of Persia* and *Noble Englishman*
Phebe, 123; see also *Beggar's Wedding*
Pleasures of the Town, see *Punch's Oratory*
Plotting Lovers, 99
Porus, 36
Prince's Ball, 7
Prodigal Son, 14, 28, 119
Prophetess, 98
Punch's Oratory, 123, 147
Punch's Politicks, 90
Purse, 68

Quaker, 65
Quaker's Opera, 30, 87, 135, 145

Rake Reform'd, 103
Rambling Lovers, 47
Recruiting Officer, 81, 83, 88, 89, 115, 147
Recruiting Serjeant, 66
Revenge, 114
Richard III, 128, 144, 147, 149
Richard Whittington, see *Whittington*
Ridotto al' Fresco, 40, 42, 158; as sub-title to *Harlot's Progress*, 39, 94
Rival Queens, 38, 41, 127, 147, 148
Robin Hood and Little John, 22, 35, 84, 89, 135, 138, 139; as sub-title to *Exile of the Earl of Huntington*, 75; to *King Edward IV*, 99, 102, 113
Royal Chace, 45
Royal Champion, 87, 138, 141
Royal Heroe, 114
Royal Revenge, 82, 138; see also *Valentine and Orson*
Royal Voyage, 7
Rum Duke and the Queer Duke, 123

Sailor's Wedding, 45
St George and the Dragon, 8, 14, 20, 136
Scaramouch Scapin, 50
Schemes of Harlequin, 53
School for a Wife, 120
Scipio's Triumph, 34–5
Semiramis Queen of Babylon, 29
Sham Physician, 103
Ship-Wreck'd Lovers, 61, 143
Siege of Barcelona, 18, 144
Siege of Bethulia, 25, 33, 35, 88, 135; see also *Judith and Holofernes*
Siege of Namur, 9–10, 136; as sub-title to *King William's Happy Deliverance*, 108
Siege of Portobello, 129
Siege of Troy, 14, 19–20, 28, 29, 54, 76–7, 80, 84, 86, 94, 95, 101, 135, 137–8, 140–1, 148, 161–5, 166
Siege of Valenciennes, 67
Simpleton the Smith, 9 n. 1
Sir Richard Whittington, see *Whittington*
Southwark Fair, 87, 135, 145
Spaniard Well Drub'd, 66, 144
Stratagems of Harlequin, 35, 88, 89, 92, 104

Tamerlane the Great, 39, 41, 54, 94, 120, 147
Tavern Bilkers, 133, 146

Tempest; or, the Distressed Lovers, 16, 61, 142, 161
Tempest; or, The Inchanted Island, 56, 147, 161
Tender Husband, 103
Thamas Kouli Kan, 48–9, 62, 143
Timur Coran, 62, 143, 168
Tipoo, 67
Tipplers, 34
Tom Thumb, 90, 147
Top of the Tree, 45
Tragedy of Tragedies, 51
Trick for Trick, 126, 148; see also *Trick upon Trick*
Trick upon Trick, 52, 57, 100, 101; as sub-title to *Country Farmer*, 97, to *Harlequin Triumphant*, 114; see also *Trick for Trick*
Tricks of Harlequin, 52
Triumph of Britannia, dance, 49
Triumph of Hymen, 62
Triumph of Love in the Temple of Apollo, 59
Triumphant Queen of Hungary, 52
Triumphs of Hymen, 107
Trojan Horse, 14, 136
Twice Married and a Maid Still, 78

Unhappy Favourite, 99, 102
Unnatural Parents, 30, 55, 86, 101, 104, 119, 125, 135, 148, 166; as sub-title to *Distress'd Virgin*, 17

Valentine and Orson, 84, 138, 139; as sub-title to *Royal Revenge*, 82
Vertumnus, dance, 127
Vienna Besieg'd, 8
Virgin Prophetess, 140
Virgin's Wish, 59
Volunteers, 54, 101
Vow Breaker, 139

Wandering Prince of Troy, 115
Wanton Maid, 52
Wanton Trick'd, 128, 149
Wat Tyler and Jack Straw, 34, 135, 137, 139, 141–2, 168
Waterman, 64
What D'Ye Call It, 78, 147
Wheel of Life, dance, 30
Whim, 68
Whimsical Battle of the Greybeards, 106
Whittington, 2, 13, 21, 55, 74, 79, 83, 90, 93, 97, 102, 124, 135, 136, 138, 139, 141, 166, 168
Whore of Babylon, 7–8, 136
Wife Well Manag'd, 54, 124, 127, 148
Winter's Tale, 16
Woman Turn'd Bully, 60
World's Creation, see *Creation of the World*
Wrangling Deities, 50